statecraft:
an introduction
to political choice
and judgment

statecraft:
an introduction
to political choice
and judgment

charles w. anderson
UNIVERSITY OF WISCONSIN—MADISON

JOHN WILEY & SONS
New York Santa Barbara London Sydney Toronto

Library of Congress Cataloging in Publication Data:

Anderson, Charles W
  Statecraft: an introduction to political choice and judgment.

  Includes index.
  1. Decision-making in political science. I. Title.
JA74.A535   320   76-22740
ISBN 0-471-02896-7

Printed in the United States of America

10 9 8 7 6 5 4 3 2 1

"The mere fact of each man's involvement, in whatever capacity, in public affairs implies each asking himself what decision is good, hearing the arguments of others and giving his own opinion when he has formed it. How then has it come about that political theory seems so little concerned to help us form the opinion which we must give?"

Bertrand de Jouvenal

"He had failed them not in honor or devotion—but in craftsmanship."

Theodore H. White on the
1972 Presidential Campaign
of George McGovern

"Before an important decision someone clutches your hand—a glimpse of gold in the iron-gray, the proof of all you have never dared to believe."

Dag Hammarskjöld

Dedicated to my teaching assistants at the University of Wisconsin, 1960–1976

D.A.	A.B.	J.G.	E.K.	I.S.
N.A.	M.C.	R.H.	R.L.K.	S.S.
R.A.	B.C.	H.H.	J.L.	S.M.S.
P.A.	C.C.	J.H.	T.Mc.	G.S.
T.B.	J.D.	M.H.	J.O.	M.S.
J.B.	N.E.	M.E.H.	D.O.	R.T.
J.H.B.	V.E.-O.	S.D.J.	R.R.	R.Y.
T.B.	E.A.F.	L.J.	S.R.	J.Z.
A.B.	B.B.G.	M.K.	L.S.	

preface

Statecraft is an old north European word for the science of government. I chose it for the title of this book because it suggests that some aspects of the practice of politics have the form of a craft or an art and that they require skill, technique, and judgment. It also implies that politics can be practiced well or poorly, that it can be done with painstaking care and creativity, or that it can be haphazard and nonchalant.

Decision making is the heart of the craft of politics. To act politically is to attempt to impose direction and form on the course of human affairs. This implies choice from among alternative possibilities. We cannot make a decision when we think there is only one course of action available to us. Understood as the craft of decision making, the object of political science is not to discover the order in human affairs but to determine what that order shall be.

As a form of human activity, politics takes place whenever there is controversy about public purposes. The first step in decision making is making up your own mind, formulating a position in the face of conflict over public policy. The second step is defending that position and attempting to have it adopted as definitive for a community.

Everyone makes political decisions. But often we do not recognize that this is what we are doing, even while we are doing it. Political activity is not confined to the affairs of government. It is present in every human association. In essence, we act politically whenever we make decisions on behalf of other people and not for ourselves alone. Politics means planning and organizing common projects, setting rules and standards that define the relationships of people to one another, and allocating resources among rival human needs and purposes. In this sense, politics takes place in families, in businesses, and in clubs and organizations. It is not only the concern of government officials.

There are many approaches to the study of politics. Most political science textbooks adopt the point of view of the detached observer. They describe the institutions and processes of government. They examine how the system "works" and how people in politics "behave." The student is encouraged to adopt the clinical frame of mind of the disinterested scientist. One gets the distinct impression that politics is something that is practiced by other people.

This book adopts the standpoint of the participant rather than the spectator. The object is not analysis of the process *by* which policy decisions are made but the process *of* making public decisions themselves. Politics here will be considered as an activity, not merely as a phenomenon to be observed.

For best results, the book should be used actively. In almost every chapter, basic dilemmas of political choice are presented. Some are case studies, and others are general problems of decision making. It is not enough simply to appreciate the complexity of these issues. The important question is how you make up your mind about these problems—and why. In politics we not only have to choose but we also have to be able to defend our convictions. Public decision making is closely related to the process of political argument. We have to make decisions on *some* basis. We have to have grounds for choice. We make cases in support of our ideas, and we are called on to justify the decisions that we make.

The book is divided into three sections. In Part One, we deal with problems of public policy—the question of what government should do. Part Two concerns political strategy, the issues that have to be faced in deciding on a course of political action. Here we deal with problems such as interest advocacy, bargaining, compromise, and coalition formation, as well as electoral campaigning and even revolutionary action. Part Three examines the subject of government organization, again considered as a problem of decision making. The question here is not *what* we decide to do, but *how* we create a process for making decisions and putting them into effect.

Throughout the book we look at the process of decision making from two different points of view. The first is that of the policymaker, the person who has the responsibility for making an authoritative commitment on public purposes. The second is that of the advocate, the person who is trying to advance a program, or a cause, or the interests of same group. Most books on policy analysis are written only from the perspective of the policymaker. But the problems of public choice have to be faced not only by those who hold authority roles in the political system but also by anyone who engages in the public debate or tries to influence the course of public action.

With the exception of international relations, most of the conventional fields of political science are touched on. The basic approach is a combination of political theory and public policy analysis. Chapters Three and Fourteen deal with fundamental questions of public law. A comparative approach is used in Chapters Nine, Thirteen, and Fifteen. Several chapters, particularly Chapters Six and Twelve, deal with public administration. The materials on American political institutions and processes common to most introductory political science textbooks are incorporated throughout, albeit from a somewhat unusual perspective.

The book is designed to be compatible with the varied skills and interests that are brought to the teaching of the introductory course in political science. The political theorist will want to give more emphasis to the explication of the normative concepts around which the analysis is built. The student of public policy may be inclined to supplement the text with more extensive case studies of public problem solving. Those who specialize in political institutions and processes will want to compare this treatment of what is at stake in making decisions about public issues with a more detailed consideration of how such issues are handled in the structural and behavioral context of American politics.

The approach is one of posing dilemmas and raising questions. Rarely if ever do I argue for a solution to these problems. Some will find this frustrating. It may seem odd to state the pros and cons and leave the matter hanging, without coming to a conclusion or resolving the dispute. At the very least, some will wonder "where I stand" on these issues. In a sense, the answer to the question is obvious. The point of view expressed in this book is that politics is essentially an act of existential choice. There are no final, definitive, "rational" solutions to political problems. However, to act politically is not *merely* a Kierkegaardian "leap of faith." Because decision making involves political argument, because it concerns giving reasons and justifying choices, politics is also a process of "reasoned discourse." It may not be possible to be completely "rational" in public decision making, but we do have to be "reasonable" about the choices that we make.

For the rest of it, my personal political beliefs and biases are relatively unimportant. Some will no doubt label the approach as "liberal" and others as "conservative." In point of fact, despite recurrent efforts by students and colleagues to inform me about my political preconceptions, I feel uneasy about identifying myself with any of the conventional labels or ideologies. In many ways, I would prefer to think of myself as a "militant moderate." I suppose I am a liberal (with a small "l") and a democrat (with a small "d"). I know I have been influenced by contemporary democratic theory, especially as expressed by writers like Robert Dahl, Charles Lindblom, and Thomas Thorson, as well as the tradition of American pragmatism and the social and political philosophy of Reinhold Niebuhr. I also know that I am not a Marxist, an Anarchist, a Rosecrucian, or a Mason, if that is any help at all.

I am indebted to many people who helped, in various ways, in the preparation of this book. First, I acknowledge my students, but most particularly the teaching assistants I have worked with in introductory courses at the University of Wisconsin over the years, who struggled with this approach to the teaching of politics, criticized it, and helped fashion it. In dedicating this book to them, collectively and individually, I am both registering appreciation for their assistance and acknowledging what I have known for some time—that my relationship with the teaching assistants has been perhaps the most rewarding and satisfying part of my work as a university teacher.

A crucial turning point in the evolution of this approach came at the University of Essex, England, where I was an exchange professor in 1971–1972. I am most grateful for the advice and friendship of David Robertson and Brian Barry who introduced me to the power of the kind of analysis that is brought to political inquiry through the examination of political language.

In revising the manuscript, I had the assistance of a uniquely talented group of readers and critics. The combination of Douglas Rae's powerful and clear mind, Gary Wynia's consistent sanity and good sense, and Booth Fowler's subtle instincts as a gifted teacher and insightful political theorist provided me with an unusual combination of advice and criticism from which I could draw. Needless to say, I alone am responsible for the use I have made of their helpful commentary.

The contribution of two members of the John Wiley organization must be specifically acknowledged. At first I rebeled against Charlotte Allstrom's forthright criticisms, but in the long run it usually turned out that she was right, and I came to adopt most of her suggestions. She was, I hope, successful as the determined advocate of the reader who is here taking on the study of politics for the first time. Wayne Anderson was all that an author could hope for in an editor—helpful, cooperative, patient, supportive, and thoroughly professional.

It pays to have a linguist as a secretary. Cheri Hannay not only typed the manuscript with astonishing accuracy and competence but corrected spelling and syntax, deciphered marginal hieroglyphics that sometimes baffled me, and generally acted as much as copy editor as typist. Jeanene Alery pitched in and did her usual excellent job in helping with the final copy.

Jeanie's contributions, as always, go far beyond unfailing encouragement and enthusiasm. I suppose that many families have to work hard at their own "domestic politics," but in ours, it comes easy.

CHARLES W. ANDERSON

Monona, Wisconsin

contents

xiii

statecraft:
an introduction
to political choice
and judgment

part one public policy: choice on behalf of other people

chapter
one
political
decisions

How do you make political decisions? How do you come to conclusions about what government ought to do—to improve the economy, to protect the environment, to combat crime, to cope with the problems of the community, the nation, the world? That is basically what this book is about.

We all think about these matters—and we all have our own opinions. But there is a difference between merely having an opinion and making a political decision. Opinions do not necessarily require thought. They can be virtually reflex reactions. But to make a decision you have to look at the various sides of the question, analyze them, and take a position after weighing the merits of opposing views. You cannot decide when your mind is already made up.

Everyone is entitled to their own political convictions. But are your convictions really your own? Or were you brought up with them? Or do they come from something you read somewhere and did not quite understand? Part of being able to make reasonable political decisions is becoming aware of your own preconceptions and biases. Politics looks easy until you realize that there is something to be decided about.

Making political decisions is a serious business because basically politics means *making choices on behalf of other people.* In politics, we are choosing not just for ourselves but for others as well. We make decisions about the rights and freedoms they will enjoy, how their taxes will be spent, how they will be protected against threats to their lives and property, what services they will receive.

Making choices for other people, deciding about policies that will

4

*public policy: choice
on behalf of other
people*

be *imposed* on them, may seem like a problem that is remote from your personal life. That is the business of the leaders of government. Politics seems much more like something that *they* do to you, rather than what *you* are apt to do to other people.

I will not try to persuade you that what you think about politics is apt to make much difference in the nation's affairs. But to think intelligently about politics at all, we have to think *as though* our ideas might be adopted as public policy, that they might become law.

What is more important, however, is that making political decisions is in fact a part of everyday life. Politics takes place not only in governments but also in businesses, universities, labor unions, churches—in every kind of human association. Whenever we serve on a committee, or manage a project, or participate in a controversy over the goals and purposes of any organization, we are making political decisions. We are making choices for other people.

Furthermore, many important political decisions are made by very ordinary people. No doubt a few readers of this book will one day run for Congress or serve as federal officials. But many more will take part in local politics, as alderpersons, members of school boards, or simply active citizens. As we will shortly see, the kinds of political issues that are decided at this level are often far from trivial or routine. And how they are decided can have a very direct and intimate impact on the daily lives of people.

the purpose
of this book

This book is about the art of making public decisions. It is not exactly a do-it-yourself manual, for politics has little in common with such subjects as small engine repair or speed reading. I cannot prescribe ten rules for making political decisions or recommend a set of steps to be followed every time you face a political dilemma. Nevertheless, there is method in thinking through a political problem to a sensible conclusion. There may not be clear-cut right and wrong answers to political questions, for politics is inherently controversial, but we do admit that there are better and worse political judgments. Public decisions can be more or less imaginative, timely, responsible, equitable, fair, realistic, and workable. Even if we cannot find indisputable solutions to political problems, we can at least try to make decisions that are more beneficial than harmful to those who will be affected by them.

The "method" I will present can be applied to all levels of political analysis. It can be used to make up your mind about the big issues of contemporary national and world affairs. It can be applied to the problems of decision making in clubs, associations, businesses, and educational institutions. It will be useful to those who hold, or are thinking of running for, local offices.

The problem of decision making is examined from the point of view of the policymaker, who must make an authoratative choice between alternative proposals, from that of the activist, who is trying to promote a program of reform, and even from that of the revolutionary, who is committed to overthrowing the existing political order. We will discuss problems of policy—what government should *do* —problems of strategy—how to advance a program in the face of hostility and opposition—and problems of political organization.

The purpose of the book is to help you in making more sensible, deliberate political decisions. Basically, we ask questions rather than give answers, for practical political judgment is mainly a matter of being able to ask the right questions at the right time. Being able to ask the right questions, as Wayne A. R. Leys says, "should unparalyze the mind at the moment of action."[1] The right questions suggest unexpected angles and perspectives that need examining. They do not give you the facts, but they suggest what facts might be important in making a decision. They do not tell you where to take your stand, but they make you ask *why* you take a particular position, and in doing so, they make you more self-conscious about decision making and better able to defend your convictions in political controversy.

A major theme in this book is the necessity for choice. Political questions are always ambiguous. Problems can be examined from a variety of perspectives. There are seldom clear-cut answers. Nevertheless, decisions must be made. Political judgment is the art of making decisions under conditions of uncertainty and incomplete information. In this book many dilemmas of public choice will be presented. Options will be delineated and arguments pro and con set forth. It is not enough simply to appreciate the complexity of these problems. The crucial question is choice. If a number of conclusions are possible, which would you adopt, and how would you defend your position?

three ordinary
political dilemmas

Consider now three problems of political decision making that might come up in any community and that would have to be settled by the kind of average people who run the affairs of local governments.

In a small town, one family decides to let their yard grow wild. They say that they prefer the natural look to well-tended grass. The neighbors complain that the yard is unsightly and that the owners ought to be required to plant and maintain a normal lawn.

At first glance, this hardly looks like an earthshaking political

[1] *Wayne A. R. Leyes,* Ethics for Policy Decisions: The Art of Asking Deliberative Questions *(Englewood Cliffs, N.J.: Prentice-Hall, 1952), p. 11.*

6

*public policy: choice
on behalf of other
people*

issue. How important, after all, are lawns compared to the big questions of inflation and full employment, peace in the Middle East and relations with the Soviet Union? But important political issues can often seem deceptively commonplace. In this case, what the city council is actually deciding about is the right of individuals to use their property as they please against the right of the community to regulate its use. Questions of basic rights, of personal freedom and public authority, cannot be trivial. If you had to make a decision in this case, what would you do—and why?

Consider a second example. You are a member of a local park commission and a tract of land, ideal for development as a recreational area, comes on the market. The price is right, and you are ready to buy. Then a delegation comes before your commission to protest. They argue that this park would be located in the richest part of town. The poorer neighborhoods, they assert, are as usual being neglected. If the city is going to build a new park it should do so where there is a real need for it.

So what should you do? Vacant land in the inner city is scarcer and more expensive than on the fringes of town where the more affluent neighborhoods are located. Should you forego the opportunity to buy the land? Would you advocate a policy of providing equal park areas in all parts of the city, though this would be much more expensive than expanding the park system by taking advantage of cheaper land? The problem is not merely one of building parks but of equal treatment and social justice.

Now consider a third case. You are a school board member. A group of parents object to the use of a certain book in an English class, claiming that it contains "dirty words," is morally objectionable and politically subversive. But the teacher, and the local newspaper, say that to ban the book would be censorship.

Of course, you do not like the idea of censorship. No government, whether Congress or the local school board, should have the right to determine what will be read or heard. But then, what authority *does* the local board have to determine what will be taught in the schools? Do professional teachers have an unlimited license to do as they please in the classroom? Has the community no power to determine the content of education provided in its schools? There is a fundamental enigma lurking just beneath the surface of the controversy. What is the relationship of the right of free speech to the idea of democratic government—the power of the people, either acting for themselves or through elected representatives, to determine what government will do. Once again, if you had to make a decision in this case, what would you do?

We will return to such cases in the pages to come. For the moment, all that is necessary is that you recognize that each requires a *decision*. A plausible case can be made on either side of each of these controversies. You may be predisposed toward one point of view or the other, but if you were actually faced with the decision, could you totally disregard the opposing point of view? Of course, no matter how carefully you considered your decision, and whatever you at last decided to do, there are those who would remain convinced that you were dead wrong.

what problem are we really trying to solve?

This chapter outlines a basic approach to thinking through political problems and making decisions about them. In the rest of the book, we will develop this approach, showing how it applies to the wide range of problems one is apt to encounter in political life.

What we need now is a point of departure. Where do you begin the process of political analysis? How can you cut into a complex and contested issue? Hearing the various arguments put forward in a heated debate, it is easy to become confused and disoriented. One can easily end up in the position of Warren Harding who once lamented, "I listen to one side and they seem to be right and then . . . I talk to the other side and they seem just as right, and there I am back where I started. . . ."[2]

In trying to make up your mind about an issue, one of the first things needed is a little room for independent thought, and one way of getting some initial leverage is to ask the question, What problem are we really trying to solve?

Carefully defining the problem to be solved, delimiting it, separating it out from irrelevancies and side issues, is one of the most important steps in political analysis. We will return to this question throughout the book. As Daniel Patrick Moynihan says, "The crucial stage in solving a problem in government is that point where one defines what kind of a problem it is."[3] The wrong statement of a problem can lead to unnecessary antagonism and conflict and programs that end in frustration. The right problem statement may generate consensus and workable policies.

Political problems are slippery. They can be formulated in any number of different ways. The seemingly obvious problem may not be obvious at all. In the case above, the apparent problem was whether the city council should buy an available piece of land to expand the park system. Quickly, however, this problem changed into another

---

[2] *Quoted in Theodore C. Sorenson,* Decision-Making in the White House *(New York: Columbia University Press, 1963), p. 42.*

[3] *Daniel Patrick Moynihan,* Coping: Essays on the Practice of Government *(New York: Random House, 1973), p. 12.*

one—whether the city should provide equal access to recreational space for all its citizens. These are very different political problems and the one we accept as the right one to work on will affect every subsequent step we take in working toward a concrete plan of action.

Consider the problem of water pollution. What problem are we actually trying to solve? At first, it would seem obvious that our goal is to clean up the water. But is our goal really "clean" water? Completely unpolluted water, after all, is nothing other than H_2O. All natural water contains some contaminants. How clean we want the water to be depends on what we want to use it for. One level of pollution is satisfactory for a ship canal, another for an irrigation ditch, another for a lake used for swimming, still another for drinking water. Sometimes it makes more sense to eliminate pollution at its source and other times it is better to clean it up after it has occurred, as when chlorine is added to a city's water system.[4]

Economics has a lot to do with the problem. It is relatively inexpensive to remove the major contaminants from a river, but the cost increases rapidly when higher levels of water purity are desired. For the discharges of beet sugar plants, for example, it costs about $1 per pound of biochemical oxygen demand to eliminate the first 30 percent of pollution, but when 95 percent of contamination has been eliminated, the cost rises to $60 per pound to clean up the rest. For the United States as a whole, it would cost about $60 billion to clean up 87 percent of all effluents, $58 billion more to clean up an additional 10 percent, and a further $200 billion to take care of the last 3 percent.[5]

Sometimes an overly rigid problem definition may make us blind to alternative, possibly better, ways of solving the problem. Planners may take as their problem statement "providing low-cost housing for low income families." They begin to consider alternative architectural styles, construction techniques, land use patterns, all with an eye to achieving the greatest economies. However, under present conditions, even the most basic housing is apt to be quite costly, and no matter how much ingenuity is applied to design and construction, low-cost housing is apt to be monotonous, cheap in appearance, and of poor quality. However, if the planner were to formulate the problem as one of "upgrading and expanding the total stock of housing," other alternative solutions to the problem of making better housing available to the poor begin to become apparent. It might be possible to encourage the construction of better, newer houses for middle- and upper-income groups. Lower-income families might then be able to take over

---

[4] *Larry E. Ruff, "The Economic Common Sense of Pollution,"* The Public Interest 19 *(Spring 1970), pp. 69–85.*

[5] *Cited in Peter Passell and Leonard Ross,* The Retreat from Riches: Affluence and Its Enemies *(New York: Viking Press, 1973), p. 43.*

the used but still substantial and desirable dwellings vacated by the more affluent. Again, whether this would be a better solution or not would require a detailed analysis. But at the beginning of the process of thinking through a political issue, we do not want to overlook possibilities, and this implies that we have to be flexible in our problem statement; we must look at the issue from various angles and perspectives.[6]

The way problems are defined in everyday political discussion is often not very helpful. We talk about "the problem of inflation." Inflation, however, simply means that prices are rising, which is a condition and not a problem. Rising prices may be a problem because they diminish the value of savings, because they make investment decisions unpredictable, or because they redistribute income in socially undesirable ways. These are possible consequences or effects of inflation, and they define the actual public problems to be solved. Controlling inflation, then, may be a means of resolving these other problems, rather than the end in itself.

Simply stating an objective does not define a problem. "Full employment" is not a problem but an aspiration. The real problem is how to achieve full employment without causing inflation, endangering the nation's trade abroad, creating further environmental deterioration, and so on. Most public policies have multiple objectives. The problem is to decide how much of one objective we want to achieve in relation to others.

We begin to talk about "trade-offs" among various policy objectives. Inflation and the level of employment are closely related. Would we be willing to pay the price of an inflation rate of 20 or 30 percent to assure that everyone who wanted a job had one? Or would we be satisfied with an unemployment rate of 4 or 6 percent if that could be achieved with a rate of inflation of 6 to 9 percent? How much would we be willing to lower environmental quality standards in order to lower costs to industry, stimulate the economy, and achieve a higher level of employment?

Multiple objectives can also be stated as constraints in defining a problem. Constraints are conditions that are attached to the primary policy goal. We want to control water pollution *without* destroying the economic viability of industries that use the lakes and rivers, or we want to have an adequate program of public welfare *without* destroying the incentive to work and *without* creating a complex system of bureaucratic regulation that interferes in the daily affairs of welfare recipients.

Every public action sets in motion a chain of direct and indirect

---

[6] *For a further discussion of this example, see Henry J. Aaron,* Shelter and Subsidies: Who Benefits from Federal Housing Policies? *(Washington: The Brookings Institution, 1972).*

10

*public policy: choice
on behalf of other
people*

effects. A thorough political analysis will try to anticipate as many of the consequences of a policy as possible, not only the direct effects but also second-level and third-level indirect effects. One begins to look at society as a complex and integrated system in which a change at any point will have some impact on all parts of the system. Of course, it is easy to become traumatized by the knowledge that "everything is related to everything else" and there is a point beyond which attempting to calculate all the consequences of a policy is simply futile. One of the indirect consequences of universal use of the automobile, as Daniel Patrick Moynihan has pointed out, is that citizens become accustomed to being arrested by armed police as a routine matter, and that may be very bad for the health of democracy. However, this is probably not a factor that will weigh very heavily in decisions about the proper mix of mass transit and automobiles in making transportation policy.

In any event, most political judgments are a matter of weighing the relative advantages and disadvantages of a proposed course of action. We consider as many important consequences as possible and try to find the *optimum* policy, that which has the greatest overall advantages and the fewest adverse effects.

Incrementalism

It is worth noting that it is often not possible to make a thorough analysis of a problem prior to taking action. Policymakers frequently have neither the time nor the capacity to "consider everything." Therefore, they evaluate only the most important consequences and consider a very limited range of alternatives, usually policies that differ only marginally from established programs. Instead of trying to define the problem to be solved precisely, and outlining and comparing a comprehensive set of alternative solutions, they look for a course of action that "will do," under the circumstances, further modifying the policy as the need arises. To proceed consciously and intentionally in this way is sometimes called "incrementalism" or "the science of muddling through."[7] Policymaking is seen as ongoing and experimental. A public decision is not made once and for all but involves a sequence of choices through time. The limitations of the first policy become the problem to be resolved at a later time.

In this style of decisionmaking, problems need not be defined fully and sharply. Sometimes it is useful to keep overall objectives and problem definitions a little vague. Political antagonists may be able to agree to support a common program for very different reasons. To try

---

[7] *Charles E. Lindblom, "The Science of Muddling Through,"* Public Administration Review 18 *(June 1959), pp. 79–88.*

to win support for a clear and unequivocal definition of a problem may create unnecessary conflict.

Incrementalism may be good advice in some situations, but it is not very helpful in others. "Muddling through" is basically a way of avoiding or postponing difficult choices. But sometimes we have to take a stand, and defend it, often in the face of uncertainty and sharply opposing points of view. The essence of political judgment is still that of making up your mind about controversial public questions. Simply being practical is not always good advice, and common sense is not always sensible. Even the most pragmatic incrementalists must delimit the scope of their problem on some basis and have some reasons for the policy choices that they make.

what standards of judgment should be applied?

We have to make political decisions on some basis. To clarify our thoughts and to weigh opposing arguments in the face of complex issues, we have to adopt some standard of judgment. Personal beliefs and attitudes will inevitably affect our political decisions. We can make judgments on the basis of our instinctive feelings or inherited prejudices, but we want to be able to do better than that. We need to become self-conscious about our basis of choice. We want to be able to choose our principles of evaluation deliberately.

We have to adopt some standard of judgment even to *identify* a problem in the first place. Not everything that happens in a society is a public problem. In order to begin thinking politically at all, we must make a distinction between "problems" and "the way things are." In any community, at any time, there are an unlimited number of things that could be done, or undone, to improve the welfare of the citizens. For a situation to be recognized as a problem, we have to show why the *status quo* should no longer be considered acceptable.

In a society that believes that "the poor are always with us"—or that they get precisely what they deserve—poverty would not be a political issue. Poverty becomes a problem when we feel that the poor have been unjustly treated or that society should be committed to greater equality among its citizens. Gunnar Myrdal, the Swedish economist, writing in 1944, described racism as "an American dilemma." It would not have been a problem in a nation that simply accepted the inferiority of a minority race. Many societies have had a permanent underclass and regarded the system as both natural and justifiable. But the American political ideology endorsed the principle of equality and the dignity and worth of each individual. There was a basic inconsistency between the belief in black inferiority and the basic norms of the political system. Racism was, for this society, an inevitable political problem.[8]

What standard of judgment we apply frequently makes a great deal of difference in the way we identify problems. For example, one could oppose further freeway construction for any of the following reasons.

1. That quiet residential neighborhoods would be disturbed and property values diminished.
2. That government should encourage mass transit and discourage the use of automobiles for environmental and energy conservation reasons.
3. That the existing metropolitan area is large enough and that further growth should be discouraged.
4. That the money spent for highways should be used instead for welfare, housing, or some other public purpose.
5. That the proposed construction would primarily benefit wealthy commuters rather than low-income groups in the inner city.
6. That it would be possible to cut taxes if proposed highways were not built.

Each of these arguments is based on a different principle of evaluation and each presents a somewhat different problem for decisionmaking. The first asks us to judge between the interests of residents and travelers. The second and third raise issues of "public interests" that may be in conflict with the desire for improved highways. The fourth and fifth address the question of the equitable distribution of public services, and the sixth raises the issue of whether it is preferable to provide expanded government services or leave more income in the hands of individuals to spend as they see fit.

standards and decision making

Now let us move from the question of identifying problems to that of decision making itself. Facing an acknowledged problem, we also have to have a basis for deciding where to take our stand.

There are many different kinds of standards that we can adopt in making decisions. We can decide on the basis of *political* criteria. We decide to adopt the policy that will best ensure our chances for reelection, that will increase our power and influence, or that has the best chance of winning a majority vote in the legislature. *Economic* criteria include efficiency, economy, or profitability. Considerations of *group or organizational interests* may be decisive. We make judgments on the

---

[8] *Gunnar Myrdal*, An American Dilemma *(New York: Harper and Row, 1944).*

basis of what will best advance the cause of a class, sector of society, industry, or association. Many standards of judgment reflect *fundamental political principles*. We decide on the basis of equal treatment or personal rights. There are also basic *procedural principles*. We agree to adopt the policy that wins the support of the majority, that is made by someone in a position of legitimate authority, or that is based on "due process of law."[9]

justifying decisions

Politics is a process of argument. We do not just make decisions; we have to give reasons for them. The judge writes an opinion justifying his or her verdict. The president explains a policy to the board of directors. The lobbyist tries to show that what will benefit his or her interest will also benefit the public.

Obviously, there are good and not-so-good reasons for political action. The president who decides to bomb a foreign country simply "because he felt like it" is unlikely to win much support. Judges cannot say that they decided for the plaintiff because the defense attorney was a loudmouthed bore. If representatives of an industry ask for a government subsidy "in order to make us richer," we may be somewhat hesitant to grant it to them.

Now it is true that there is a certain refreshing candor about reasons such as these. We often rightly suspect that statements of principles are afterthoughts, designed to rationalize a decision that was made on other grounds. Of course, a good political analyst will look behind formal political arguments. What are they getting out of this? is a question that should always be asked. However, oddly enough, even a shrewd assessment of the personal motives of others is not much help in making public decisions. The industry may want a subsidy in order to make more money, but that does not answer the question of whether such a subsidy should be granted. We can simply assume that some private interest lies behind every case for public action. The important question is whether individuals have a *right* to what they are after, or whether it would be good public policy to give it to them.

A distinction has to be made between private interests and public problems. Politicians may be fundamentally interested in getting reelected, but that is their problem; it is not a public issue. Or the problem facing our glorious leader is that an angry mob is beginning to gather at the gates of the palace. Once again, that is his* personal

---

* *Throughout the book, I will occasionally use the impersonal pronouns "he", "him" and "his" simply for reasons of style and accepted English usage. If any reader is in danger of assuming that only men can appropriately participate in politics I suggest that the pronoun be mentally translated "he or she", "him or her" each time that it occurs.*

[9] *This is similar to the classification of standards of judgment in James E. Anderson,* Public Policy-Making *(New York: Praeger, 1975), pp. 15–18.*

14

*public policy: choice
on behalf of other
people*

problem. The public issue is whether they have a *right* to assemble, or whether government is *entitled* to disburse them with force, and whether their grievances are *justified* or not.

It is not enough for a group that thinks its taxes are too high simply to demand that they be changed. It has to show *why* its burden of taxation is unfair, and to do that, it has to appeal to some standard of evaluation that is recognized as appropriate in the society for judging the propriety or impropriety of tax assessments.

Political argument is not merely a process of persuasion. People can be induced to change their minds in all kinds of ways, including emotional appeals, force, and intimidation. The problem of political judgment is to find good reasons for public action. When we face a difficult decision, we evaluate rival arguments, looking for relevant grounds on which to base a choice. When we come to a conclusion and have taken a position on an issue, we have to be able to defend it against legitimate criticism. As Brian Barry says, "if you *have* reasons, you must be able to *give* reasons."[10]

Not only do we have to distinguish between private interests and public problems but also between private reasons and public reasons for political action. Just because you like something is no reason for imposing it on everybody. This seems to be one of the most frequent errors in political argument. For example, I recently served on a committee to reconsider the content of the introductory political science course in my university. One student member argued for a certain approach to the course, because she had "gotten a lot out of it." But this argument failed to impress anybody. One person's satisfaction is not sufficient reason to create a requirement. Questions of whether a certain course provides a prerequisite foundation for more advanced courses or skills needed by professionals in a field may not be decisive, but they do address the *public* issue.

One test of any standard of judgment is whether it can be applied consistently. The idea of "positive discrimination" means that anyone who has suffered prejudice or deprivation for some reason that they had no control over—race, sex, and the like—ought to be treated more than equally in public policy until they can catch up with the norm. But does this mean that anybody who can claim some social disadvantage is entitled to special treatment? Left-handed people, tall people, and fat people all have special problems in our society. Does the principle mean that anyone who can claim some kind of disadvantage is entitled to special treatment? If not, on what grounds do we create "affirmative action" for women but not for fat people? When is prejudice or depri-

---

[10] *Brian Barry,* Political Argument *(New York: Humanities Press, 1965), p. 2. This book is excellent on the entire question of political evaluation.*

vation *relevant* for making distinctions between categories of people in public policy and when is it not?

It is for all these reasons that basic political principles are important in public decision making. Concepts like rights, freedom, equality, justice, and democracy are commonly used in defining public problems and evaluating and justifying policy choices. For the moment, such words may seem no more than lofty abstractions. Part of the purpose of this book is to turn them into sharp-edged tools for political analysis. The reason for emphasizing basic principles is not to make politics more high-minded but simply that practical political judgment cannot do without them.

To summarize then, we use standards of evaluation and political argument in decision making for the following purposes.

1. *To define our own position.* Amidst the bombardment of rival appeals, demands, and attempts to persuade, we have to decide what counts as a good reason for public action and what does not. We have to evaluate the claims that others make in the political process. We have to answer the question of *why* we decide as we do.
2. *To make claims and proposals for public action.* It is not enough to simply demand action from government. We have to make a case in support of our interests and ideas, showing why it would be good public policy to adopt them. The advocate in politics has to think not only for himself and the group he represents but also for the policymakers and the community as a whole.
3. *To justify decisions we have made.* Public decisions have to be defended. Authority that is unexplained is arbitrary. People may accept the decisions of public officials out of respect for authority or fear of coercion, but in the long run, support for government depends on the belief that the decisions of those in authority are reasonable, fair, and in the best interests of the community.

who bears the burden of proof?

In clarifying your thoughts about a controversial political argument, it is frequently useful to ask the question, Who bears the burden of proof?

It is impossible to be completely neutral and objective in making political decisions. We cannot simply weigh all sides of the argument. We have to weigh them against something. Political judgment presupposes some standpoint.

16

*public policy: choice
on behalf of other
people*

A scientific experiment begins with a hypothesis, a theory about how things are expected to work out. The experiment either confirms or rejects the hypothesis. Political arguments often begin from a presumption, a rule that normally decides the case. Those who choose to think otherwise must give reasons. They bear the burden of proof.

For example, a jury in a criminal case is not expected to make a perfectly neutral, impartial decision. Instead, it is expected to have an initial bias in favor of the defendant, to start from the presumption of innocence. The defendant does not have to prove anything. It is the prosecution that has to make an argument—to prove guilt "beyond a reasonable doubt."

A person who believes that "that government is best which governs least" does not have to be persuaded that cutting the public budget or reducing the size of the bureaucracy is a good thing. Rather, he has to be given reasons for new public programs that are strong enough to override his initial presumption. The person who believes strongly in equality does not have to be shown why it is desirable to provide the same public services to everyone. Rather, he has to be given reasons for making distinctions between people in different categories and situations.

To consciously think through the question of burden of proof is often a useful point of departure for political decision because it makes you aware of preconceptions, of implicit biases and assumptions. It makes it possible to decide deliberately among alternative standards of judgment. But what is more important is that the question opens the possibility of political argument. There might be good reasons to do otherwise. You might be persuaded to accept a different perspective on the problem. To act "purely on principle" can be arbitrary and self-righteous. But to have a basic standpoint, which is applied flexibly and reasonably depending on the circumstances, recognizing the potential validity of opposing views, is pretty much what good political judgment is all about.

Many political arguments, often the most important ones, concern where the burden of proof should be located in the first place. In America, there has been a strong presumption historically in favor of the rights of private property. People should be free to do as they please with their property unless there are compelling reasons to restrict or regulate this right. Socialists feel that the presumption should be reversed, that for private property to be legitimate, it must be shown to be socially useful. There usually is a limited right of private property in socialist states, and there frequently are areas where small private enterprise is free to operate; but these are exceptions and not the rule, and such exceptions generally reflect a conscious policy decision, based on grounds of social utility.

Similarly, there has long been an implicit presumption in American public policy that natural resources should be put to economic use as quickly and efficiently as possible. This has been our basic approach to the settlement of the public lands, the exploitation of minerals and water resources. Those who advocated conservation and the preservation of environmental values had to show that there might be public interests to be weighed against economic development. Today, there are many who believe that the burden of proof should be the other way around, that those who exploit natural resources should be called upon to demonstrate that their activities are compatible with protection of the environment.

We face the most perplexing problems of political judgment when the basic decision-rules of society are themselves the subject of controversy. In most normal, routine decisions, however, the burden of proof is pretty clear. For example, the most basic presumption in political argument is that rules ought to be followed. It is the person who breaks the law or deviates from recognized regulations who has to give an explanation. Nevertheless, understanding rules as presumptions is of great importance. Rules state what is normally to be done, but there may be good reasons for not following them in particular circumstances. Arbitrary and excessively rigid enforcement of rules is a perversion of political judgment as is blind obedience to orders. In every organization, there must be some latitude for discretion, for interpreting rules to fit particular circumstances. But the official who exercises discretion must be able to justify the action. As Carl Friedrich says

It will be generally assumed that a person vested with the power to exercise discretion will be able to give reasons for what he has done. This aspect is particularly evident where a superior gives a subordinate discretion. He will ordinarily assume that the subordinate will use good sense, experience, stick to established precedent and so on. But he will also expect the subordinate to "explain," if for any reason he finds that the decision made ought to be subjected to review. The superior will rarely be satisfied with an explanation such as "I just felt that way" or "my instinct told me this was the right man," let alone an explanation which would say "I liked his face" or "she had such a lovely voice."[11]

ideology and decision making

Ideologies are relatively coherent systems of beliefs, values, and standards of political evaluation. Ideologies can provide the individual with broad guidelines that can be applied to all kinds of political

[11] *Carl J. Friedrich, "Authority, Reason and Discretion" in Carl J. Friedrich, ed.* Authority *(Cambridge: Harvard University Press, 1958), p. 42.*

18

*public policy: choice
on behalf of other
people*

decision-making situations. In a sense, ideologies are political decisions made at the wholesale rather than the retail level. The truly committed Marxist sees all problems as manifestations of class conflict. The orthodox liberal may interpret every public issue from the viewpoint of the realization of individual rights or freedom. The consistent conservative takes as his or her primary value the preservation of established customs and traditions.

Ideological thinking has both advantages and disadvantages in political decision making. It does provide a consistent frame of reference for defining problems, making evaluations, and justifying decisions. On the other hand, ideology may lead to excessive rigidity or narrowness in political thinking. We may fail to see alternative perspectives on problems or the validity of appraising a political situation from some other point of view.

People vary greatly in the way they use ideology in decision making. Some profess that they endorse no ideology but make judgments on a practical, case-to-case basis. Many of us would prefer not to associate ourselves with a particular doctrine, and we are quite truthful in saying that we can see good points in a variety of opposing theories. However, there is some pattern in everyone's beliefs, and often we are simply unaware of where our basic political attitudes come from. John Maynard Keynes once wrote

> The ideas of economists and political philosophers . . . are more powerful than is commonly understood. Indeed the world is ruled by little else. Practical men, who believe themselves to be quite exempt from any intellectual influences are usually the slaves of some defunct economist. [12]

Other people may endorse an ideology but be relatively open and pragmatic about its application. And, of course, there is often a difference between the abstract principles that people avow and the way they make decisions in practice.

Formal political ideologies, like Marxism, liberalism, and conservatism, are not the only structured systems of political evaluation. A profession can provide a framework of standards for interpreting public affairs that is as comprehensive as any political ideology and often just as rigid and doctrinaire.

Doctors, lawyers, social workers, military officers, policemen, forest rangers, and other professionals all develop, through specialized training, certain habits of thought and sets of principles for making judgments. Like ideologies, professional standards provide a frame of reference for decision making, but they also may create blind

[12] *John Maynard Keynes,* The General Theory of Employment, Interest and Money *(New York: Harcourt, Brace and World, 1936), p. 384.*

spots. Lawyers tend to think in terms of legal rights and obligations. Economists focus on the criteria of economy and efficiency in making policy evaluations. Both of these are appropriate standards for public choice, but they are not the only standards. The lawyer who sees all decisions as questions of legal rights or the economist who sees all decisions as questions of efficiency is acting much like the Marxist who sees all problems in terms of class conflict. Engineers may go about thinking through political problems in the same way that they go about building a bridge. The mechanical approach to problems may leave them insensitive to the feelings of those they are working with or make them less able to see that the best solutions to political problems are frequently compromises and accommodations rather than logical, systematic designs.

Ideological labels are apt to be confusing. There is no agreement among scholars on how ideologies should be classified, and the names of ideologies mean different things in different parts of the world. For example, in America, "conservatism" means what most Europeans would call "liberalism." Since America had no medieval tradition, no monarchy, aristocracy, or established church, essentially what was to be conserved was the nineteenth-century tradition of individual freedom, self-reliance, and minimal government. In the same way, Americans use the term "liberal" to identify a position that most Europeans would describe as social democracy or perhaps socialism. Despite such confusions, it is possible to give a rough idea of the basic values of the most familiar American ideologies.

It is useful to see ideologies as a way of defining the burden of proof. Conservatives will endorse some proposals for change if they feel there is a strong case for them. Likewise, liberals value many established institutions and practices. John F. Kennedy, whose basic values were liberal, was fond of Chesterton's saying, "Don't ever take a fence down until you know the reason why it was put up."[13] To see ideology as establishing presumption rather than arbitrary dogma helps make the actual use of ideology in decision making more comprehensible.

American conservatism or "classic liberalism" places high value on individual freedom. Unless compelling reasons can be given for public action, individuals should be left to do as they please. "The burden of proof for intervention rests always with the state."[14]

In classic liberalism, political authority *itself* needs to be justified. Grounds have to be given for the free and autonomous individual to

---

[13] *Arthur F. Schlesinger,* A Thousand Days: John F. Kennedy in the White House *(New York: Fawcett World Library, 1965), p. 105.*

[14] *Franz L. Neuman, "The Concept of Political Freedom,"* Columbia Law Review 53 *(November 1953), p. 904.*

20

*public policy: choice
on behalf of other
people*

consent to the power of government. The problem of political obligation is central to liberal theory. Why should I obey the commands of government? is a question that requires a rational answer. Government is envisioned as arising out of a contract between the people to form a state. Hence, government must demonstrate that its actions are consistent with that contract, that they are constitutional and lawful.

Government exists to protect the rights of individuals. The classic good reason for interfering with one person's liberty is to protect the freedom of another. Law is justifiable when it protects an individual against injury from another, but "victimless crimes" (such as public drunkenness or requiring that seatbelts be worn in automobiles) are often questioned. The American conservative's credo is: when in doubt, leave people alone to work out their own solutions to problems.

The American conservative is a strong believer in the free enterprise system. The individual choices of consumers and producers in the marketplace is a better way of making economic decisions than state intervention and planning. Nonetheless, the conservative recognizes that there are exceptions to the rule. There may be compelling reasons for government to intervene in the economy, to preserve competition against monopoly, for example. Even Adam Smith, the intellectual father of capitalism, recognized that government economic activity is legitimate when a persuasive case can be made that private enterprise is unwilling or unable to do the job.

Classic liberalism has very much influenced American political ideas. Strong cultural and legal precedents exist in favor of the civil liberties of the individual, the rights of private property, and noninterference in the economy. The problem in American political argument has normally been to find reasons sufficient to justify public action.

American liberalism is the ideology that is normally associated with the activist wing of the Democratic party, with figures like George McGovern, Hubert Humphrey, Morris Udall or the Kennedys. Whereas the conservative is predisposed in favor of established institutions and practices, that things should remain as they are unless there are overriding reasons for social experimentation, the reform liberal sees change as desirable. The way the reform liberal puts the question of burden of proof was perhaps best stated by Robert Kennedy: "Others ask why; I ask, why not?" The *status quo* need not be accepted as the norm. It must be justified. The burden of proof is on those who are skeptical of change.

Within the common liberal tradition that unites both American conservatives and reform liberals, there is a tension between the values of liberty and equality. All liberals endorse both, but classic liberals tend to emphasize the former and reform liberals the latter.

For the activist liberal, inequalities—of rights, opportunities, wealth, income, advantage—have to be justified. The presumption is equal treatment. The disadvantages of racial and ethnic minorities, of women and other special groups, are *prima facie* problems calling for public response. Disparities of political power and influence should be rectified—the liberal is likely to take the principle of "one person, one vote" quite seriously. Increasingly, reform liberals are concerned about disparities of wealth and income in America—the fact that the top 10 percent of the population receive 29 percent of the income, while the bottom 10 percent receive only 1 percent. It is not that reform liberals necessarily want absolute equality of income (though a few do think this way), but rather that they suspect that many such disparities cannot be justified, that they do not result from differences of skill, initiative or hard work, but from differences in initial advantage or simple luck. In short, they assume that there can be no good reasons for the existing pattern of income distribution and that the burden of proof belongs to the one who would defend manifest instances of inequality or discrimination.

Again, all liberals have common values. The classic liberals are not impervious to arguments for equal rights and equal treatment. However, at the margin, they insist that the case for the desirability of government action to rectify injustices must be proved, while the reform liberal feels that the defender of the *status quo* bears the burden of proof. Similarly, the reform liberal acknowledges the validity of the principle that government action must be shown to be constitutional and lawful, and that basic individual rights cannot be weakened except for exceptionally good cause.

Radicalism is a word that embraces a variety of ideological positions. There are many forms of radical thought in America, including Marxism, the "New Left" of the 1960s, and some forms of contemporary populism. Although there are vast differences between them, one persistent theme has been important in American public debate in recent years. The "system" is repressive and exploitative. The basic institutions of the political and economic order, particularly big government and big corporations, do not serve to further individual purposes. Rather, they exploit and dominate individuals, making them part of a brutal and impersonal machine, dedicated to its own purposes, its own power, and its own indefinite expansion. The individual is powerless in the face of gigantic concentrations of power and wealth. Technology and the complex organization are not instruments of human purposes; instead, people are "used" by such institutions—human beings are shaped to fit the needs of technology and bureaucracy.

From this point of view, the burden of proof is on the establishment to justify its existence—to give convincing reasons that it should not be regarded as corrupt, exploitative, and inhumane. Radicalism assumes that the system is controlled by an unresponsive, interlocking elite of top power holders, themselves the victims of a system that forces them to pursue the goals of ever greater growth and ever

22

*public policy: choice
on behalf of other
people*

expanding power. Reform cannot come from within the system. The framework of liberalism is itself part of the repressive apparatus. What is required is a complete restructuring of the social order.

summary

To a certain extent, the groundwork for political decision making can be prepared in advance. We can become self-conscious about our biases and preconceptions and about the nature of our political ideology. We can learn to distinguish between private and public reasons for political action.

The initial purpose of such questions as

What problem are we actually trying to solve?
What standards of judgment should be applied?
How can I justify my position?
Who bears the burden of proof?

is simply to establish a standpoint for evaluating a political controversy. We need not sustain our first approximate answers to these questions to the bitter end. In the course of time, we may revise our initial estimate of the situation. Like scientific hypotheses, our first standpoint for political evaluation may be corrected and improved, perhaps reversed, in the light of evidence and argument.

However, we will continue to use these questions as we probe deeper into the problems of political decision making. This chapter has introduced a basic approach to thinking through complex political issues. Now we must begin to explore the various forms that political problems and political arguments can take. At the end, we should have a fairly comprehensive view of what the art of making considered political decisions is all about.

for further reading

Anderson, James E., *Public Policy-Making* (New York: Praeger, 1975). This is an excellent introduction to the entire decision making process. It deals with the study of public policy, with the identification of problems, policy formulation and adoption, and the assessment of policy impact.

Barry, Brian, *Political Argument* (New York: Humanities Press, 1965). A fine example of tough-minded reasoning about the use of basic principles of evaluation and the justification of decisions.

Although it is well-written, it will be hard going for most beginners.

Benn, S. I., and R. S. Peters, *Principles of Political Thought* (New York: The Free Press, 1958). A good discussion of basic principles and their application to decision making. It is a work in political philosophy, but its practical importance is apparent. Easier than Barry and somewhat more comprehensive.

Leys, Wayne A. R., *Ethics for Policy-Decisions* (Englewood Cliffs, N.J.: Prentice-Hall, 1952). This book on applied ethics makes an excellent follow-up to this chapter. It deals with major systems of ethical thought, from utilitarianism to Marxism, and applies them to case studies. Although the case materials are dated, this is not a major liability for the reader.

Mitchell, William, and Joyce Mitchell, *Political Analysis and Public Policy* (Chicago: Rand McNally, 1969). An introductory text that approaches political decision making from the viewpoint of political economy. More formal and abstract than the present book, but in many ways similar and complementary.

Rivlin, Alice N., *Systematic Thinking for Social Action* (Washington: The Brookings Institution, 1971). Very good on the subject of problem identification and policy analysis in general. The author participated in the planning of the War on Poverty, and her examples are drawn from this experience.

Vickers, Sir Geoffrey, *The Art of Judgment* (New York: Basic Books, 1965). The best comprehensive treatment I know on public decision making, especially on the question of problem definition. The author is British, and the case studies will be unfamiliar to most Americans, but this does not detract from the overall theory and approach.

chapter
two
role and
responsibility

When faced with a political decision, it is important to ask the question, What am I expected to do about this problem? *To whom* and *for what* am I responsible? The answer to this question is seldom obvious.

Responsibility is a standard of judgment that has to be applied in making political decisions. Usually we are called upon to make decisions because we have been elected or appointed to a leadership role. Others expect us to make decisions in their behalf. We are in some sense responsible to them for our choices and actions. The question is what this responsibility means in practice.

In this chapter, we discuss responsibility in relation to two closely associated ideas: community and authority.

The problem of community is that of deciding whose interests we will take into account when we make public choices. We may have been elected to represent a small group within a larger organization. Are we then responsible only for advancing the interests of this group or for the impact of our decisions on the community as a whole? This is the question of responsibility *to whom?*

Authority means that we are empowered to make some kinds of decisions but not others. Within the limits of our authority, others agree to be bound by the commitments we make for them. What then are we *entitled* to do about a public problem? This is the problem of responsibility *for what?*

What we decide to do about a public problem depends in part on how we understand the role we are playing in the political process. There is an old saying in politics that "where you stand depends on where you sit." Those who speak for an aggrieved minority may feel that their responsibility is to fight for the rights of the disadvantaged. The chairman of the committee they are working with may be trying to contrive a compromise that will be generally acceptable. The chairman thinks that the militant activist is rash, arrogant, and excessively demanding. The militant thinks that the chairman is hypocritical, unprincipled, and trying to duck the issue. But were their positions reversed, each might act exactly like the other.

Political decision making takes place in a context of institutions, roles, and relationships. The standards of choice and judgment that we will apply to a certain extent come with the job. Judges and attorneys are supposed to make decisions according to the rules of law. Managers in companies are expected to make decisions according to stipulated rules and procedures. Every political role has its own code of decision making, its own canons of performance.

However, there is more to politics than simply playing a role. The important question is how the individual decides to act out the part he or she is called upon to play in the political process. Assessing one's responsibility in political activity is itself a problem of decision making. It is a matter that often calls for deliberate choice and judgment.

Should the labor leader work to get the best wages and benefits possible for the members of his union, using all the powers and resources at his disposal to achieve this end? Or should one who occupies this role consider the impact of a proposal on the company, on consumers, on the health of the nation's economy? To whom and for what is this person responsible?

In a company, the labor relations manager and the treasurer may disagree sharply over a plan to close down a plant. The job of one is to prevent trouble with the unions and that of the other is to balance the books. Each is *expected* to evaluate the problem from a different point of view, applying different standards of judgment.

But is the treasurer of the firm only responsible for the profit and loss statement? Or should the treasurer also be concerned about the future of employees if a plant is closed down? It becomes apparent that the problem of role and responsibility is part of the whole question of identifying and defining public problems that we discussed in the last chapter. The answer we give to the problem of responsibility in part determines our response to the question, What problem are we actually trying to solve? Perhaps the problem the treasurer should be addressing is not simply how to make the best profit, but how to make

26

*public policy: choice
of behalf of other
people*

a profit *without* causing unnecessary hardship for the firm's employees.

In answering the question of responsibility, we cannot rely entirely on what other people think we are supposed to do. "Responsibility" is not merely "responsiveness." Opinions about the responsibilities of leaders are often divided. Most political roles have multiple and ambiguous expectations attached to them. Some expect the chairman of a committee to be an active and forceful leader. Others think the chairman should be relatively passive, simply presiding over meetings. You cannot please everybody, and in politics it is seldom worthwhile even to try. Responsibility is appraised from different points of view. To the members of a union, the labor leader who compromises too readily with management is considered "irresponsible." But business executives and public officials also talk about "responsible union leadership," and by this they mean a willingness to be moderate in making demands, taking into account the problems of the industry and the economy as well as the wishes of their members.

In defining responsibility, we cannot take our cues simply from the attitudes of the people around us or, for that matter, from the statement of duties that goes with the office. Adolph Eichmann thought he was only doing his job when he presided over Hitler's "final solution" to the Jewish question. President Nixon's principal advisers thought that their primary duty was loyalty to the president, and on that basis they commissioned and later concealed the Watergate break-in and other crimes.

There are no easy answers to the problem of defining responsibility. Nonetheless, it is a question that has to be considered carefully whenever we accept a political office or assume a political role. Like ideology, our conception of responsibility is a "background choice," a fundamental, basic judgment that will influence all the decisions we subsequently make. The conception of responsibility we bring to a political role is an important part of "leadership style," the distinctive, personal mark that characterizes a political performance.

responsibility and
the representative

To see the dilemmas of responsibility that have to be faced in normal, everyday political activity, let us focus on one political role, that of the representative. Serving as a representative is a very common political role. It includes legislators, members of councils and committees, leaders of interest groups and associations, in fact anyone who is selected to speak for others in the policymaking process. Most of the readers of this book will eventually represent somebody, somewhere. But what you are expected to do when you serve as a representative is often far from clear.

Let us assume that you have been elected to a student-faculty committee on curriculum reform. What are you expected to do as a member of this committee when a major policy question arises? Should you put forward your own ideas and make up your mind on the basis of the facts and evidence and what seem to you to be the relevant standards of evaluation that should be applied to the case? Or should you take the matter back to your constituents, discuss the pros and cons with them, find out their opinions, and defend the majority position whether or not it corresponds with your own views? What do you answer in such a situation if you are asked whether you are "merely speaking for yourself" or if your views *really* represent student opinion?

How you answer this problem depends on which of two basic standards of responsibility you adopt. On the one hand, it can be argued that the representative simply "stands for" the constituency. We can call this the *delegate* view of the function of the representative. The job is to speak for the views of the electors. Representatives do not speak for themselves; they speak for others.

Those who support the delegate view of representation argue that if government is to be democratic, if it is to rest on "the will of the people," there should be no significant difference between the pattern of opinion in a representative assembly and in the population as a whole. The legislature should be, as far as possible, a mirror of the opinion of the community.

On the other hand, representatives can be seen as *trustees.* They are charged with looking after the interests of their constituents and of the society as a whole. They must use their best judgment in making decisions. They are responsible *for* the welfare of the community not merely responsible *to* the electors. They may vote against the expressed wishes of their constituents if they feel it is in their best interest.[1]

The problem becomes more complicated when we realize that the representative is making policy not merely for his own constituents, but for the entire community. The congressman is elected in a specific district, but makes decisions for the entire nation. In effect, the representative participates in making policy for people who have had no part in electing him.

Should the congressman decide primarily on the basis of what is good for the district or for the nation as a whole? If he or she is a strong advocate of economy in government and trying diligently to cut defense spending, what should be done if the opportunity arises to build a giant military installation in the district, one that will provide a large number of civilian jobs and considerable prosperity to the con-

---

[1] *For a detailed examination of this question, see Hannah F. Pitkin,* The Concept of Representation *(Berkeley: University of California Press, 1967).*

28

*public policy: choice
on behalf of other
people*

stituents? Should he or she vote against appropriations for the facility (assuming he thinks it is not vital to the security of the nation) or is it simply "good politics" to support funding for the installation while trying to cut the defense budget in other areas? Is the primary responsibility of the representative to do the best for constituents, or for a conception of the national interest?

Student representatives face a similar problem. They can see the curriculum committee as something like a bargaining relationship, with students and faculty on opposite sides; the problem is that of extracting the maximum concessions for those they represent, for the students. Or the committee can be envisioned as a legislative body, faculty and students sharing a common responsibility for solving a public problem of the university. Which concept of responsibility the members adopt can have a pronounced impact on the kind of policies the committee generates.

The problem comes up in many contexts. Today, there is a great deal of discussion of the idea of "corporate responsibility." Should the leaders of business enterprise think of their responsibility as primarily that of doing what is best for the stockholders, which normally means making the best profits? Or should they endorse a larger concept of responsibility, balancing shareholder interests against the welfare of their employees, consumers, and the "public interest"?

Opinion on this issue is sharply divided. On the one hand, some feel that the single-minded quest for profitability has led to many of the evils of our economic system—environmental deterioration, the irrational overproduction of unimportant goods that have high profit margins (like cosmetics) while many human needs are neglected.

On the other hand, many raise the question of the right of corporate management to make public decisions. Managers are not elected officials. They have great power, but what gives them the authority to decide what is best for the nation or the communities in which they operate? That is the responsibility of government. It is up to labor unions, not paternalistic management, to look after employee interests. Businessmen should stick to business, and desirable economic policy best emerges from the confrontation of pluralist interests, of bargaining and accommodation between business, labor, and government, each "responsible" for distinctive community interests.

Political science offers no sure guidance on the question of whether the representative should act primarily as a trustee or a delegate. (The debate goes back at least to the seventeenth century.) Some claim that the best public decisions emerge from hard bargaining, compromise and accommodation among strongly partisan spokesmen for rival interests.[2] Others believe that statesmanship re-

---

[2] *For an eloquent defense of this position, see Charles E. Lindblom,* The Intelligence of Democracy *(New York: The Free Press, 1965).*

quires detachment and impartiality, with the "public good" rather than "private interest" being the primary criterion of choice.

responsibility and community: the "we" and the "they"

When we enter into a political decision-making situation, we have in mind a certain group of people to whom we are responsible, whose interests we are trying to advance. Other people will be affected by our actions, but they appear in our mind's eye as forces to be reckoned with, as antagonists, or perhaps we do not take them into account at all. In getting a perspective on a political problem, it is worthwhile to be aware of how we define the "we" and the "they." This can make a great deal of difference in our definition of the problem to be resolved—and our conception of responsibility.

Consider, for example, the difference between the following sentences:

All Americans are entitled to equal rights.
We must do something about the condition of the poor.
(Why? Perhaps so that *they* will not burn down *our* cities or overthrow *our* system of government.)

We reveal some of our most fundamental political attitudes when we use these words in political argument, and for this reason, it is worth being closely attentive to how they are used by other participants in the political debate. For the city council, "they" may be the federal bureaucracy. It becomes apparent that federal programs are not seen as part of a collaborative effort to solve local problems but rather as interference in local affairs. To the faculty, "they" may be the student body or its representatives. It is not then "we," the university as a whole, that forms a community of interests. The militant labor leader does not feel great concern about the interests of management in defining a policy position. "They" are only interested in driving down wages to the lowest possible level, and the leader intends to try to prevent "them" from doing that to "us."

How the basic community, the fundamental human solidarities, is defined by leaders can have important consequences. In the mid- to late-1960s, a sharp cleavage developed in the American civil rights movement. The early leaders of the movement, the National Association for the Advancement of Colored People (NAACP) and the Southern Christian Leadership Conference under Martin Luther King, stressed the identity of black people with other Americans. Their goal was integration for those who had previously been excluded from the mainstream of American society.

For King in particular, racism was a national problem. The relevant community was envisioned as the United States. The relevant

30

*public policy: choice
on behalf of other
people*

"we" was not the black minority but all Americans. Race had been the historic divisive factor in the nation's life. The ideals of the American nation could not be realized so long as there was hatred and hostility between black and white. Racism degraded both the majority and the minority culture. Only when the races could see one another as brothers and fellow citizens could either win true freedom or dignity. To achieve this objective, it was necessary to stimulate the moral sense of the majority, while bringing a sense of dignity and worth to the minority. The indicated strategy was a movement dedicated to non-violent, passive resistance. Only politically organized moral force could create a permanent change in American values and beliefs.[3]

In the mid-1960s, however, after facing disillusionment and violence in the early civil rights marches and demonstrations, many black leaders began to perceive the problem differently. Peaceful protest and civil disobedience were not effective strategies. The white man was not responsive to moral appeals. The black American must now define the "we" as his own people and white Americans as "the others" whose assistance and support was neither expected nor desired.

Blacks had to look after their own interests. The appeal was made to "black pride" and "black power." For Stokely Carmichael, this meant that the movement could not count on alliances or coalitions with sympathetic forces in the white community. Blacks had to establish a power base of their own, one with which the white society would have to reckon.[4]

> Black Power seeks to correct the approach of dependency, to remove that dependency, and to establish a viable psychological, political and social base upon which the black community can function to meet its needs.

Historically, black Americans had been taught to see white culture and values as "good" and their own customs and heritage as something to be despised. Through "black pride," the minority race would begin to find worth in their own characteristics, their own ways and traditions. Afro-American history, literature, music, and art were to be taught in the schools. "Black is beautiful" became a slogan of the time. For the Black Muslim movement, the search for a separate cultural identity had to go further. Christianity and Western civilization were the religion and culture of enslavement. Islam was the true religious and cultural heritage of the Afro-American.

Our conception of community has an important bearing on how

---

[3] *See David L. Lewis,* King: A Critical Biography *(Baltimore: Penguin Books, 1970); and Martin Luther King, Jr.,* Why We Can't Wait *(New York: American Library, 1964).*

[4] *Stokely Carmichael and Charles V. Hamilton,* Black Power *(New York: Random House, 1967), p. 86.*

we define political responsibility. In the United States, poverty is officially defined (as of 1975) as a family of four, living in an urban area, with an income of $5038. Families below that level are generally entitled to welfare benefits. This might seem a totally inadequate standard of living, but in many parts of the world it would be considered relative affluence. The *average* family income in many parts of Africa and Asia is no more than $200 to $400 per year, and poverty means bare subsistence if not starvation. How we conceive of the problem of poverty, and our responsibility in relation to this problem, has much to do with the part of the human race we are thinking about at the time.

Political decision making often involves drawing lines. In solving problems for some community, we define other groups as antagonistic, nonantagonistic, or irrelevant. Human conflict is fundamental to politics, but the terms of conflict need not be taken for granted. Enemies and allies do not just happen. To a large extent, they are intentionally chosen.

It might seem that the more inclusive the definition of the community, the better. Decision makers are responsible for the consequences of their actions. They should try to assess the impact of policy on all affected interests. The aim should be to achieve the "greatest good for the greatest number." Even if we think of politics simply as the pursuit of power, it is better, generally, to have more allies than enemies. But this is not always the case. Sometimes the job is to defend the interests of a particular group that is under attack. Whether we are trying to protect the rights of the few or the many, we often have to decide that we are against *somebody*. We often cannot avoid taking sides. Part of the problem of responsibility is to do this deliberately.

responsibility and authority

Another question that has to be asked as we evaluate our responsibility in a political situation is, What authority do I have? What am I entitled to do about this problem? The treasurer of an organization who decided to take funds set aside for a party and spend them on food parcels for the poor would probably not be applauded for an act of generosity. The treasurer is responsible for the custody of funds but has no authority to determine their use. Interestingly, despite the fact that this decision was one of charity, we would probably call it an immoral act.

The authority of an office may be stated in the constitution or bylaws of an organization. Or it may simply be a matter of custom and tradition. Authority states both the right of an individual to make decisions on behalf of others and the limits of that right.

There is an important distinction between power and authority. Power can be based on simple coercion. The despot who terrorizes a population into submission is exercising power but not authority.

32

*public policy: choice
on behalf of other
people*

Authority means that a people has entrusted specific individuals with making decisions for the group and has committed itself to be bound by those decisions.

Authority sometimes attaches to an individual. Spontaneously, a group acknowledges someone as their leader and willingly accepts his or her guidance in common projects. It is equally likely that authority is vested in a role and not a specific person. Authority goes with the office. In effect, we agree to treat *anyone* who occupies that role as though he or she had the attributes of natural leadership. Ernest K. Gann commented on the authority relationship that exists between captain and first officer in the cockpit of an airliner:

> The rules are fixed and catholic. I am, in *all* eventualities, supposed to know more than he does, a theory we both secretly recognize as preposterous.[5]

Sometimes, one's authority to act in a political situation is clear and compelling. But often, authority becomes a problem of choice and judgment. How complex the problem of what you are entitled to do can become is illustrated in the following case study.

the d.a.'s dilemma

Put yourself in the position of a young, liberal activist who has just been elected prosecuting attorney in a university community. Among your beliefs is a strong commitment to the idea that possession of small quantities of marijuana should not be a crime. (Let us assume that this is happening in a jurisdiction where marijuana possession has not yet been decriminalized.) Marijuana, you believe, is no more dangerous than such widely used drugs as alcohol, tobacco, and tranquilizers. Furthermore, you feel that marijuana use is a "victimless crime" that affects no one but the user. Many of your followers support you on this issue. The question is, what are you entitled to do about it in this official capacity?

State's attorneys normally have considerable latitude in bringing charges and prosecuting criminal cases. They can be vigorous in the enforcement of some laws and lax with regard to others. They can bear down heavily on repeated violations and be lenient with first offenders. Prosecuting attorneys can undertake investigations of their own into criminal activities. They do not have to wait for a citizen to bring charges. Often, they are elected officials and normally, they work with minimal supervision from higher authority. But the question is, can the prosecuting attorney simply overlook violations of the marijuana possession statutes and not prosecute such cases?

---

[5] *Ernest K. Gann,* Fate is the Hunter *(New York: Simon and Schuster, 1961), p. 4.*

What we think about this problem depends on the standard of evaluation we apply to the problem of authority. We could argue that laws against marijuana possesion are simply "bad laws" and ought not to be enforced. Every state and community has laws on the books that have fallen into disuse. In some states, there are still laws that make adultery a criminal offense, but they are hardly, if ever, used. By simply not enforcing laws, police and prosecutors help weed out archaic and unreasonable laws. In not enforcing the marijuana possession statutes, the district attorney is simply following an established and useful custom.

The response to this, of course, is that prosecutors are not entitled to decide what is "good law" and "bad law." They are law enforcement officials and not legislators. Although they have some discretion in their work, the grounds for using that discretion should be the quality of evidence available in a particular case and the characteristics of the offender. Prosecutors have no authority to nullify the law.

A second way of approaching the problem would be to claim that prosecutors are responsible for the efficient conduct of their office. They have to set priorities. They have limited resources of time and personnel. They are *entitled* to concentrate on really serious offenses against persons and property and to devote less attention, perhaps to neglect, minor offenses such as marijuana use. State's attorneys are responsible for the safety and security of the community and this implies that they have to make judgments about which crimes are more important to prosecute. This kind of argument is probably more compatible with the idea of authority than the first, but it is also something of a rationalization. It is true that prosecutors have to make a decision that some offenses are more important than others, but does this mean that they are entitled to decide not to enforce the marijuana statutes at all?

There is a third line of argument that could be used. Law enforcement officials should be responsive to the attitudes, customs, and opinions of the community, and we are assuming that in this particular city, there is no strong desire to enforce the law against marijuana possession vigorously. Obviously, police and prosecutors must use common sense. Respect for the law in general requires that the average citizen see the law as generally reasonable and fair. Only a zealot would rigidly enforce the marijuana statutes in a community that did not regard use of the drug as a serious matter.

Nonetheless, if we admit that prosecutors should be responsive to community sentiment in matters like marijuana use, we must also accept the actions of those prosecutors who enforce the law more severely against racial minorities, transients, or the poor than against the "respectable" members of the community if *that* is their understanding of local sentiments and customs.

In deciding what you would do and how you would justify your

34

*public policy: choice
on behalf of other
people*

actions if you were the district attorney in this case, it is worth bearing in mind that the problem is not whether marijuana should be legalized or not, but what authority a prosecuting attorney has to do something about that issue. To whom and for what are you responsible in this situation?

responsibility and moral choice

Fundamental moral dilemmas arise in politics when what we *ought* to do comes into conflict with what we are *expected* or *entitled* to do.

We can hope that we will never have to face the really agonizing moral choices of politics. With luck, we will never have to decide whether to resist a brutal totalitarian regime or submit to it for the sake of our families and associates. (One of the most degrading aspects of totalitarianism is that it forces people to make this choice.) However, the ordinary moral dilemmas of everyday politics can also be perplexing. We have to be able to make the distinction between the trivial corruptions and petty venalities that are present in every human organization and truly important issues of conscience. We cannot be in a constant state of indignation about human frailty. Some corners are always going to be cut. We weigh them as part of the price of any public action. But there are times when one has to say "enough."

When we decide that we face an issue of conscience, we also have to decide what to do about it. There are three courses of action that are worth considering.

Resignation in Protest

One of the most straightforward responses to a situation in which you find yourself responsible for policies with which you fundamentally disagree is to resign in protest, giving a full public statement of the reasons for your misgivings. In effect, what you do is shift your role in the political system from public official to critic. The alternatives are not very promising. Either you have to assume responsibility for a policy you believe to be basically wrong, or you use your position to undercut the policy surreptitiously, which, of course, you are not entitled to do. However, in a democratic society, opposition to policy from outside the government is both legitimate and expected.

In Great Britain, resignation in protest is a well-established and honorable custom. When a cabinet minister quits, he is almost expected to give a detailed explanation of why he can no longer be identified with official policy. In many cases, such actions not only do not destroy the individual's political career but may even, in the long run, positively advance it. In America, oddly enough, the tradition seems to be the contrary. One study shows that of 389 federal executives who resigned voluntarily between 1900 and 1969, 355 remained silent, while only 34 went public with some vocal and sustained protest.[6] Why this contrast should exist is not immediately apparent. It may be that the sense of "team loyalty" has different connotations in Great Britain than in the United States. However, it is more likely that this is simply a difference in the institutions and historic traditions of the two nations. In any event, the situation may be changing. "Going public" after resignation may be increasing in American public life. During 1969–1970, three senior officials of the Nixon administration quit and publicly stated the nature of their dissent from official policy.

Whistle Blowing

Often, the first to become aware of corruption, mismanagement, or unethical conduct are not top officials and policymakers but individuals located deep within government or corporate bureaucracies. The inspector on the assembly line becomes aware of a critical design defect in an automobile that makes it unsafe; the policy analyst finds a large cost overrun on a government contract; the accountant discovers a possible misappropriation of funds. What is the right course of action for the employee who learns about a pattern of systematic racial or sex discrimination in hiring practices, the connection between government contracts and campaign contributions, the knowing nonenforcement of laws against industrial pollution or pesticide control, or the suppression of serious health hazards to employees in a factory?

Such situations raise important questions of responsibility. Does loyalty to the organization come before obligation to the larger society? How far should the individual go in trying to set matters straight within the organization before "blowing the whistle" on illegal or corrupt practices? When is it appropriate to act anonymously so as to avoid reprisals, "leaking" the story to a sympathetic journalist, tipping off a legislator, or some public interest lobby? When should one take matters into one's own hands, acting overtly and publicly?[7]

One of the more famous "whistle blowers" of recent years was Daniel Ellsberg, who released the classified Pentagon papers on the Vietnamese war to *The New York Times*. The Ellsberg case raises a further question about the responsibility of the individual in such questions. The release of classified papers was in itself an illegal act. Was it nonetheless justifiable? Many acts of whistle blowing will, at the least, involve breaches of confidentiality. The individual has to face the

---

[6] *Edward Weisband and Thomas M. Franck,* Resignation in Protest: Political and Ethical Choices between Loyalty to Team and Loyalty to Conscience in American Public Life *(New York: Grossman, 1975).*

[7] *A recent book discusses many of these questions in detail. See Ralph Nader, Peter Petkas, and Kate Blackwell, (Eds.),* Whistle Blowing *(New York: Grossman, 1972).*

36

*public policy: choice
on behalf of other
people*

question of when and if it is wise to use means that may in themselves be wrong to right a greater wrong.

The person who reveals corporate or governmental misdeeds is likely to be subject to harassment and reprisal. Ernest Fitzgerald, the Defense Department analyst who disclosed that cost overruns on the Lockheed C-5 were running 100 percent over the original contract and reported similar problems with the Minuteman missile program, was the target of a concerted effort to ease him out of public service. His performance ratings declined. He was given less important assignments. In a sense, the Defense Department tried to isolate him when he would not resign. Eventually, he ended up dealing with the cost problems of bowling alleys in Thailand. One of his assistants was reassigned, the other ordered not to report to Fitzgerald but to go directly to higher military officials. Eventually, his position was "abolished." Despite civil service security, he was, in effect, fired.[8]

This raises the question of the responsibility of other parties to the whistle blower. The person who reveals corruption and malpractice is often vulnerable and alone. Professional colleagues, public officials, legislators, labor unions (in the case of workers who disclose industrial defects, illegal pollution, etc.) have a responsibility to defend the person who faces such issues of conscience and acts on conviction. The Nader organization's Conference on Professional Responsibility has made strong recommendations that codes of professional ethics and the law be developed to make clear that the individual has both the right and the responsibility to put loyalty to moral principles and the law above loyalty to any person, party, or organization.

Civil Disobedience

Resignation in protest is basically an alternative to be pondered by the public official who faces a dilemma of responsibility. Whistle blowing is an option for the employee or administrator. Civil disobedience is a course of action that applies more to the situation of the citizen or protest leader faced with the problem of obedience to unjust laws. All three, it should be noted, are in a sense remedies of last resort, to be applied only after normal channels of protest, argument, and appeal have been exhausted or proved unworkable. But in considering when the use of such remedies is appropriate, we help to clarify the issue of responsibility.

All three of these strategies apply to the person who faces a dilemma of responsibility. The revolutionary is in another situation, and we will come to that problem later on. The revolutionary feels no

---

[8] *Ibid.*, pp. 39–54.

obligation to the political order of the society. Hence, he faces no moral quandary. The problem is only how to topple an illegitimate regime and replace it with a new political system. However, practitioners of civil disobedience acknowledge an overall responsibility to the laws and the structure of authority in society. The problem is what to do in the face of *particular* policies that they cannot conscientiously obey.

Civil disobedience has had an important part in contemporary history. It played a role in the civil rights movement and in protest against the Vietnamese war. The subtle philosophy of civil disobedience has been developed historically in the writings of Henry David Thoreau, Mohandas Gandhi, and Martin Luther King.

Practitioners of civil disobedience recognize that it is a potent political weapon, one that can very easily get out of control. To incite others to disobey the laws can lead to riot, violence and insurrection. This is not the objective of civil disobedience. The leaders of nonviolent movements have always tried to instill great discipline in their followers. Gandhi called off his protest marches when they erupted in violence. The early leaders of the civil rights movement carefully instructed their lieutenants and followers in the philosophy and practice of nonviolence. Practitioners of civil disobedience acknowledge that they are breaking the law. They must submit to arrest and not resist the authorities. They must recognize that their noncompliance with law is selective, not general. In the Birmingham civil rights protests, marchers were instructed to scrupulously obey a local ordinance against jaywalking, to stop for traffic lights, and to stay on sidewalks and not walk on lawns. At issue was the exercise of the right of peaceful assembly, and the issue would only be obscured if the principle of disobedience to unjust laws was confused with disobedience to law in general.

The willingness to face arrest and imprisonment resolves the basic contradiction of believers in civil disobedience. Would not society break down completely if each individual could decide for himself which laws to obey and which to ignore? Although the practitioner of civil disobedience bases his action on a higher moral principle and wants to bring pressure to bear on the ethical sensitivities of the society to change unjust laws, he can also recognize that civil disobedience is fundamentally an act of individual conscience. The individual can decide for himself when he faces a conflict between conscience and civic obligation, so long as he is willing to accept the consequences of his actions.

It should be acknowledged that leaders of nonviolent protest movements have recognized the political power of civil disobedience. For a powerless minority, passive resistance to some extent nullifies the coercive powers of the state. Massive noncompliance with laws poses a problem for policymakers. Filling the jails with militants eventually becomes absurd. Although the civil disobedient argues that he will not use force or coercion to change the law but only nonviolent appeals to the moral sentiments of the people, such strategies of the civil rights movement as economic boycotts against department stores and city bus systems had devastating economic consequences and were recognized as potent tactical weapons.

conclusion

Political decisions are made in the minds of individuals. But politics is a collective activity, and every public policy is the result of the efforts of many different people. Some are allies and collaborators. Others are antagonists. Some are specialists. Each has a role to play in the process.

From the moment that we become active in politics, we face important choices about the part we will play in the political drama. The questions of responsibility—what am I expected to do and what am I entitled to do?—can help clarify our conception of our relationship to the decision-making process. We can ask the further question of the relevant community to be taken into account—how the "we" and the "they" of politics are to be defined—and we can explore the moral dimensions of the situation in which we find ourselves.

These are questions that have to be asked by the elected official, by the activist advocate of a cause, by the expert consultant, by the public administrator, by the person who simply finds himself accepted as a leader in a group or organization.

Our answers to these questions will have an important bearing on our "style" of leadership. They will also affect the approach we take to the work of decision making. How we define problems, what standards of judgment we will apply, will in part be determined by our answers to the problem of responsibility. Furthermore, thinking through the problem of role and responsibility gives us a better understanding of what other participants in the political process are doing and provides us with a basis for evaluating their actions.

for further reading

Bell, David V. J., *Power, Influence and Authority* (New York: Oxford University Press, 1975). A short elementary analysis of these basic concepts of politics. Relates authority to the use of political language and the idea of political argument.

French, Peter (Ed.), *Individual and Collective Responsibility: The Massacre at My Lai* (Cambridge: Shenkman, 1972). A collection of thoughtful essays based on one of the most important moral issues of the Vietnam war.

Gandhi, Mohandas K., *Non-Violent Resistance* (New York: Schocken Books, 1951). A classic treatise on civil disobedience.

Gustafson, James F., and James T. Laney (Eds.), *On Being Responsible: Issues in Personal Ethics* (New York: Harper and Row, 1968). Essays, many by prominent theologians, on responsibility, not only as a political problem, but a personal and social one as well.

King, Martin Luther, "Letter from Birmingham Jail" reprinted in Theodore Lowi, *Private Life and Public Order* (New York: W. W. Norton, 1968).

King, Martin Luther, *Stride Toward Freedom* (New York: Harper and Bros., 1968).

King, Martin Luther, *Why We Can't Wait* (New York: Harper and Row, 1964). Together, these three give a good idea of King's philosophy of nonviolent political action.

Nader, Ralph, Peter Petkas, and Kate Blackwell (Eds.), *Whistle Blowing* (New York: Grossman, 1972). Good case studies and practical advice for the would-be whistle blower.

Pitkin, Hannah F., *The Concept of Representation* (Berkeley: University of California Press, 1972). A thorough, rigorous examination of the responsibility of the representative.

Spiro, Herbert J., *Responsibility in Government: Theory and Practice* (New York: Van Nostrand Reinhold, 1969). A useful introduction to the problem of political responsibility.

Stiehm, Judith, *Non-Violent Power: Active and Passive Resistance in America* (Boston: D. C. Heath, 1972). A short, well-written introduction to the major issues and philosophies of civil disobedience.

Weber, Max, "Politics as a Vocation," reprinted in Karl de Schweinitz and Kenneth W. Thompson (Eds.), *Man and Modern Society* (New York: Henry Holt, 1953) pp. 643–50. A classic essay on statecraft, with much to say about the problems of authority and responsibility.

chapter three
rights and regulations

In the next three chapters, we discuss three basic problems of decision making. To each, we apply a specific standard of judgment. The first is making rules and regulations and how this affects the *rights* of people. The second is the question of how far government should go in regulating and directing human affairs. This raises the issue of *freedom*. The third problem is that of distributing resources among the competing needs and desires of individuals. Here we have to talk about *equity* and *fairness*, *equality* and *justice*. Taken together, these three cover the commonest and most fundamental forms of political controversy. In each, we try to illustrate how basic political principles can be used to identify and define political problems and to reason toward concrete policy positions.

how decisions affect rights

Every political decision establishes rights or affects them. When an organization decides to publish a journal, every dues-paying member has a right to receive it, unless there are specific provisions to the contrary. If we make a law providing that women have equal rights in employment, the employer *no longer* has the right to pay women less than men for the same work.

Today the question of rights seems a particularly important focus of political argument. We talk about the rights of minorities, of women, of consumers, of defendents, of prisoners, of those committed to institutions. The right to work, to strike, to privacy, to a good environment, to medical care, to welfare are all extensively debated issues. We claim rights to free speech, to access to the files that government agencies or credit bureaus may have about us, to refuse military service, to walk safely on the streets. Some argue that even trees and other natural objects should have rights.[1]

But what are rights? What are we affecting when our public actions touch on other people's rights or establish them?

Rights are Freedoms

Having a right opens up a sphere of unencumbered action for the individual. If you have clear title to a piece of property, you can use it, sell it, lend it, or give it away, entirely at your own discretion. You do not *have* to exercise a right. You do a duty. In the United States, voting is a right. You can go to the polls or stay at home. In many European countries it is also a duty. The citizen can be fined for failure to vote. (This accounts, in part, for the fact that participation in elections is often higher in Europe than America.)

Rights are Entitlements

A right may be a *claim* against some other person not to interfere with your purposes or positively to assist you in achieving them. When we invoke a right, we are doing something more than asking for permission or a favor. We are asserting that another person is required to do our will. We are entitled to expect a certain performance from him.

Rights, in this sense, are commands. They are a form of power over the actions of other people. To appeal to rights is to use strong language. Normally, we do business with others through polite requests. It is only when we encounter resistance that we escalate and invoke a right. Notice how this develops in the following conversation.

Since the passage of the Buckley amendment to the 1974 Education Act, students have the right to see any records kept by school authorities that might be used in evaluating them for outside parties—grade transcripts, letters of recommendation, and so forth. When a student goes to a university records office to see the files, the exchange with the clerk might go something like this:

S. "I'd like to see my file."
C. "I'm sorry, I can't do that."
S. "But I've got a right to see my file."

---

[1] *See the list in Richard E. Flathman (Ed.),* Concepts in Social and Political Philosophy *(New York: Macmillan, 1973), p. 436. On the question of the rights of trees, see Christopher D. Stone,* Should Trees Have Standing? Toward Legal Rights for Natural Objects *(Los Altos, Calif.: William Kaufmann, 1974).*

42

*public policy: choice
on behalf of other
people*

C.   "Well, you've got no right to come barging in here demanding that I drop everything to take care of you."
S.   "Then who should I see?"
C.   "The dean is the only person who is authorized to take materials out of the files."
S.   "Well, I'm an authorized person too—I've got as much of a right to see my files as he does."

Note the confrontational style of the argument—the invocation of "right" and "no right." This exchange goes beyond the usual pleasantries that we use in transacting daily business. Usually, we only assert rights in a situation of conflict.

Rights have corresponding duties

The rights of one person appear as obligations and restraints to someone else. Freedom of choice disappears when you have a duty corresponding to someone else's right. You have *no right* not to make good on a lawful debt. No matter how good it would make you feel, how much it might advance your pursuit of happiness, or how fitting the deed might seem, you have *no right* to dump a load of dead fish in the executive offices of a corporation whose factory pollutes a stream that runs past your house.

Like a complex traffic system, rules establish "rights-of-way" for individuals through the maze of transactions that take place in organized society. According to John R. Commons, when we make rules, we are laying down principles for the guidance and restraint of persons in their relations with one another. We can talk about the basic patterns of these relationships by using four common English verbs.

1.   *Rules that specify what a person "must" or "must not" do.* You must possess a license before driving a car. You must not drive it on sidewalks.
2.   *Rules that define what a person "may" do.* I may enter into a contract with you. I do not have to. I am free to do so or not as I see fit. The rule defines a right, an area of discretion or freedom. But once I have made a contract, I *must* fulfill it, or you *may* sue me (at your discretion, you do not have to) and a court will compel me to make good on my promise.
3.   *Rules that define what a person "can" do.* Here we begin to talk about rights to free action that will be underwritten by the power of government. You *can* (have the right to) compel me to pay a lawful debt, and you *can* go to court to get me to do so.
4.   *Rules that specify what you "cannot" expect government to back you up in doing.* In this sphere, you operate at your own risk. You *may* buy a piece of property next to mine, but I *may* build a

drive-in restaurant on my land, and you cannot compel me to tear it down in the absence of relevant zoning ordinances.[2]

Another distinction that can be made is between negative rights and positive rights. There are, for example, four kinds of rights that can be established by public action.

1. *Negative rights against government interference.* Governments, like individuals, are the bearers of rights and duties. The concept of limited, or constitutional, government means that the functions and purposes of the state are spelled out in advance. Where government has the right to act (where it *may* make policy), the individual has a duty to comply. Where the individual has a right to free action, the government has a duty to refrain from interference.

   Most of the provisions of the Bill of Rights of the American Constitution are stated as prohibitions on government action.

   Congress shall make no law respecting an establishment of religion, or prohibiting the free exercise thereof; or abridging the freedom of speech . . . (First Amendment).

   The right of the people to be secure in their persons, houses, papers, and effects, against unreasonable searches and seizures, shall not be violated . . . (Fourth Amendment).

   These are restraints on government action, but they are not promises to assist the individual in achieving his purposes.

2. *Negative rights against interference by other individuals.* Most of the criminal law, and much of civil law as well, is concerned with restraining individuals from interference with the freedom, security, and possessions of others. Laws against theft or larceny are duties corresponding to the right to use and freely dispose of property. Laws against pollution imply a right of individuals to enjoy clean and attractive surroundings without interference.

3. *Positive rights to action by other people.* Government may also invest individuals with the right to expect a specific performance from someone else. Laws governing the health and sanitation of restaurants and public accommodations in effect mean that customers are entitled to expect certain standards of cleanliness from the owners of these establishments.

[2] *John R. Commons,* The Legal Foundations of Capitalism *(Madison: University of Wisconsin Press, 1968), pp. 6, 28–32, 65–142.*

44

*public policy: choice
on behalf of other
people*

The citizen has a right to service from a public utility, and this service can only be terminated under specified conditions. The company cannot decide for itself to stop the supply of electric power to low-volume users because it is more profitable to serve major industries.

4. *Positive rights to action by government.* Any law, regulation, or policy in effect creates rights for citizens to expect some specific performance from government. If you retire at age 62, and have participated in social security, you have a right to benefits. You have a right to deduct legitmate business expenses from your income tax. You are entitled to police and fire protection—the chief cannot whimsically decide not to respond to calls from your neighborhood. If you are accused of a crime, you have the right to counsel, and if you cannot afford to pay for an attorney, the government has a duty to provide one.

Rights are seldom simple. Usually they are embedded in complex relationships with other rights and duties. For example, there is no single right of property. Property, in fact, includes a wide variety of rights and duties that may attach to the ownership of things. Property rights can be temporary, as in the case of patents and copyrights, or permanent, as in the case of land. You can own a piece of property and have the right to use it but not to sell it, or destroy it, or give it away—if, for example, you put it up as collateral for a loan. Duties as well as rights come with property ownership. You must maintain and use your property so that it will not cause injury to others. There is no "absolute" right of property. The use and disposition of property is normally highly regulated. John Locke thought that property was an "inalienable" right, but in the United States, the state has the right of eminent domain and may require the sale of property to the government if it can be shown that the property is needed for some legitimate public purpose.

a checklist of questions for decision makers

From the point of view of the policy maker, the essential problem is to determine what rights and duties would be created as a result of public action. Any political decision will, in fact, establish rights and duties, but unless we think self-consciously about this, we may create situations that are indefensible later. In political argument, we will eventually be called upon to justify the entitlements and obligations we create.

Whenever we make any kind of policy decision, there are certain questions that can be asked that help clarify the issue of rights and obligations.

1. *What rights are we creating and on whom are we imposing duties?* We have to be very clear about how we define the beneficiaries of a right and about who bears the burden of seeing that a right is realized. If a woman has a right to procure an abortion, does a doctor have the duty to perform one? Under current American law, doctors are not obligated to perform abortions, but hospitals may be required to make their facilities available for abortions. The hospital bears a duty, but the doctor does not, with respect to this right.

Even the most innocuous of local ordinances probably should be analyzed in this way. Let us say that as a member of a city council we are writing new health regulations for restaurants. What rights of the businessman should be taken into account? Can we require the owner to open the premises for inspection except during business hours? What rights does the owner have to make appeals against the rulings of inspectors? Who will have the duty of deciding such appeals? What rights will citizens have to make complaints under the ordinance? Who will have the responsibility of responding to such complaints?

Frequently, making decisions about rights takes the form of deciding about conflicts of rights. We face the problem not of who has a right and who does not, but of which right should be superior. Consider the following mildly excruciating example, again from the point of view of a member of a city council.

Mr. Johnson has a house with a lovely view and Mr. Berg, his neighbor, builds a high fence on his property that partially obstructs the view. Johnson argues that he bought his land primarily because of the view, and that he has a right to it. He claims that the view is *part* of the property, as much as the trees, the land, as much as any feature of the property that made it desirable in the first place. By building the fence, Berg reduced the value of Johnson's property. He has infringed on Johnson's rights, has caused him injury through his actions, and should be required to take down the fence.

In response, Berg argues that he has a right to privacy. Johnson's house is so situated that he can look right into Berg's windows and yard. As far as views are concerned, Berg considers Johnson's house an architectural monstrosity and wants it hidden from view. There is no local law that actually prohibits a fence of this height and therefore Berg can do as he pleases. The fence is attractive and well-constructed. It is not an eyesore. Berg claims that he is asserting a right identical to Johnson's. He has the right to an attractive and desirable property.

Let us ask three different questions about this case.

First, how would you decide the conflict as it is presented?

Second, if the city were to draft a new ordinance regulating fences, how should it deal with the problem of these rival rights in drafting a general rule that would apply to all future situations?

Third, would your views be any different if Berg's fence was already up when Johnson bought his lot? Would Johnson's case that

Berg should remove the fence be stronger or weaker? Why?

Our reflections on this problem lead naturally and inevitably to a second question.

2. *What should count as an injury?* Almost everything we do has some impact on someone else. Life is full of inevitable frictions and tensions, compromises and accommodations between people. Which of these are important enough to be defined as matters that require regulation, as an area where rights and duties must be spelled out? Many of our actions are seen by others as working against their interests and purposes. Are we then to be restrained from doing anything that someone else could conceivably construe as being to his disadvantage? Before we create a rule, we must first decide that there are good reasons for imposing an obligation where once there was an area of free choice.

If one business executive is more successful than another and drives the second out of business, the competitor has obviously been injured, but we are unlikely to argue, in our economic system, that the bankrupt party has a right to remain in business, and that the competitor has the obligation to enable a rival to prosper. However, if a monopoly is created and the monopolist uses this power to drive up prices, we might argue that a significant injury has been done to consumers and that the government has an obligation to restore competition or to regulate the business so that it will obtain no unfair advantages.

Let us return again to the example we discussed at the beginning of the book, the case of the family who decided to let their yard grow wild while all their neighbors kept neatly tended lawns. What injury does this family do to anyone else, and is it important enough to regulate? It is one thing if the "naturalized" yard spawns noxious weeds, such as poison ivy, deadly nightshade, and ragweed, which might cause illness or suffering to hay fever victims. But what if the family promises to keep their back-to-nature movement within bounds and roots out such plants? The neighbors might protest that it is a nuisance to keep their lawns clean of the prairie grasses, sumac, and other plants that propagate from the wild yard. Is that point strong enough to restrain the family from adopting their own style of landscaping? Or it might be argued that the natural yard detracts from the neat, tidy, and uniform appearance of the street in general and, as such, reduces property values and the enjoyment that everyone in the community derives from the attractive appearance of the town. Like ugly factories and garish neon signs, it is an environmental issue, the right of people to live in aesthetically pleasing surroundings. But is this "environmental insult" (in the eyes of some—others find the yard interesting) sufficiently grave that it overrides the rights of individuals to plan the landscaping of their own home?

(We can, of course, ask the question the other way around. Is the right of the property owner so important that it overrides the right of the community to plan its overall appearance. It all depends on where we place the burden of proof—on the side of community interest or individual right.)

There is a further problem here. Whichever way we decide the case, how do we formulate our policy as a general rule? For example, if we side with the property owners, how do we distinguish their case from that of the individual who simply lets the yard go, to become generally rundown? Actually, it takes a lot of work to achieve an authentic natural look and the effect can be quite attractive. If we do not want to require "well-tended grass lawn," what standard should we apply? To say "well-tended natural look" may not be good enough, for the slovenly gardners can claim that their yard is just as natural as the other, and who decides what "well-tended" means?

If we decide the other way and insist on a uniform standard of grass lawns, are we going to prohibit people from filling their front yards with trees, ornamental shrubs, and flowers? Do we need a committee to decide what is and what is not good landscaping? If so, who is going to sit on the committee? Who has the *right* to decide such matters of taste?

This last problem takes us to the next question for those who must make decisions about rights and regulations.

3. *How have we defined the groups to which rights and duties apply?* In the above case, we are trying to establish a distinction between the person who carefully creates a natural yard and one who just lets his property run down. The problem of making defensible categories is central to the creation of rights. In the first chapter, we mentioned the problem of "affirmative action." If we believe that women, blacks, chicanos, native Americans, or other minorities should have special rights, how do we deny them to others who claim a similar social disadvantage, such as fat people, or tall people, or left-handed people?

When we create rights and duties, we also establish categories of "persons" (in the legal sense, this includes organizations as well as individuals) to whom they apply. We believe in "equal rights" but we do not all have the same rights. Landlords and tenants, workers and employers, buyers and sellers, professors and students all have different rights. The important point is that rights must apply to anyone in a similar situation and that such limitations and differences as we establish must be relevant and rationally defensible. For this reason, it is worth taking some care in how we define the categories we establish.

Today we have become accustomed to thinking that race and sex are not relevant categories for making distinctions between the rights of individuals. In fact, this principle is so firmly ingrained in our minds that we seldom stop to consider why such discrimination is indefensible. The fact is that discrimination on grounds of race and sex is not only degrading to the people concerned but it is also illogical.

48

*public policy: choice
on behalf of other
people*

Why is sex not a relevant category for discrimination in employment? Some would argue that sexual equality should not apply to such jobs as fire fighting. Why? Because women are not strong enough to carry people from burning buildings. But, in that case, the relevant test is strength and not sex. There is no reason to presume in advance that in the pool of applicants for any fire fighting job, the women will not turn out to be stronger than the male applicants.

In recent years, there has been a great controversy about research into the genetic basis of intelligence. Some scholars have suggested that intelligence may be correlated with race, and that blacks may, on the whole, have lower intelligence than whites. This whole line of thinking has aroused great horror in some circles, and there have been suggestions that such research be suppressed. However, the fact of the matter is that the issue is irrelevant to the question of racial discrimination.

Even if it did turn out that intelligence is inherited, and that high intelligence is more common in the white than in the black race (for which there is no convincing evidence one way or the other), the finding would have no importance for the question of equal rights. Rights pertain to individuals and not to races, and we *already* know that there are many blacks of high intelligence and whites with low IQs. In any statistical distribution, there are people at the top and at the bottom. Even if scores on IQ tests were relevant to some distinction of right and opportunity (itself a highly questionable proposition), we would still have no grounds for discrimination on the basis of race. In any group of people we are concerned with—applicants for jobs or educational opportunities—the smartest might turn out to be the blacks and the least intelligent the whites. Once again, the relevant differentiator is intelligence and not race, and intelligence is a function of the individual and not the group.

Establishing defensible categories that define the beneficiaries of rights is often very difficult. When the War on Poverty was created in 1963, the Council of Economic Advisers picked $3000 as the "poverty line." Families below that level were entitled to benefits. However, poverty is not a simple phenomenon, and the poor appear in very different situations and have very different needs. Farm families may need less cash income than city families, and large families are obviously in a different situation than small ones. Over the years, more sophisticated definitions of poverty—of the right to welfare—have been established. Family size and place of residence are now taken into account in defining the poverty line.[3]

Nonetheless, there are still difficulties in defining the category of

---

[3] *Alice M. Rlvlin,* Systematic Thinking for Social Action *(Washington: The Brookings Institution, 1971), p. 10.*

"poverty" that establishes an entitlement to certain rights. Medical or graduate students, for example, may be the heads of families below the poverty line. They are young, and their low incomes are temporary. They are in effect "deferring income" in the expectation of higher earnings later in life. Are they then "in the same situation" as the truly impoverished? Should they be entitled to food stamps, rent subsidies, and other welfare benefits?

4. *Do we have the authority to regulate in this case?* Finally, in making rules that affect rights and duties, we have to make sure that government itself has the right to legislate in a particular field and that such action would not interfere with the rights of individuals *against* government action. Here we see the close relationship between the ideas of right and authority, which we discussed in the last chapter. In effect, this is another way of asking What am I entitled to do? when we face a decision-making problem. This is an important question, and we will return to it later in the book.

rights and the advocate

So far, we have been looking at the problem of rights and duties from the point of view of the decision maker. But the issue can also be approached from the standpoint of the advocate. How do you make a case that you, or some group you are concerned about, ought to be the beneficiaries of a right? What grounds are appropriate in arguing for the recognition of a right?

If you are threatened with expulsion from a university, you might want to claim a right to a hearing before an independent panel. On what do you base such a claim? If there is a regulation providing for such hearings, the matter is quite simple. A category exists (students) that is entitled to a right (hearing). You are a member of the category, therefore appropriately entitled to the right. But what if no such regulation exists?

You might appeal to precedent. If it has been the custom in the past to provide a hearing if a student requests one, there is a strong case that you should be granted an appeal, even if there is no written rule. The burden of proof is clearly on the administration to give grounds for denying your request. But what if there is no precedent? How do you go about claiming that such a right *ought* to exist?

There is a school of thought called "legal positivism" that argues that rights are a legal and not a moral concept. The only rights that exist are those that government will enforce. Rights are established by law. No law, no right. Nonetheless, the structure of rights is constantly changing. We do, in fact, *claim* rights long before they are recognized in law. In appealing for the recognition of such potential rights, we must make a case that goes beyond established rules and usages. We move

50

*public policy: choice
on behalf of other
people*

to a new level of argument—that of "fundamental fairness" and "natural law."

Fundamental Fairness

In appealing to fundamental fairness, we are saying, in general, that the rules should be logically consistent, that like cases should be treated alike and different cases differently. Our sense of injustice is aroused when people in the same situation are treated differently—as, for example, when the courts let a famous person off with a suspended sentence and send a poor offender to jail for the same crime. That deep-rooted human instinct is also outraged when obviously significant differences are ignored in making rules. It would strike us as "unfair" if special programs for the blind or deaf were eliminated on the grounds that all people should be treated equally. The handicapped, we feel, have a *right* to special assistance.

In arguing for fundamental fairness, we frequently are asserting that rules should be consistent with the higher-order norms of the system.

All people are entitled to equal protection of the laws. If we cannot make an exception for blacks, we cannot make an exception for women.

All people are entitled to a fair trial. We do have separate systems of juvenile courts, since children are not legally responsible for their actions as adults are. But we cannot justify denying children the basic rights of "due process of law," such as the right to counsel, to confront accusors, to cross-examination of witnesses, when they come before the juvenile authorities. (It is interesting that such rights have only very recently been recognized in American law.)[4]

It is a basic principle of the common law that an individual should be responsible for the damages that his actions inflict on others. There may be no specific law that protects a farmer against pollution from a factory that ruins his crops. But should not the farmer have a *right* against the factory owner in this case? Would it not seem fair that he should be able to call upon government to restrain the factory owner from causing him harm or to collect compensation for the damage done?

In all these areas, the structure of rights has changed fundamentally in the last generation. Rights of individuals have come into existence where there were no clearly defined rules before. In each case, the reformers argued that the law should be made consistent with its own fundamental premises. And the battle is far from over. New questions are constantly being asked and new areas of rights explored.

---

[4] In re Gault *387 U.S. 1.*

For example, some argue that we should look further into the question of the rights of employees and students. The loss of a job or expulsion from school can be extremely harmful for the individual. There should perhaps be some protection against the arbitrary authority of employers and university officials. Perhaps the individual should have a legal right to have a formal statement of reasons if he is fired or expelled and an opportunity to publicly respond to charges made against him.

Natural Rights

Beyond fundamental fairness, appeals for the recognition of new rights may be made on the basis of "natural law." There are rights that people ought to have simply because they are human. This is at once the highest level of argument about rights and duties and the most treacherous, because everything depends on the assumptions that are made about human nature. Arguments about natural rights are inherently debatable, for there are many different conceptions of what is essentially natural, or human.

For example, it could be argued that there are certain rights that are necessary to the full development of the human personality. There are universal human needs—food, shelter, safety, a measure of privacy, affection, and respect from one's fellows. The Universal Declaration of Human Rights (adopted by the United Nations in 1948) holds that all people have a right to an adequate standard of living, to work and leisure, to education, to security in sickness and old age, and to participation in artistic, scientific, and cultural activities. It is the obligation of governments to work toward the realization of these rights for all their citizens.

On the other hand, a social Darwinist would assert that natural selection and the "survival of the fittest" characterize the natural order, and that the state ought not to interfere with the natural competition among individuals for supremacy. Human progress requires that the most able, the strongest, and the best be given the widest scope of freedom, that the domination of some and the submission of others is the natural order of human existence.

The authors of the Declaration of Independence believed that "man is endowed by nature with certain inalienable rights." Jefferson thought these included life, liberty, and the pursuit of happiness. Locke also mentioned property. What they meant was that no rational person would submit to authority unless these rights could be better protected by government than by the individual acting for himself. Believing that legitimate authority rests on voluntary consent, they pictured an autonomous person in the "state of nature," before the creation of civil society, deliberating on whether or not to create a government. He might conclude that collective security was desirable to secure his freedom and property against the intrusion of others.

52

*public policy: choice
on behalf of other
people*

However, if government itself becomes oppressive, the individual would have been better off—or at least as well off—coping for himself.

The only legitimate purpose of government then is to secure the personal freedoms of the individual. The only limitations of freedom that a rational person will accept are those necessary to secure the reciprocal rights of other individuals. Generally, though not always, this conception of natural rights is used to support claims to rights *against* governments. It provides a theoretical underpinning for arguments that government's role should be strictly limited, that the state should take on no purposes of its own nor attempt to define what is in the best interest of the people.

As you can see, arguments about natural rights can start from very different premises and lead to contradictory conclusions. For this reason, we might be tempted to dismiss this form of reasoning as at best idle theorizing and at worst chicanery and illusion. Nonetheless, the idea that there is a ''higher law'' beyond the conventions, working rules, and operating compromises of any particular political order has been a consistent, nagging theme that runs through all the history of Western civilization. Plato and Aristotle, the Roman jurists, the Christian theologians of the Middle Ages, the rationalists of the Enlightenment, and many modern political theorists have all suspected as much. The thought that there are certain needs and concerns that are universal in the human experience, that there are standards of judgment against which the law itself may be judged, is not an idea that can be dismissed lightly. Whatever interior urge impels us to say ''I have a right'' or ''That is unfair'' seems to come from a source in ourselves different from personal self-interest or public practicality, for when we say such things, we mean something quite different from ''I would like'' or ''They won't stand for it.''

And, as a practical matter, we will have to make up our minds about arguments from natural rights, for they are very much part of political discourse. How do you, after all, decide that genocide or exploitation is a bad thing, and the preservation of wilderness worthwhile, if you believe that all values are relative and a mere matter of social convenience?

In any event, appeals to natural right are a common, not an extraordinary, part of political discourse. When people assert claims to rights, they often do not call upon established rules, precedents, or fundamental fairness to support their case. They talk in terms of right and wrong. Often the fundamental assumptions they are working from are implicit or inarticulate. They appear as ''feelings,'' but if you pry and prod a bit, feelings can usually be expressed as reasons. We cannot arbitrarily dismiss this ordinary way of making political judgments on the ground that moral language is often unsystematic and unsophisticated. The committed skeptic, in particular, must recognize the right of those who make moral arguments to be heard and, for that matter, taken seriously.

conclusion

In our age, the problem of rights seems to have become, once more, a central topic of political controversy and decision making. Perhaps this is a consequence of the highly organized, interdependent world we live in. In an earlier time, rights did not have to be as specific or detailed. We did not have to rub against one another so much nor were we as dependent on one another. In the early stages of the creation of industrial society, the task was to organize people, as rationally and efficiently as possible, to get the job done. Now we have begun to suspect, perhaps, that complex organization has become our permanent condition, and so we look once more at the structure of relationships we have created, to see if we can make them a more comfortable, secure, and acceptable environment for the individual. So we begin to ask, not only whether organizations are efficient at achieving their purposes, but what individuals have a right to expect from them and from each other. Perhaps in this way we begin the task of turning a system into a civilization.

At all levels of politics, public decision making has much to do with defining rights and duties. New rights are constantly being discovered and asserted, old rights more clearly delineated and detailed. Structuring rights and duties is a fundamental problem in any political organization. In fact, from a normative point of view, rights and duties are what organizations are made up of. Social roles are defined by the expectations—the entitlements and responsibilities—that attach to them, and roles are the basic building blocks of social organization. In this chapter, we have taken up some of the questions that should be considered when we make decisions about rights, but as we shall see, the concept of rights colors every aspect of public decision making.

for further reading

Benn, S. I., and R. S. Peters, *Principles of Political Thought* (New York: The Free Press, 1958), Chaps. 4, 7. The best short general discussion of the nature of rights I know. Chapter 7 is on property rights.

Brant, Irving, *The Bill of Rights: Its Origin and Meaning* (New York: New

54

*public policy: choice
on behalf of other
people*

American Library, 1967). A basic introduction to American constitutional rights.

Finnis, John (Ed.), *The Rights and Wrongs of Abortion* (Princeton: Princeton University Press, 1973). A serious, thorough discussion, though abstract and philosophical, of the crucial issues of rights in the controversial area of abortion. Those interested in this subject probably should also read the Supreme Court's decision which legalized abortion, *Roe v. Wade* 410 U.S. 113.

Friedman, Wolfgang, *Legal Theory* (London: Stevens and Sons, 1953), Third Edition. A good survey of various conceptions and systems of natural law.

Gellhorn, Walter, *Individual Freedom and Governmental Restraints* (Baton Rouge: Louisiana State University Press, 1956). On the problem of structuring rights and regulations.

Hand, Learned, *The Bill of Rights* (Cambridge: Harvard University Press, 1958). Another good book on basic constitutional rights.

Rodgers, Harrell R., and Charles S. Bullock III, *Law and Social Change: Civil Rights Laws and their Consequences* (New York: McGraw-Hill, 1972). It is one thing to declare a right, it is another to determine what difference it makes in the life of individuals and society. This book is a good study of the impact of civil rights laws.

Schiengold, Stuart A., *The Politics of Rights* (New Haven: Yale University Press, 1974). On the relationship of rights and political activism. The use of rights and the law by advocates of social reform. Rights as a standard of judgment in public policymaking.

Shapiro, Martin, *Freedom of Speech: The Supreme Court and Judical Review* (Englewood Cliffs, N.J.: Prentice-Hall, Inc., 1966). A good introductory study of the first amendment right of free speech.

Strauss, Leo, *Natural Right and History* (Chicago: University of Chicago Press, 1953). An excellent discussion of the idea of natural rights by a major political theorist. Traces the evolution of the concept in Western political thought.

Westin, Alan P., *Privacy and Freedom* (New York: Atheneum, 1967). A discussion of the right of privacy.

chapter
four
freedom
and control

In making decisions about rights, we are doing nothing less than staking out the scope and limits of individual freedom. It seems strange to talk about freedom as something that is created by governmental authority. We often associate freedom with the absence of restraint and supervision. But freedom is an issue of political order. It does not connote its absence.

The issue of freedom is central whenever we make decisions about rights. However, there is another way in which public decision making affects individual freedom. Whenever we make a policy choice, we are, in effect, deciding how much events will be controlled and regulated by government authority, and how much they will be left up to the voluntary initiatives of individuals and their spontaneous adaptation to the acts of one another.[1]

We have entered upon a big and basic problem. The question of whether we should have free enterprise or state planning, government regulation or private initiative, has divided people as much as or more than anything else in the political universe. But the fact is that this is not an either-or choice. Freedom and control can be mixed together in an infinite variety of combinations. There has never been a "pure" free enterprise system nor an absolute system of complete state regulation and control. Furthermore, this is not only a question of how we set up

---

[1] *On the idea of spontaneous mutual adaptation as a form of political organization, see Michael Polanyi,* The Logic of Liberty *(Chicago: University of Chicago Press, 1951); and Charles E. Lindblom,* The Intelligence of Democracy *(New York: The Free Press, 1965).*

56

*public policy: choice
on behalf of other
people*

the structure of a political system as a whole. Every time we make a political decision, we have to consider the problems of freedom and control.

When we face a public problem, there are really only four sorts of things that we can do about it. These are our basic alternatives. Which we will decide to employ depends largely on how much freedom and how much compulsion we think is appropriate in the particular situation.

1. *Market mechanisms.* We can let the outcome depend on what individuals decide to do, without any interference or direction from government.
2. *Structured options.* We can create government programs or activities that individuals are free to use or not as they see fit.
3. *Biased options.* We can devise incentives or deterrents, so that individuals will be guided, voluntarily, toward the desired ends of public policy.
4. *Regulation.* We can directly control, setting up constraints and imperatives for individual action, backed by the coercive powers of government.

These four possibilities, in their many permutations and combinations, are the basic tools of the trade of statecraft. These are the things we can do, through government, to solve problems. We will build our discussion around the implications of each for the value of freedom.

market mechanisms: voluntary choice and individual initiative

One crucial question is whether to choose at all. In the absence of conscious and deliberate public decision, problems somehow solve themselves. Some kind of order eventually emerges.

There is a logical limit to rush-hour traffic congestion, which comes when no vehicle can move. At this point, in fact, far short of it, some individuals will come to feel that the frustration is not worth the effort; they will rearrange their schedules, find alternative routes, take the bus, or stay home altogether. There is a rough kind of justice in this process. Those who leave the highway first will be those who need it least, those who do not have to be in a particular place at a particular time or have the ingenuity to find a better way to reach their destination. Traffic congestion will eventually stabilize just short of the point where movement becomes totally impossible.

In one respect, politics is much more like medicine than architecture: one can hasten natural processes, help them along, direct them to useful ends, but one cannot defy them altogether. As Sir Geoffrey Vickers commented, "The sole purpose of human intervention is to regulate the relationship at some level *more acceptable to those concerned* than the inherent logic of the situation would otherwise provide."[2]

For this reason, and also as a safeguard against unnecessary meddling, a good question that can be asked about any public problem is, How would things work out if no action were taken at all? This question compels one to think about the natural course that events would take if people were left to work out their own solutions, and it provides a useful standard against which to measure desirable public intervention, if any is required at all. Some kind of balance and equilibrium will eventually be achieved. The question is, would that be good enough?

For example, the seating arrangements in a large lecture hall will take care of themselves if the professor makes no definite assignments. The first to arrive will choose their seats from the almost unlimited options available, and normally the seats near the aisles will be the first chosen. Those who come later will eventually have to decide whether to scramble over those already seated or (in my university at least) sit on the floor. A stable pattern—a kind of order—will emerge, with most aisle seats taken, empty seats in the middle, and some sitting in the aisles. This may seem irrational, and seating assignments might appear to be an obvious improvement. But unless the assignments were made so that those who came first were required to occupy the center seats with aisle places reserved for those who had to rush in just before the bell, there would still be a lot of scrambling and inconvenience. Sitting on the floor might be less embarrassing and disruptive than broken-field running to comply with the dictates of authority. It is not altogether obvious that the voluntary scheme makes less sense than arbitrary assignments.

The historic assumption of liberalism is that leaders do not necessarily know what is better for the people than the people do themselves. It is assumed that individuals are the best judges of their own interests. In societies where the language of political argument comes from liberalism, there is a bias in favor of individual initiative and voluntary organization. The burden of proof falls on the proponent of government intervention to show that public planning and control can achieve a better outcome than spontaneous mutual adjustment.

The classic example is, of course, the free market economy. For the founding fathers of liberal political economy, Adam Smith, David Ricardo, and James Mill, the distribution of goods and services was

---

[2] *Sir Geoffrey Vickers, The Art of Judgment (New York: Basic Books, 1965). Emphasis in the original. The example of traffic congestion is also taken from Vickers.*

58

*public policy: choice
on behalf of other
people*

better organized through the interaction of buyers and sellers in competitive markets than through any central decision about what should be produced and sold.

The logic of the free market is ingenious and perennially fascinating. Where producers are free to make anything they think they can sell at a profit and consumers can choose from among a wide array of goods and services, the total, cumulative production of society will reflect individual wants and needs with considerable accuracy. No one decides what people should have. If, on the whole, the members of one society are more interested in food than housing, and in another, more interested in housing than food, one will produce more food and the other more housing. (This happens to be the case in comparing France and Britain. The French spend a higher proportion of their incomes on food and the British spend more on housing.)

It is the presence of alternatives, and the fact that every decision has to be weighed against all other decisions, that makes the whole thing possible. No one can coerce anyone else, for everyone can take their business elsewhere. Sellers cannot determine what will be produced or fix prices at their own discretion, so long as there is a competitor who might find it advantageous to make a more attractive product or sell at a lower price. On the other hand, consumers cannot ask the impossible. No seller will agree to prices that drive him into bankruptcy. The employer cannot exploit the employee who is free to work elsewhere. But wages are "controlled" by the decisions of employers as to what additional employees are worth to them.[3] The system comes into balance, an "order" is created, at just that point where prices reflect what consumers are willing to pay and sellers find it worthwhile to produce, where wages are based on what employees are willing to work for and what employers find it profitable to pay.

Yet, the system is never static. There is a constant built-in force for improvement and progress. Each competitor has an incentive to get a larger share of the market by making a better product or adopting less expensive methods of production. And, it is further argued, the whole system results in greater justice than the wisest ruler could devise. No political judgment is made on what different individuals should receive in relation to one another, what they deserve in view of their different contributions to society. Rather, the reward of each individual depends on what others are willing to pay for his services. If 100,000 people are willing to pay $1 each to see a basketball star play, then he is entitled to an income of $100,000. If no one is interested in buying hand-dipped candles, there is no reason why society should support those who want to make them.

---

[3] *For a well-argued and ingenious defense of "pure" free enterprise, see Milton Friedman,* Capitalism and Freedom *(Chicago: University of Chicago Press, 1962).*

Such is the case in the abstract for the pure free market system. Unfortunately, such a system only works as perfectly as its proponents claim it would under the most restrictive of conditions.

First, there must be choice among relatively equivalent commodities. The consumer must be free to do business elsewhere, and the choice to do so must be relatively costless. (If there is only one clinic in a small town, and the next doctor is fifty miles away, is the individual really "free" to choose a personal physician?)

Second, there must be freedom of entry and exit in all markets. Without government regulation, the only protection the individual has against the power of monopoly or oligopoly is that a new firm could easily decide that it would be advantageous to compete against the artificially controlled prices of existing competitors. The classic political economists visualized a world of small businessmen and craftsmen, where it would be relatively easy for someone to set up a new shop or enter a new trade. In a world of giant corporations and trade unions, this condition is often very hard to realize. Unions control access to the "market" for many forms of labor. Similarly, many areas of manufacturing industry are dominated by a small number of giant firms. There are four major automobile companies in the United States, and while the number of large petroleum companies has grown from seven to eighteen in the past generation, it is still very difficult for a new firm to amass the capital, organization, and technical skill to enter such an industry. Furthermore, firms in such industries often work together in a variety of ways to prevent new competition.

Third, and this is the most controversial, there must be relative income equality among all consumers. If this is not the case, the rich are "freer" to bid for goods and services than the poor. The cumulative product of goods and services does not represent the aggregate of individual needs and wants but is biased in favor of what the wealthier need and want. It is probably obvious that the production of yachts in the United States is higher and the production of cheap housing lower than it would be if all consumers had relatively the same power of choice in the marketplace.

Some contemporary economists, especially John Kenneth Galbraith, argue that modern industrial society is anything but a reflection of the free, voluntary choices of producers and consumers. Rather, in an economy dominated by large corporations and trade unions, organizations, and not markets, make the decisions on what will be produced, at what prices, and what wages will be paid. The direction of the economy is set, not by what people want and need, but by what can be produced at a profit. "Wants" are created, by advertising and mass marketing. Corporations decide what they can produce and sell profitably, and then induce consumers to buy. Galbraith may or may not be right in his analysis, and there are good grounds for skepticism of it, but it is a sophisticated argument against concluding that the

60

*public policy: choice
on behalf of other
people*

modern "free enterprise" system fully reflects the autonomous, voluntary choices of those who participate in it.[4]

Nonetheless, in many areas of the modern economy, the market system works approximately as the model provides. And in many areas of policymaking, relying on market effects is an option that should be taken seriously.

For example, take the problem of price and wage controls. Many see government regulation of prices and wages as a necessary remedy for inflation. However, if such controls were applied over an extended period of time, we would eventually have to face the problem of how to make decisions on the relative value of different goods and the income of various occupations without reference to the market.

How could this be done? How would we decide how much to pay miners in relation to garbage collectors, doctors in relation to auto mechanics? Either the outcome would eventually depend on the political power of different groups, or we would need some standard for comparing the value or difficulty of different jobs. But it is difficult even to imagine a standard that would be generally acceptable.

We might begin by trying to assess the relative difficulty of various jobs. Perhaps we would try to measure the number of calories expended per hour in different kinds of work. But in that case, we might end up paying ditchdiggers more than brain surgeons. We might then want some measure of concentration and intensity of effort. Possibly this could be done by measuring brain waves or by some other device. But this still does not seem satisfactory. We feel that skill and responsibility should count for something in establishing relative salaries. How then do we compare the relative skills exercised, say, by a gem cutter and a surgeon? If we used years of training as a criterion, we might decide to pay the doctor more than the brilliant novelist who had little formal education. Responsibility is also difficult to measure. Which is greater—the responsibility of the journalist who has to get the facts straight in a story of national importance or that of the airline captain who is responsible for the safety of his passengers? And if we adopt the criterion of social value, someone will have to decide whether society needs cello players more than police officers, or motel keepers more than accountants.[5]

Obviously, setting wages and prices equitably under a system of comprenensive controls would be a staggering task. For this reason, many feel that despite its imperfections, the market is a better way of

---

[4] *John Kenneth Galbraith,* Economics and the Public Purpose *(Boston: Houghton Mifflin, 1972). See also his* The New Industrial State *(New York: Houghton Mifflin, 1967), esp. pp. 350–68.*
[5] *An interesting discussion of the difficulties of setting relative salaries under price and wage Controls in Britain is found in Aubrey Jones,* The New Inflation *(London: Deutsch, 1973).*

making such decisions than any system of conscious planning and regulation.

structured options

It might seem that freedom is most perfectly realized when people are left alone to do as they please without any interference from government. However, that is not always the case. Freedom of choice implies, at the least, that there be something to choose between. As the Danish poet, Piet Hein puts it

> People are meant to hold various views;
> which has been construed to mean
> That rulers should give them the freedom to choose
> And one thing to choose between.[6]

One choice that decision makers have is to let people work out solutions to their own problems through the market mechanism or some equivalent form of private initiative. The second possibility is for policy makers to create options for individual choice. In this case, the outcome still depends on the voluntary choices of individuals. However, policymakers specify what the alternatives will be.

A university curriculum follows this approach. One could imagine a pure free market university. On registration day, each professor might set up a stand and advertise his wares. "Practical politics at cut rates." Students shop around for the best buys. In fact, what happens is that the administration and faculty plan a system of course offerings. Students choose from the array of options offered. In the long run, such a system is somewhat responsive to consumer demand. Some departments expand, some will contract, and some will eventually be abolished in response to student interest. However, the program is not a pure free market system. It will continue to reflect a conscious decision by policymakers as to what ought to be taught.[7]

Many public programs are based on a system of structured options. In the Community Action Programs of the War on Poverty, federal policymakers were aware that it would be very difficult to define a single policy that would assist the poor. Needs varied greatly

---

[6] *Piet Hein*, Grooks 5 *(Garden City, N.Y.: Doubleday, 1973), p. 43.*

[7] *In the modern economy, most market choices are, in fact, between structured options. In buying insurance, mortgaging a house, shipping goods, or making an employment contract, you do not usually strike an individual, tailormade bargain with the producer. Rather, your choice is between various versions of a standardized contract—you choose plan A, B, or C, and there is little opportunity for the individual to modify the terms presented to him. See Wolfgang Friedman,* Law in a Changing Society, Revised Edition *(Baltimore: Penguin Books, 1972), pp 130–131.*

62

*public policy: choice
on behalf of other
people*

from area to area and group to group. Also, it was clear that little could be accomplished without the active cooperation of the poor themselves. Therefore, a virtual shopping list of potential projects was created and neighborhood organizations were invited to apply for the kind of program they felt would best meet their needs. Day-care centers, clinics, recreational facilities, and neighborhood renewal projects were among the programs eligible for federal funding.

Similarly, in the Chilean agrarian reform of 1967, the issue arose of whether the land expropriated from large *haciendas* would be distributed to peasants in the form of collective or individual farms. The issue was a heated one, socialists and liberals holding strongly opposing views. Finally, it was decided to let the choice rest with the farmers themselves. In the first stage of the reform, the land would be organized in collective farms. However, after the peasants had gained experience in working for themselves, they could decide either by vote of the entire community or individual free choice whether to continue farming in common or divide the land into individually owned plots.

Many social programs contain structured options. Most Americans over 65 are eligible for Medicare, which provides hospital services, but they must choose whether or not to participate in Medicaid, which provides physician's services, out-patient care, and diagnostic services.

Whereas in the United States, social security provides a flat sum to everyone who is covered upon retirement, in many European nations, the individual can choose from a variety of plans for old-age insurance, some of which pay far higher benefits than the basic rate. The idea is to enable people, if they choose, to maintain a higher standard of living in retirement.

In facing a complex or controversial issue, where the policymaker is reluctant to lay down a single rule for everyone, a program of structured options is frequently desirable. The policymaker does not have to decide what is best for everyone. A policy of structured options really combines public planning with market mechanisms. There are two decision points in making public policy. The first is when the policymaker lays down the basic alternatives. The second belongs to the citizen, who chooses among the options available. The nature of public policy depends on both decisions. Those options most preferred receive the bulk of government funding. However, significant minorities are not forced to conform to the will of the majority. And alternatives that are not viewed with favor by the citizens are dropped from the agenda.

Making Decisions About Public Services

The creation of structured options as a form of policymaking is not limited to the kinds of programs suggested by the examples described above. In fact, almost every public service that is not compulsory or obligatory is of this type. When government establishes libraries, parks, and athletic facilities or sponsors orchestras, art galleries, or public television stations, it is creating an option that individuals are free to use or not as they wish. And the extent to which an activity will be supported, or whether it will continue to be supported at all, depends on both the individual demand for it and the judgment of the policymakers on the desirability of the activity.

One crucial decision that every policymaker eventually faces is whether or not to expand the range of public services that government provides.

Let us say that you are a member of a city council, and a group of music lovers proposes that the city subsidize the formation of a local symphony orchestra. The proponents argue that having the opportunity to hear good music would obviously enhance the quality of life in the community. It offers an option, a choice for individuals, that did not exist before.

However, a conservative faction of taxpayers responds that if the community as a whole was really enthusiastic about symphonic music, an orchestra could be self-supporting, and there would be no need for public sponsorship or subsidy. They hint that what the music lovers really want is for the citizenry as a whole to support them in their own particular interest. If they really want a symphony that badly, they should be willing to pay for it. They go on to intimate that since the music lovers are mostly the richer people of the city, to support an orchestra out of general taxation would mean using the taxes paid by the average citizen to support a service for the rich.

The music group responds that public sponsorship of the orchestra would stimulate a more general interest in music, that this would enrich the lives of those who have not had the opportunity to hear good music, and that as more people got interested, the orchestra would become self-supporting. Without public subsidy, the cost of tickets would be so high that many people who wanted to attend the symphony would be excluded for economic reasons. Public sponsorship is preferable to private initiative because the service would be more generally available to the members of the community. The symphony would in effect be a public service, like a library or a park.[8]

If you were faced with this decision, what would you do, and how would you justify your decision?

A distinction can be made between negative and positive freedom. Negative freedom is freedom *from* interference in one's own affairs. Positive freedom is freedom *to* do something. To be free to get a

---

[8] *For a detailed analysis of this problem, see Brian Barry,* Political Argument, *pp. 214–22.*

64

*public policy: choice
on behalf of other
people*

good education, to enjoy rewarding work or leisure activities, means that society must organize to make these opportunities for self-fulfillment available. However, the question then arises of when is it appropriate for government to create options for the expression of individual interests.

There are three questions that can be asked when we face decisions about creating new public programs or services:

1. Is there a public interest in the project?
2. Is the project worth the expense and effort?
3. Who will pay for and who will benefit from the project?

1. Is the project one that it is appropriate for government to undertake? In our society, it is often said that public action is desirable only when private initiative is unwilling or unable to provide a service. This is often taken to be a conservative principle, since it seems to mean that, at the margin, private initiative is to be preferred to government action. In practice, this idea does not limit the scope of government action very much. It seems to mean that any project that is not created by private action is an appropriate subject of governmental initiative.

Another principle that can be applied is that there ought to be a public interest in the project, that it ought to benefit all the members of the community. Some feel that government action is most appropriate in the provision of "public goods," those services where it is difficult or impossible to isolate the specific beneficiaries or users of a service. Police and fire protection are often cited as services of this type. Every citizen benefits from having these services available, whether he uses them or not. It would seem silly to support a police department by charging fees for services rendered. (If you are burglarized, and the police apprehend the thief, you pay for the restoration of your property; otherwise, you do not.) Everyone benefits from the presence of police patrols as a deterrent to crime. Similarly, if you subscribe to the fire service and your neighbor does not, and your neighbor's house catches on fire, you would have to wait until the blaze reaches your house before anything would be done about it.

However, in practice, it is very hard to determine when a particular service is in the public interest and when it serves the specific interests of a particular group. Does the symphony orchestra benefit only music lovers or the citizens in general? Every government sponsors projects that are of particular interest to some citizens, though they also enhance the life of the community as a whole. In judging whether there is a sufficient public interest in a project to justify its being undertaken by government, we have to calculate the direct benefits to the specific users and the community as a whole, and make up our minds about the question of whether there is a sufficient case for supporting the project out of public taxes, through government action.

2. In a world of scarce resources, government cannot support every project that some group wants, and that might conceivably benefit the entire community. We have to assign priorities. Money used for one project cannot be used for another. We have to calculate the "opportunity costs." What alternative activities will be lost if we decide to support one specific project? The more public services are provided, the higher taxes will be, and there is some limit beyond which people will resist further taxation. It is hard to say precisely where this limit is, but resistance by taxpayers to further expansion of the manifold services of the welfare state is becoming apparent.

There are some who argue that the provision of services by the modern state has gone about as far as it can go. We have come to expect that government will guarantee full employment and a high, stable standard of living; that it will provide security for old age, sickness, and injury; that it will ensure a decent environment and a constant supply of energy; that it will provide educational opportunities to everyone and be the patron of science, culture, and the arts; that it will provide a multitude of services to specialized groups and interests. Furthermore, we expect all these things to be made available universally, to all citizens. In our time, the state has experienced a "revolution of rising expectations." We expect extensive services of the state as a matter of right, of entitlement. We are quick to criticize government when it falls down on the job. It may be that the demands for public services have become excessive, that government is facing a "fiscal crisis." Large cities have gone to the brink of bankruptcy, legislators find popular resistance to increased taxation, and government deficit spending is a spur to inflation and diminishes capital resources available to private enterprise. We may in the future have to give serious thought to our priorities. We will have to define standards for deciding which claims to new or expanded services to accept and which to reject.[9]

3. The question of who should pay for a service, and who will benefit from it, is often particularly useful in deciding how a public service should be financed. It is not necessary that every project be supported out of general taxation. We can also apply "users fees" to the provision of a service. In the United States, most public highways are built from money received from gasoline and auto registration taxes. The theory is that those who use the roads ought to pay for their construction and maintenance. Similarly, most public universities charge tuition, and public campgrounds are in part supported by fees. These are charges on those who actually use the service.

---

[9] *See Daniel Bell, "The Public Household,"* The Public Interest 37 *(Fall 1974), pp. 29–68; and* James O'Connor, The Fiscal Crisis of the State *(New York: St. Martin's Press, 1973).*

66

*public policy: choice
on behalf of other
people*

It is possible to combine users fees and support from general taxation, depending on how much we feel that a service is of benefit to a particular group and how much we feel that it benefits the community at large. Thus, in public universities, tuition normally covers only part of the cost of education, the rest being made up through public subsidies.

We often feel that it is desirable to supplement users fees with direct subsidies in order to make a service more widely available. If we based higher education completely on tuition charges, only the relatively wealthy could afford to attend universities. When we decide that it is not appropriate for universities to completely "pay their own way," we are saying that there is a public intrest in providing access to educational opportunities to all qualified students, that it is appropriate for all members of the community to share the burden of financing this service, whether they directly use it or not.

Some public services are obligatory. Every home has to be connected to sanitary sewers, and homeowners must pay for their construction and upkeep for reasons of public health. Here we are interested in *discretionary* public services, those that people can use or not as they so desire, and their implications for the value of freedom. A society that is rich in freedom is one that provides a wide variety of opportunities for the expression of diverse interests and talents. This positive sense of freedom cannot be achieved if we simply leave one another alone, if we do not interfere in each other's affairs. It implies participation, and the intentional creation of collective undertakings. Freedom of choice implies that there will be something to choose between.

To what extent is the structuring of options for individual self-expression a public responsibility? Is the good society the one that provides the largest range of opportunities, that is rich and vital in its activities, where there is always something going on? As you travel around, you become aware that the quality of public life in some communities is enriching and satisfying, while in others it is narrow, mean, and constricted. To a large extent, the difference depends on the relative value that people put on the things of public life and the things of private life. For some, parks, cultural activities, civic affairs, and ceremonies are an important dimension of freedom. For others, life is circumscribed by the household and the family. They cherish the freedom to go their own way. It is hard to say that one or the other of these is the higher value of freedom. But which spirit prevails in a community makes a great deal of difference.

Biased Options

As we move along the continuum from freedom to control, there is another stopping place where the exercise of public authority can be made compatible with the value of individual choice. In a program of structured options, the policymaker lays out the possibilities for individual action but is neutral about the outcome. In a program of biased options, the deck is stacked in favor of some alternatives. The policymaker structures incentives and deterrents to guide individuals in the direction of the objectives of public policy. The individual is still free to defy the wishes of policymakers, but does so at a price.

For example, if the objective is to keep people from smoking or drinking, one alternative is to outlaw the sale of cigarettes and liquor. Another is to raise the taxes on those products to the point where people might drink or smoke less. Whether or not to drink or smoke is still a free choice for the individual, but the option to do so has been made considerably less attractive.

The structuring of incentives and deterrents is an important aspect of policymaking. Modern economic policy rests on the idea that it is possible to reconcile a certain measure of government planning and management of the economy with a free enterprise system by using the government budget and the monetary system to influence the choices of producers and consumers.

Thus, in a period of recession, the normal tendency of business is to cut production and lay off employees, which may only aggravate the economic slump. In response, government may increase its own spending. This puts people to work and provides more money for consumers. Alternatively, government may lower interest rates. This makes it easier for business to get credit for expansion. The business owner is still free to expand production or not at will, but the context of decision has changed. With cheaper credit and increasing demand, there is an incentive to increase production and hire more workers. Conversely, in a period of inflation, government may cut spending, raise taxes, increase interest rates, and restrict the money supply in an effort to "dampen" excess demand.[10]

Incentives may be used for a wide variety of public purposes. To encourage the use of mass transit and discourage automobile use, government might subsidize a bus system to make fares as cheap as possible and increase the charges on downtown parking meters. The two policies might be linked together, revenues from parking meters going into a special fund to support the bus system.

To control industrial water pollution, the government could make pollution a criminal offense and fine or imprison the violators. Or it

---

[10] *Some good sources on government economic policy include David J. and Attiat Ott,* Federal Budget Policy *(Washington: The Brookings Institution, 1963); Joseph A. Pechman,* Federal Tax Policy *(Washington: The Brookings Institution, 1965); and Paul A. Samuelson,* Economics: An Introductory Analysis *Seventh Edition (New York: McGraw-Hill, 1967), pp. 316–58.*

could impose a tax on the use of public rivers for the discharge of industrial wastes. The use of the river is no longer free to the businessman, and if the cost of this "user charge" is high enough, he has a real incentive to install pollution abatement equipment.

There are many different ways of creating incentives and deterrents. Government can directly subsidize a desired activity. Or it can use the taxation system to encourage or discourage individual choices. For example, money earned from investment may be taxed at a lower rate than regular income, as an incentive for people to put their savings to productive use. Interest paid on home mortgages is deductible from federal income tax, a form of incentive to home ownership, and an indirect way of assisting the construction industry.

Many public policies contain unintended incentives and deterrents. For example, Aid for Dependent Children (ADC) was a welfare program created in the 1930s to provide assistance to mothers and children in case of a father's death or a broken home. However, in the early 1960s, it became apparent that when the primary wage earner, traditionally the father, was unemployed and could not find work, this program created a real incentive for the father to desert his family when they could be better provided for on welfare. For women already receiving ADC payments, there was an incentive not to marry. People could live together and continue to receive payments, but if they married, assistance would stop. Until the program was reformed to provide assistance for poor, but complete families, the unintended consequences of a program originally designed for widows was to produce a variety of incentives against the maintenance of normal family units.

Similarly, regulatory policies may create unintended incentives. In the 1970s, the federal agency that regulates airlines, the Civil Aeronautics Board, calculated the profit that an airline might make as a percentage of invested capital. This meant that the more airplanes that an airline bought, the higher its profits could be. The result was that the airlines, which were restricted from competing by cutting fares or offering different services, found that the best way to compete was to buy more planes and fly more frequent schedules. The result was that many routes were saturated with flights, many planes flew with many empty seats, which was inefficient, uneconomical, and wasted fuel.[11]

Whenever you are considering a policy proposal, it is worth asking the question, What incentives and disincentives does it contain? Who will benefit from them? What choices are individuals being encouraged to make as a result of this policy, and what would be the

---

[11] *Roger G. Noll,* Reforming Regulation *(Washington: The Brookings Institution, 1972), pp. 17–18.*

overall consequences for society if a large number of people made that choice? Are the incentives implicit in the program compatible with the objectives of the policy?

For the policymaker, the creation of biased options may be an unusually subtle instrument of public action. Rather than the simple "yes-no" solution of a regulation or a rule, they provide a high degree of flexibility. One can vary the amount of a subsidy or a tax so that the precise degree of a desired effect can be achieved.

Is the idea of biased options compatible with the principle of freedom? To be sure, the outcome is still dependent on the free choices of individuals. However, in extreme cases, such as a prohibitively high tax on liquor or cigarettes, they may be tantamount to compulsion. (It could be argued that a law is no more than an extreme form of a biased option. You are still free to choose to commit murder, but if you do, you have to calculate the desirability of this choice against the chances of imprisonment or execution.)

There is another problem to be considered. Incentives and deterrents affect different groups differently and may be unfair to people who are not in a position to take advantage of them. The incentive to home ownership created by federal tax deductions of interest paid on home mortgages benefits the middle class, who are more likely to be homeowners, and does not benefit renters, who are likely to come from lower income groups. Similarly, the lower rates of taxation on income derived from investment are really only available to those who have savings to invest.

If we decide to discourage liquor consumption through high taxes, or gasoline consumption through high prices, it is likely to be the poor who will be affected the most. A doubling in the price of gasoline may serously affect the options of a low-income family, but the wealthy may not be very much concerned. The society as a whole may conserve petroleum, but it will be the poor who will be responsible for most of the savings. For many of the common incentives and deterrents created by public action, the freedom of choice available to the individual will depend on the size of his income.

Regulation

The fourth possibility then is that government decides which actions will be permitted to the individual and which will not. Freedom of choice is defined and delimited by law, rules, and regulations. The outcome no longer depends on the response of individuals to the options offered by public policy. Individuals are required to act in certain ways.

The case for regulation seems most compelling when basic rights

70

*public policy: choice
on behalf of other
people*

are at issue. We do not offer people incentives to respect the lives, property, and freedoms of others; we require them to do so. To abstain from murder is not an option. It is an obligation.

The case for regulation is also strong when important community interest is at stake. Governments do not offer people the option of taking a driving examination; they require licensing in the interest of public safety. We do not give people cash subsidies to keep their property in good repair; we compel them to do so, so that harm does not come to other individuals.

There is one other area where the idea of freedom of choice seems untenable. This is the case where individuals will automatically benefit from a public service whether they pay for it or not and might think it in their self-interest to avoid contributing to the provision of a service from which they will benefit. This is called the "free rider" problem, and the example that is usually given is collective bargaining.

If a group of workers join a union and pay dues to provide for bargaining with management, and agree to withhold their labor if necessary, they will benefit in higher wages, *but so will every other worker, whether he is a member of the union or not.* The individual might then calculate that it was to his advantage to receive the benefits of collective bargaining but avoid the costs. He will continue to work while the others are on strike, and at the end, his wages will rise with those of the striking workers. He will come out ahead, and get a "free ride." This is the logic underlying the idea of the union shop, where every worker employed by a firm is required to join the recognized union.[12]

The principle can be applied to such public services as police and fire protection, and to some forms of social insurance. One reason that social security is obligatory is that the individual might calculate that it was not worthwhile for him to save in his working years for old age, for the community would take care of him in any event. After all, what is society going to do about its destitute elderly citizens? It could be argued that they *ought* to have provided for their retirement, but if they, in fact, do not, will they simply be left to starve? However, if welfare payments are given to any impoverished older person, then any individual could calculate that it was not worthwhile to save for old age. In effect, he would be maintained by those who paid taxes *and* had put aside money for their retirement. Hence, the only conclusion seems to be that people must be required to insure themselves for the time when they will no longer be able to support themselves.

[12] *Mancur Olson, Jr.,* The Logic of Collective Action *(Cambridge: Harvard University Press, 1965).*

Whenever we face a public decision, we have to decide how much we want the outcome to depend on the voluntary choices of individuals and how much we want to direct, channel and control individual activities. Any problem, as we noted, will somehow solve itself. The idea of public action is to direct individual choices toward a better outcome than would be achieved if each person decided for himself how best to cope with the situation.

Between a policy of laissez-faire and direct governmental regulation and control, there are other options for public action that are compatible with the principle of freedom of choice. Often, what we are doing in making public policy is expanding the range of free choice available to the individual by providing options that did not exist before. In much of modern life, our choices are between planned, authoritatively determined alternatives. We do not commission an automobile maker to build a car custom-made to our specifications. We choose from the models available. Similarly, we choose from the programs of study offered by public schools and universities and from among the recreational and cultural activities offered by public institutions.

Another possibility for public action is to leave the final outcome up to the choices of individuals, but to direct them toward preferred choices by establishing incentives and deterrents.

When we are deciding what to do about a public problem, it is worth considering each of these four alternatives and assessing the advantages and disadvantages of each. For example, consider the following modes of response to the "energy crisis."

If the problem is to induce people to conserve energy and at the same time develop new or alternative energy sources, one answer might be to let nature take its course. As fossil fuels become scarcer, prices will rise, and people will automatically begin to cut down on wasteful energy use. Higher prices will provide incentives to energy producers to explore new energy sources, previously neglected because they were uneconomic. The situation will take care of itself, in time.

Perhaps, though, we could hasten the process by public encouragement of the development of alternatives to the scarce and depletable fossil fuels. Government could structure options, providing funds for research and development into various forms of nuclear power, wind, solar energy, coal gassification, and so on. As each of these energy technologies developed, market forces would determine which was the most useful, desirable, and economical. All that government would do is assure that the alternatives become available.

Or we could accentuate the effect of market forces by imposing taxes as an incentive to energy conservation and providing subsidies for the development of new energy sources. We could give the market process some direction, deciding which energy uses would be most severely penalized and which would be spared from absorbing the full impact of rising prices. We could direct investment toward those energy sources that seemed the most promising or desirable.

Finally, we could impose direct regulations, rationing gasoline, heating fuel, and industrial energy according to some conception of need and social value. We could require the diversion of investment to alternative energy sources, prohibit the use of dangerous or polluting fuels, or require automobile manufacturers to meet certain standards of fuel economy in building new cars.

As we consider these separate options, and various combinations of them, we begin to see that the position we adopt and advocate depends on one fundamental assumption. Does the better policy result from conscious, deliberate public planning and decision—from choice on behalf of others—or does it arise from the cumulative effect of individual choices by consumers and producers, each calculating his own needs and interests in the light of general conditions of supply and demand.

for further reading

Barry, Brian, *Political Argument* (New York: Humanities Press, 1965). The chapter on freedom is complicated, but helps to clarify a number of muddled ideas about the concept.

Bell, Daniel, "The Public Household," *The Public Interest 37* (Fall 1974), pp. 29–68. On the question of how many public services a modern society can afford to provide.

Berlin, Isaiah, *Two Concepts of Liberty* (New York: Oxford Univerersity Press, 1958). Here a crucial distinction is made between positive and negative freedom.

Dahl, Robert A., and Charles E. Lindblom, *Politics, Economics and Welfare*, Revised Edition (New York: Harper and Row, 1976). An elegant discussion of alternative forms of regulation and control and their implications for democracy and freedom.

Friedman, Milton, *Capitalism and Freedom* (Chicago: University of Chicago Press, 1962). A very readable defense of freedom of choice and market forces in many areas of public policymaking.

Galbraith, John K., *Economics and the Public Purpose* (Boston: Houghton Mifflin, 1972). A brilliant discussion of where market effects work and where they do not in modern industrial economies.

Hardin, Garrett, "The Tragedy of the Commons," *Science 162* (December 13, 1968), pp. 1243–48. An example of a logical situation where relying on market effects can lead to a situation which no one would rationally prefer—where market forces are inapplicable in achieving public ends.

Kneese, Allen V., and Charles L. Schultze, *Pollution, Prices and Public Policy* (Washington: The Brookings Institution, 1975). A discussion of the use of incentives and user charges in federal pollution control policy.

Mill, John Stuart, *On Liberty* (New York: Liberal Arts Press, 1958). The classic liberal analysis and defense of the value of freedom.

Okun, Arthur, *Equality and Efficiency: The Big Tradeoff* (Washington: The Brookings Institution, 1975). A discussion of the choice between market forces and the establishment of rights as different methods of public policy.

Stewart, Michael, *Keynes and After* (Baltimore: Pelican Books, 1967). The best introduction to the thought and impact of John Maynard Keynes I know. Keynes is father of the theory that modern capitalist economies could be managed through the careful use of incentives and deterrents to affect the behavior of consumers and producers.

chapter five
justice and distribution

What is justice? This sounds like a philosopher's question. Yet it is also a problem we have to face in making public decisions. Every public policy benefits some people more than others. Tax advantages for business investment may legally be available to everybody, but only the relatively wealthy are apt to be in a position to take advantage of them. Affirmative action programs help minorities and women and discriminate against white males. Even policies that apply equally to all citizens in fact treat people differently, for human needs and interests are infinitely diverse. A uniform system of education benefits some people and frustrates others.

The problem of justice, equity, or fairness—terms that we will use synonymously—is important whether we are creating rights, making rules, or allocating resources. Who will bear the costs of government programs? How will benefits be distributed? Every time we make a public decision we have to ask the question, Is what we are doing fair?

ideas of justice

Throughout history, various definitions of the concept of justice have been proposed.

The ancient Greeks thought that justice meant "to render to each his due."

Some equate justice with simple impartiality, as in the expression, "justice is blind."

Justice has been defined as "treating like cases alike and different cases differently."

The contemporary American philosopher John Rawls has proposed a definition of justice that is being widely discussed and debated. Rawls argues that the most reasonable principles of justice would be those that all would assent to in the "original position," before society was formed, and before people had any knowledge of their place in society, their social class or status, their talents and abilities, or their psychological makeup. Rawls' two principles of justice are

1. Each person has an equal right to the most extensive scheme of equal basic liberties compatible with a similar scheme of liberties for all.
2. Social and economic inequalities must meet two conditions: they must be (a) to the greatest expected benefit of the least advantaged members of society and (b) attached to offices and positions open to all under conditions of fair equality of opportunity.[1]

The difficulty with all such formal definitions is that they are exceedingly abstract and general. It would be very hard to determine how to apply them in particular situations. Rawls himself agrees that his general principles of justice are not much help in deciding concrete cases.[2]

The legal scholar Edmund Cahn once made the interesting observation that we may not be able to define justice, but we certainly know what injustice is. If I were to say, at the beginning of a course, "All students will write one paper," and then, randomly selecting one student, go on to add, "But *you* will write two papers," you would have a very simple reaction. You would call my decision unfair. What is more, you would get angry. Your reaction would not only be intellectual but also emotional. The "sense of injustice," as Cahn calls it, is not just a reasoned judgment. It is a visceral, psychological reaction. We seem to have tapped a basic human instinct.[3]

However, were I to say, "All students will write one paper but those enrolled for honors credit will write two," the response would be different. If everyone does the same work, but some receive honors credit and some do not, *that* would be considered unfair. Establishing relevant distinctions and rationally defensible categories is an important part of the problem of justice, just as it is essential in the definition

---

[1] *Johns Rawls,* A Theory of Justice *(Cambridge: Harvard University Press, 1971). Rawls' book is detailed and closely reasoned. A better introduction to his ideas is his article "Justice as Fairness" in Peter Laslett and W. G. Runciman (Eds.),* Philosophy, Politics and Society, Second Series *(Oxford: Basil Blackwell, 1967), pp. 132–57.*
[2] *John Rawls, "Concepts of Distribution Equity: Some Reasons for the Maximin Criterion,"* American Economic Review *64 (Spring 1973), pp. 141–46.*
[3] *Edmund Cahn,* The Sense of Injustice *(New York: New York University Press, 1949).*

76

*public policy: choice
on behalf of other
people*

of rights. The abstract principle, "Treat like cases alike and different cases differently," captures at least one important dimension of the problem of justice.

criteria of justice

The question of fairness is part of many kinds of decisions. Public officials and managers of private firms have to decide how much employees should be paid in relation to one another. Should police earn more than fire fighters or should they be treated equally? Should faculty salaries be based on publication and scholarly research, or teaching performance, or experience and seniority? Should family responsibilities and personal circumstances be taken into account in making salary decisions? Should a professor with four children be paid more than a single person even though the bachelor is a better teacher? Or should all college teachers be paid the same, whatever their needs, talents, or accomplishments?

We do not often want to leave such decisions entirely up to the market. In fact, the laws of supply and demand normally operate with little precision in establishing relative salaries in public service or large companies. People compare their salaries not only with what others in the same occupation are earning in society at large but also with people in different occupations in the same organization. Demands for higher pay are based not only on market forces but also on conceptions of relative equity among those who work for the same firm. But, do we really want to base the pay of public administrators or faculty members on what they could get if they threatened to go elsewhere? Does this not mean that the largest rewards would go to those with the least loyalty to the government or the university? Might not others threaten to quit because they felt "unfairly treated" in comparison to those who could make the most extravagant demands?

Or take another problem. Assume you are a member of a welfare board. How much income should a destitute widow, an orphan in a foster home, or a blind person receive? Should assistance to those dependent on public welfare depend on the effort they make to become self-sufficient, on their productive contribution to society? In that case, we would want to increase welfare payments the more the handicapped person earned from outside employment, and welfare benefits usually work the other way around—the more you earn, the less assistance you receive.

Or should welfare be based on need? Should a welfare recipient receive enough to provide a decent minimum standard of living, adequate food, housing shelter, and medical care? But what if it is proposed that those dependent on public welfare through no fault of their own be paid enough to take an annual vacation in Florida, on the ground that were they not handicapped, they certainly would earn enough through normal employment to be able to enjoy such an experience? Should welfare recipients' budgets include a liquor allowance? Or should a person on welfare not drink? What is fair treatment for those dependent on public assistance and what the taxpayers will stand for may be entirely different things.

There are basically three criteria that can be applied to making decisions on comparative fairness.

1. *Desert.* We treat people unequally because some deserve more than others. It is only fair that those who assume larger risks, responsibilities, who are more productive or skillful, earn more than those whose performance is average or below average.
2. *Need.* We treat people differently because they have different needs. Those with family responsibilities should perhaps receive higher incomes than single persons.
3. *Equality.* It is just that all people be treated in the same way. All people who do the same work should receive equal pay. It is not fair to pay women less than men for the same job.

The three criteria are complex and contradictory. The real problem is how to decide when to apply one rather than another to a problem of distributive equity.

income distribution

J. Kenneth Jamieson, president of the Exxon Corporation, earned $677,000 a year in 1976. The average industrial worker earns about $12,000 annually. A surgeon may have an income of about $80,000 a year, as may a senior airline captain. Some experienced professors earn about $30,000. Are these disparities in income justifiable? On what grounds can we defend them, either absolutely, or in relation to one another? Is it true that Jamieson is, in some sense, worth sixty times as much to Exxon as a refinery worker? How do we decide that he is not worth twice as much or one hundred times as much?

In all industrial societies, income is unequally distributed. In the United States, the top 5 percent earns more than twice as much as the bottom 20 percent of all income earners. The top 20 percent earns more than the bottom 60 percent although the latter group contains three times as many people (see Table 1).

Are such inequalities in income distribution a public problem or are they not? Should government consciously undertake to redistribute income toward greater equality? Or is the prevailing distribution of income in some sense justifiable, and would it only lead to greater injustice if government attempted to make income distribution more equal or "rational"? Who bears the burden of proof? People who believe that all departures from absolute equality must be defended or

78

*public policy: choice
on behalf of other
people*

table 1
family income in the United States in 1972

Families	Percentage of Income
Lowest fifth	5.4
Second fifth	11.9
Third fifth	17.5
Fourth fifth	23.9
Highest fifth	41.4
Highest 5 percent	15.9

Source. Statistical Abstract of the United States: 1974, p. 384.

those who believe that anyone who proposes to make income distribution more equal must justify his position? To answer these questions,
we need to apply some criteria of fundamental fairness.

The Question of Desert

Society can reward people unequally in many different ways. There
can be differences of status, prestige and respect. But here we are
mainly concerned about differences in income. When is it fair for some
people to be paid much more than others?

To ask What do people deserve? is not a simple question. The
concept of desert has to be broken down and analyzed, because there
are really a variety of different principles that are subsumed under this
heading.

Compensation. We might decide to treat people unequally on the
grounds that they deserve compensation for the risk, sacrifice, danger,
or unpleasantness of their work. We might agree that a person was
entitled to a higher return if the chances of bankruptcy were one in two
than if it was an investment in a sure thing. Perhaps the oil "wildcat-
ter" deserves to "strike it rich," for the risks of coming up with nothing
but a dry well are very great indeed.

We might decide that people are entitled to unequal income on the
grounds of greater *effort,* if they work longer hours or exercise greater
diligence. In effect, we are compensating them for the loss of leisure
that others enjoy.

We might argue that some deserve higher incomes on the grounds
of *deferred gratification.* The doctor, lawyer, or professor might defend
his or her above-average income on the grounds of the very low
income received during the years of education. Incidentally, it is very
easy to estimate how much compensation a person is entitled to based
on this reason alone. If the average industrial wage is about $12,000,
and the duration of professional education about nine years, counting
both undergraduate and advanced training, the professional's deferred income is at most $108,000, if we ignore interest. In other words,
this is what such a person would have earned by entering the labor

force directly from high school, as a semiskilled worker. Averaged over a working lifetime of forty years (the professor or lawyer would graduate at about age 26) this amounts to about $2500 a year. Hence, it would be fair, on the basis of deferred gratification alone, to pay doctors or professors about $14,500 per year, perhaps $18,000 if we considered interest. How then do we account for the fact that most trained professionals earn far more than this?

We might feel that it is necessary to compensate people whose work is dangerous, dirty, or unpleasant. Should a miner earn more than a bus driver on this basis? A high steel worker more than a carpenter?

Superior Performance. Do we really believe in the principle of "equal pay for equal work"? Should all doctors, architects, corporation presidents, stonemasons, or cooks be paid the same? Or should people be rewarded for excellence, for superior performance?

Note that effort and excellence are different principles of justice. The student who appeals a grade on the grounds of hard work on a wrong-headed paper (while a friend, who got a higher grade, dashed off a brilliant essay in an evening) may be in the same position as the bus driver who claimed overtime pay for taking a bus from Chicago to Albuquerque when the schedule called for a trip to Denver. Obviously it takes longer to drive to Albuquerque than to Denver, but rewarding effort without considering accomplishment may be completely unfair.

However, the idea of using performance alone as a standard of reward raises one serious question. Should people receive higher incomes simply because they possess an unusual talent or above-average intelligence? These are innate characteristics, something the individual can do nothing about. Is it fair to reward those who are simply lucky enough to have a gift for science, music, or administration more highly than those who do not?

Nonetheless, we are inclined to believe that excellence and achievement should be rewarded in some way. It does not seem fair for two people to be treated the same, though they work the same hours and put in the same effort, when one demonstrably does the better job.

Productivity is a standard that is frequently used in justifying income differentials in modern industrial society. The worker who produces more is entitled to the higher wage. Wage increases should be related to productivity. If industrial wages rise in excess of productivity, the result would be inflation. In countries that have adopted income policies—wage controls as a means of trying to control inflation—this standard is frequently used in making public decisions about what workers in different industries ought to be paid.

The effect is that workers in highly productive industries, usually those using advanced technologies, earn more than those in declining industries. There are many who assert that this is as it should be. The standard of equity is that people are paid in relation to their contribu-

80

*public policy: choice
on behalf of other
people*

tion to the total product of society. Furthermore, in a free market system, labor will move from the less productive to the more productive sectors of the economy. People will not be encouraged to remain in backward industries when they could earn more, and their labor would be worth more, in the more dynamic sectors of the economy.

However, the standard of productivity, if applied universally, raises some serious questions of equity. It is very hard for workers in some industries, particularly in the service sector, to raise their productivity. A dentist can only treat so many patients; increasing productivity in education usually means simply increasing the size of classes. (In public universities, improving "productivity" is often a euphemism for simply cutting the budget.)

Furthermore, to what extent do productivity increases represent a contribution by the worker, in terms of skill or effort? They may result from the introduction of laborsaving equipment or the improved organization of work, which may be due to management rather than labor. Does the worker *deserve* to benefit from such improvements, unless they also mean a greater exercise of skill, effort, or concentration on his part?

Social Benefit. Should people be rewarded in proportion to their contribution to society or to the welfare of others? This looks like a principle that would be very hard to apply in practice, for it seems to imply that somebody would have to decide whether policemen or artists, advertising executives or stockbrokers, contributed more to the common good. Nonetheless, if we are to justify existing income inequalities, we would probably have to appeal to a principle of this type.

On what basis does a president of a major corporation deserve to earn as much as sixty times more than an industrial worker? It would be hard to claim that the president works sixty times as hard or puts in sixty times the hours. The question of whether the president is sixty times as good at his job as the lathe operator is at his is never asked. To justify the high incomes of executives and leaders, we would probably have to appeal to the idea of *responsibility*. Those who must make decisions on which the welfare of others depends should be highly rewarded. But just why should the political arts—making choices on behalf of others—deserve greater reward than other kinds of accomplishment or skill? Is the work really so unpleasant that high inducements have to be offered for people to accept executive positions? Is it that the consequences of a mistake could be so grave—are we really rewarding risk rather than responsibility? How would we go about defining an equitable relationship between the salaries of managers and workers?

Of course, it is possible to appeal to the logic of the marketplace in justifying income differentials. In a competitive society, people get what others are willing to pay for their services. People capable of managing a large corporation are in scarce supply and there is a lot of demand for their services. In the same way, only a few have the talent to be a doctor, scientist, or architect. Income levels are determined by the laws of supply and demand. Of course, we still have to ask the question of whether those who command a scarce ability *deserve* to have a higher income than the average person. Does society really have to pay unusually high wages to those with special aptitudes to induce them to use them? Either we must justify the high incomes of top managers and professionals on the basis of effort, sacrifice, risk, or performance, or we must admit that such incomes are based simply on market power, that those who command a special talent can hold out for the highest bidder.

Furthermore, if we were to justify income differentials on the basis of the market, we would have to be persuaded that the market actually did operate freely and openly in setting income levels. This would mean that there were no artificial scarcities, created perhaps by restricting entry into some professional fields. We would also have to assume that salaries were really set by the laws of supply and demand and not by agreement among the practitioners of a field. And we would have to believe that no groups were systematically disadvantaged in the competitive struggle.

The Idea of Equality of Opportunity

There is a historic belief in American society that unequal rewards are justified on the basis of equality of opportunity. People who work hard, demonstrate talent and ability, put out more effort than colleagues, will get ahead. On the whole, it is held, the society rewards merit, rather than inherited position, social class, or status. The only policy problem is to assure that everyone has an equal start in the competitive race. Unequal rewards can be justified if they obviously arise from the differences in ability and effort and not the accident of being born into the right family or social class. In America, there has long been a strong faith that universal education was the basis of equality of opportunity. If all have a fair chance to develop their aptitudes and talents, what they make of these abilities in later life is up to them.

Discrimination is an important problem for a society that believes in equality of opportunity. If it can be shown that there is a systematic bias against racial or ethnic minorities, or women, in competing for the positions of privilege and prestige that society has to offer, then the entire justification for income differentials based on merit alone is called into question. The society is unjust, by its own chosen standard. White males have had the advantage of an artificial scarcity of talent. They have not really had to compete against all who have unusual ability or are willing to work especially hard. Blacks, Mexicans, Indian Americans, and women have been handicapped in the competitions. It

82

*public policy: choice
on behalf of other
people*

is apparent that race affects income. In 1973, the median income for white families was $12,595, while for black families, the median income was $7596.[4]

Race and sex both limit income potential. For the same work, women and nonwhites have usually been paid less than white males, as Table 2 makes clear.

In recent years, many have come to doubt whether education is a sufficient remedy for the problems of inequality of opportunity. Even the best schools may not be able to overcome initial disadvantages of family background, cultural deprivation, and the like. The famous Coleman report attempted to demonstrate that even when educational quality is held constant, children from families with higher incomes, higher status, and living in better neighborhoods had higher levels of education achievement.[5]

Hence, creating equality of opportunity has become a complex policy problem. If we are to insist that income differentials can be justified if they arise from real differences of merit and not of initial advantage, what is required of government to assure that all get a fair start in the race of life? Universal education alone may not be sufficient. Sex and race discrimination are obviously a problem. But if family and social background are also crucial, is it necessary for society to assure that each person has adequate nutrition and health care, the chance to grow up in a good neighborhood, perhaps some guaranteed level of income in the first place, if we are to remain consistent with our own criterion of justice?

An important issue of fundamental fairness arises in connection with efforts to remedy race and sex discrimination. If people have been treated unequally in the past, is it fair to treat them more than equally until they catch up, to compensate them for past injustices? This is the

table 2
weekly earnings by race and sex in 1971

	White		Nonwhite	
Occupation	Male	Female	Male	Female
White collar	$199	$114	$156	$115
Blue collar	152	88	120	81
Service workers	132	72	105	70
Farm workers	80	68	61	58

Adapted from Kenneth M. Dolbeare and Murray J. Edelman, *American Politics: Policies Power and Change,* Second Edition (Boston: D.C. Heath, 1974), p. 88.

[4] Statistical Abstract of the United States, *1974, p. 383.*
[5] *James S. Coleman,* Equility of Educational Opportunity *(Washington: Government Printing Office, 1966).*

question of "Affirmative action" or "reverse discrimination." If justice means treating like cases alike and different cases differently, it can be argued that those who are victims of discrimination are in a special situation, one that calls for special assistance from government, assistance that is not made equally available to all citizens. The opposing view would be that justice is satisfied if all people are treated alike, without regard to such irrelevant characteristics as race and sex.

Let us assume that a university maintenance crew has never employed a nonwhite or a woman. The university claims that it does not practice discrimination, rather, no qualified minority candidate has ever applied for a job. Should the university then be required to discriminate in favor of nonwhites or women until they make up a specified proportion of the crew? Discrimination does not have to be overt after all; it can take subtle forms. Perhaps minority group members simply assumed they would not be welcome on the crew. Perhaps they had no opportunity to learn a craft, or perhaps they were discouraged from joining the union. Should government then act to break this self-perpetuating cycle? If so, what do we make of the argument of the rejected white male applicant who claims that he was discriminated against on the (irrelevant) grounds of race and sex?

Egalitarianism.

There are some who believe that equality of opportunity, as it is understood in the United States, does not justify existing income inequalities, that it is not an adequate standard of justice. They argue that justice requires a more equal distribution of income itself.

Christopher Jencks, for example, claims that there is no evidence that those who get ahead in American society deserve to do so, that they win their high positions on the basis of unusual ability or effort. Rather, success is a product of many factors, not the least of which are aggressiveness, contacts, simply being in the right place at the right time, or luck. The grand prizes in our society do not go necessarily to those who deserve them. Who wins and who loses has a lot to do with initial advantages and disadvantages, and after a certain point, it is simply a random process.

Income differences cannot be explained as a result of schooling. Education is not an adequate means of creating equality of opportunity. Given all the factors that influence success, the only way to create real equality of opportunity would be to create a greater equality in the distribution of income itself, which would assure that people were free to choose the opportunities they want.[6]

---

[6] *Christopher Jencks,* Inequality: A Reassessment of the Effect of Family and Schooling in America *(New York: Basic Books, 1972). See also Lester C. Thurow, "Education and Economic Equality,"* The Public Interest 28 *(Summer 1972), pp. 61–81.*

84

*public policy: choice
on behalf of other
people*

Egalitarians may also argue that the idea of equality of opportunity is a socially demoralizing doctrine. It leads to the belief that those on top are there because they deserve to be. They are worthy, they have proved themselves through ability and effort. By the same token, those on the bottom can explain their fate as resulting from a lack of ability or worth. They are there because they are not as good. They are unworthy. But they have no right to complain. In a meritocracy, virtue is rewarded, and they are not among the virtuous.

The Criterion of Need

We may or may not want to defend differences in income on the grounds of desert, but what happens when we apply the criterion of need? Those who favor income redistribution frequently assert that though people may differ greatly in ability, dedication, and ambition, their basic needs are very much the same. To lead a decent life everyone must have adequate nutrition, shelter, clothing, education, and health care, at a minimum. One can argue about what standard of living is necessary for a decent, respectable way of life, but it is really not impossible to define. The United States Department of Health, Education, and Welfare does it all the time in setting the "poverty level." This definition of poverty relies on accepted standards of nutrition; the costs of housing, clothing, and the like; allowances for recreation, appliances, education, and health.

So we can raise the question of whether a minimum income is a human *right,* something that people are entitled to without taking into account their abilities, efforts, or accomplishments. In a society that has enough abundance to go around, is it fair for some part of the population to live in poverty?

This puts the basic policy question squarely. Is the income distribution in a society a public problem, one that government should do something about, in the name of fundamental fairness? Should government consciously attempt to redistribute income toward greater equality?

The issue of income distribution is a large and complex problem. However, this is not an issue that can be avoided, for it bears on every decision we make about the system of taxation or the distribution of benefits from government programs.

progressive taxation and justice

Who should bear the burden of government? How should the costs of providing public services be distributed? This is a decision we must face whenever we create a public program, whether in government or a private organization. Should all members of a political science associ-

ation pay the same dues, or should there be special "student rates," on
the assumption that students have lower incomes than faculty members, and that it is only fair to charge them less? (The question of justice
and incentives, again, are different. We might want to offer special
rates to students as an inducement to them to join, without considering fundamental fairness.)

There are three basic ways of organizing a system of taxation.

1. *Equality of contribution.* Everyone pays the same. A poll tax is
   like this, or a flat fee for membership. Such taxes are usually
   called regressive, for they impose a greater burden on the
   poor than the rich. A flat, $1000 tax on each household would
   represent 10 percent of the income of a family who earned
   $10,000 but only 1 percent of the income of a family making
   $100,000. Sales taxes are usually considered mildly regressive.
   They impose a flat rate, say 4 percent, on everything pur-
   chased. It is true that the rich buy more than the poor, hence
   pay more in taxes, but the poor consume a higher proportion
   of their incomes, the rich saving and investing more, and
   consequently such tax tends to weigh more heavily on those
   with lower incomes.

2. *Proportionality.* As Irving Kristol points out,[7] when the income
   tax was first proposed in the nineteenth century, the idea was
   that a proportionate tax would be more equitable than a flat
   rate tax as a way of raising revenues. Taxation should be by
   "ability to pay," that is, proportionate to income. Hence, a tax
   rate of, say, 15 percent of income would achieve the desired
   result. A person with an income of $100,000 would pay $15,000
   in taxes, one with an income of $10,000 would pay $1500. The
   object was to achieve fairness, not a redistribution of income.

3. *Progressive taxation.* The idea of a progressive tax is that the
   more you earn, the more you should pay in taxes. Hence, a
   progressive tax system would levy a rate, say, of 25 percent on
   all income up to $10,000. The rate would increase by incre-
   ments. Between $10,000 and $15,000, the rate might be 29
   percent, and so on, with income above $100,000 taxed at a rate
   of 70 percent. (This is approximately the way the present
   federal income tax works.) Remember that this does not mean
   that a person earning more than $100,000 pays a rate of 70
   percent on all income, but only on the proportion that is over
   $100,000. He or she pays 25 percent on the first $10,000, about
   30 percent on the second $10,000, and so on.

[7] *Irving Kristol, "Taxes, Poverty and Equality," The Public Interest 38 (Fall 1974), pp. 3–28.*

86

*public policy: choice
on behalf of other
people*

Critics of the progressive income tax, like Kristol, argue that such a tax cannot be justified on the grounds of basic equity, but only as a means to income redistribution. To support such a tax, one must believe that the rich are, in some sense, not entitled to their high incomes, and that it would be desirable public policy to transfer some of the income of the rich to the poor through the intermediary of government.

Another way of putting this would be to say that the rich do not *need* their high incomes as much as the poor need theirs, and that it is fair to charge them more of that part of their incomes which would not go to cover basic needs (food, shelter) to pay for government services.

Hence, our attitude toward progressive taxation depends in large part on whether we think existing income differences are justified or not. If the rich *deserve* their high incomes, if they are a just reward for unusual effort, risk, sacrifice, or performance, then it is not fair for government to take a disproportionate share of them in taxation. As Kristol would say, the money does, after all, belong to the individual and not to the government. Disproportionately high rates of taxation, if the individual truly deserves the income, are tantamount to theft.

On the other hand, if we feel that it is the responsibility of government to meet human needs, that fundamental fairness requires that all citizens have adequate food, shelter, education, health care, and the like, then it is appropriate to charge those who have more than they can consume in order to meet these needs. Or, if we agree with Christopher Jencks, that the "grand prizes" in our society result from luck or initial advantage rather than skill, effort, or performance, then the rich are not entitled to their high incomes, and it is appropriate for government to reduce the "unearned increment" and redistribute it toward the end of greater income equality.

Progressive Taxation and "Loopholes"

The fact of the matter is that the taxation system of the United States is not progressive. Very few, if any, rich individuals pay the full rates that appear in the income tax schedules. Many giant corporations and millionaires pay no federal income tax at all in many years. What we have achieved in practice is more like a system of proportionality. In fact, each quartile of the population pays about 25 percent of their income in taxes.

The reason for this is the system of deductions and exemptions —some would call them "loopholes"—built into the tax structure. Investments are taxed at a different rate from regular income. Charitable contributions, business expenses, investments in municipal bonds, and certain kinds of trusts are not taxable at all. Such deductions are defended as incentives—the special rates on investments are an inducement for people to put their excess earnings to productive use in the economy rather than spending them for luxuries; the deductions for charity are an incentive for people to contribute to worthwhile projects.

However, critics argue that the system of tax incentives is often unfair because many of these legitimate deductions are only really available to those with very high incomes. Investing in municipal bonds, establishing "tax shelters" through trusts and foundations, is not the sort of thing that the average wage earner is likely to do. He has enough trouble just making ends meet. His income is fully taxable. The rich person can deduct large portions of his income. The intent of the progressive income tax is thereby nullified.

However, many of the "loopholes" in the federal income tax system were put there for reasons of fundamental fairness. The largest allowance in the system is the exemption for dependents. At present, you can deduct $675 from your income tax for each person who is dependent on you for support. The idea is that the needs of large families are greater than those of single people, and it is unfair to tax them at the same rate.

A tax system without such loopholes might be basically unjust. Consider deductions for business expenses. Is it fair for a mechanic who works for a large firm and has his equipment provided to pay the same tax as one who must provide his own tools and materials? The two might have the same gross income, but they are obviously not in the same situation.

The great complexities of the American taxation system are a source of annoyance and frustration to citizens—particularly around April 15. Those who can afford a skilled tax lawyer seem to be able to "get away with murder." It would seem so simple to do away with all the intricate provisions of the tax code, all the exemptions and deductions, and simply tax everyone at a single proportionate rate. But would such a system be fair? Might it not impose burdens and create advantages that are indefensible?

Whenever we make a public decision, we have to ask the question, Who will bear the costs? Is it fair that all should pay equally? If not, what are defensible grounds for making distinctions? The principle of justice—"treat like cases alike and different cases differently"—is a fundamental standard to be applied to such decisions.

The problem of welfare: incentives and equity

Let us now look at the question from the other side. In appraising the fairness of any public action, we have to ask not only who bears the burden but also who receives the benefits. In a society where income is unequally distributed, should all benefit equally from government expenditures? Or should government attempt to create greater equal-

88

*public policy: choice
on behalf of other
people*

ity or justice by transferring income or wealth from the richer to the poorer members of the community? This brings us to the important question of welfare policy.

Welfare has always been a controversial issue. Virtually no one is satisfied with the present system of welfare in the United States. People talk about "welfare cheaters" and the "welfare mess." Why is it so hard to define a satisfactory welfare policy? Why is welfare such a complicated issue? Why is it so hard to reform? Some suggest that the hardheartedness and selfishness of a prosperous society is at fault. Others say that the problem is that starry-eyed reformers keep trying to press for an egalitarianism that most of the society does not want.[8] In fact, as we shall see, welfare is a complicated issue because it raises fundamental questions of fairness and justice.

Throughout most of the nineteenth and twentieth centuries, the objective of welfare policy was neither to redistribute income nor to provide assistance on the basis of need alone. The idea that government should try to eliminate poverty by providing aid to those with low incomes is of relatively recent origin. Rather, the principal purpose of public welfare historically was to assist those who could not be expected to support themselves. The criterion of justice that was applied was not *need* but *desert*. The "deserving poor" were those who were impoverished through no fault of their own.

The basic presumption of public policy has been that people are responsible for their own support. Both Marxist and liberal states define work as a duty of the citizen. The problem of welfare policy, then, is to establish categories of legitimate dependency. The fundamental question is, *When is the individual properly exonerated from responsibility for his own maintenance?* The seriously handicapped or disabled are an obvious category. So are dependent children. But after that, the matter is apt to become controversial.

From this point of view, the most serious problem of injustice is that those who could provide for themselves might prefer to live off welfare. The riddle of how to prevent people from taking unfair advantage of public assistance has profoundly influenced welfare policymaking in all Western societies.

For example, old age might be considered a legitimate condition of dependency. A decent society should honor and respect its elders and provide for their security in later life. However, most Western societies have seen the problem differently. A responsible individual should not become a burden on others. He or she will save in his working years to provide for his retirement, or the family should be responsible for maintaining the elderly, not the society as a whole.

---

[8] *Bill Cavala and Aaron Wildavsky, "The Political Feasibility of Income by Right," Public Policy XVIII (Spring 1970), pp. 321–54.*

It would be unjust for those who did prudently plan for their retirement to have to pay for the support of those who frivolously "spent it all." It would be unfair for families willing to support their parents and grandparents to have to pay taxes to provide for those who did not. What then should public policy be toward the impoverished elderly? It would be indecent simply to ignore their misery. However, if public assistance were made available to anyone who fell into poverty in later life, no one would have an incentive to save for old age.

Out of logic like this, the basic approach of Western societies to old age dependency emerged. The individual is not *entitled* to support in later life, rather the individual is *required* to save for retirement through compulsory social insurance.

The modern "welfare state" then is based on a distinction between conditions of dependency that are covered by direct assistance, such as physical handicap, and those that are covered by social insurance, such as old age, unemployment, industrial accidents, and health care (which is available only to the elderly in the United States), where the individual—sometimes with his employer or the government—is required to contribute to secure himself against the threat of loss of earning power.

The most persistent issue of welfare policy has been how to avoid creating situations where the individual would rationally prefer welfare to work. Sometimes the solutions to this problem have seemed worse than the evil of poverty itself. The British, in the nineteenth century, adopted the principle of "less eligibility," which meant that public assistance should never appear more attractive than the least desirable job in the economy.

The result was the workhouse. To many, the purposes of this institution were essentially altruistic and humanitarian. The causes of poverty lay in the individual and not the social order. Destitution was caused by bad habits. If the poor could be taught punctuality and discipline, cleanliness, morality and skill, they would become self-supporting. It was better to place the poor in such redeeming institutions than simply to support them through the dole. However, the workhouse could not be made too attractive, not actually desirable, lest people come to prefer it to normal employment. As a consequence, life in the workhouse became grim, regimented, spartan, and horrifying. It became a fate to be avoided at all costs.

The workhouses have long since vanished, but the essential dilemma of public policy remains. How provide assistance to those authentically in need, yet create no positive incentive to prefer welfare to work?[9]

[9] *On the history of welfare policy, see Gaston Rimlinger,* Welfare Policy and Industrialization in Europe, America and Russia *(New York: John Wiley, 1971); and Hugh Heclo,* Social Politics in Britain and Sweden *(New Haven: Yale University Press, 1974).*

Poverty and Welfare

The Great Society program in the United States in the 1960s marked a basic change in our philosophy of welfare policy. Poverty itself became recognized as a condition of dependency, one in which the individual is entitled to public support. The criterion of justice changed from desert to need. The only test of eligibility for public assistance is income itself. The poor are entitled to benefit from special programs whatever the cause of their poverty.

This is a basic redefinition of the problem of welfare policy. It rests, in part, on the idea that society, and not the individual, is responsible for poverty. It means that income inequality is recognized as a public problem, one that government should do something about. And this new conception of welfare raises its own problems of social justice.

During the 1960s, a variety of programs were created that made benefits available to low-income families (those whose earnings fell below the official poverty level, about $5000 for an urban family of four in 1976). Among these were:

1. Direct cash assistance,
2. Rent subsidies,
3. Medical care (Medicaid),
4. Food stamps.

This system has become highly controversial, and many of the objections to it reflect arguments about fundamental fairness.

First, it is argued that the poor themselves are treated unequally. Those with low incomes are "in the same situation," yet, depending on where they live, those with the same incomes may receive very different benefits. Benefits vary with the specific policies of state and local governments. Some of the poor live in areas where subsidized housing is available, while others do not. Some states provide rather generous medical care programs, some provide very limited programs, and a few provide none at all.

Second, the complex regulations of modern welfare programs expose the poor to a degree of government regulation not experienced by other citizens. The poor are recognized as a "separate category." A social stigma attaches to the welfare recipient.

The present welfare system requires a large bureaucracy to administer it. It is expensive and inefficient. Furthermore, it is subject to a number of abuses. The food stamp program, in particular, has been used by many who are far from poor.

A Minimum Guaranteed Income

Many have suggested that these problems could be overcome if government provided income, rather than particular services, to those in eed. One way to do this would be through a negative income tax. Above a certain income level, the individual pays taxes to the government. Below that level, the individual would not pay taxes but would receive a check from the government representing the difference between his actual income and the minimum guaranteed income. Hence, if the poverty level were $5000 for a family of four, a family with an income of $3000 would receive a payment of $2000 from the Internal Revenue Service. The system, it is argued, would be easy to administer. Basically, the IRS would be the welfare system. No one would know who was on welfare and who was not. There would be no requirements to meet, no forms to fill out, no "special government" for the poor. The system would be simplicity itself.

Justice and Income Maintenance

However, whether the approach be that of providing special services to the poor or one based on a guaranteed income, any policy of income maintenance raises basic problems of fundamental fairness.

The first problem of justice is that of income redistribution itself. We have already raised the issue of whether it is fair for a society to commit itself to transferring income from the better-off to the less-well-off. Our first response to the idea of income maintenance depends on our answer to the question of whether income differentials are justified or not.

However, perhaps the more serious question arises when we compare the situation of those directly above the line of eligibility for income support with those below it. The crucial question of justice may be not whether a program of income maintenance is fair to the rich, but whether one can be devised that is fair to the working poor.

Consider the following example. Let us assume that two people are working at the same job, but one works part time and earns an annual income of $3000 and the other works full time and earns $8860. Let us assume, for the sake of simplicity, that both pay a tax of 25 percent on their earned income.

Now the low-income worker might be eligible, in some of the more generous states, for a variety of benefits from present programs. The individual might receive:

Direct cash assistance	$3600
Medicaid worth	1000
Rent and food subsidies worth	1260
Total welfare benefits	5860
Earned income	3000
Gross income	8860
Tax on earned income	750
Effective income	$8110

92

*public policy: choice
on behalf of other
people*

On the other hand, the full-time worker, not receiving welfare be
nefits, would pay tax on his full income.

Gross income	$886
Tax	222
Effective income	$664

In short, it is possible for the part-time worker to realize a highe
standard of living than the full-time worker.[10]

The same problem exists in any known program of negative in
come taxes. We have to draw the line somewhere, and those im
mediately above the line, who pay taxes, will compare their earning
with those below the line, whose incomes will be brought up to a leve
very close to that of the fully self-supporting through income mainte
nance payments. We might argue on the basis of need that a certain
minimum income is necessary to sustain a decent way of life, but the
self-supporting full-time worker will be apt to ask whether his part
time co-worker *deserves* to receive approximately the same income tha
he does.

The problem involves not only fairness but also the incentive to
work. Under any scheme of income maintenance, might not a person
rationally prefer to receive welfare payments rather than increase his
work effort? Welfare specialists talk about the high "implicit tax" rates
on those who raise their income levels above the poverty line. The
person earning $3000, whose income totals $5000 including welfare
payments, and who takes a job paying $6000, not only pays tax on his
higher income but also *loses* $2000 in benefits otherwise guaranteed
Many income maintenace programs have very high implicit tax rates.
Some estimate that the tax rate for present cash assistance programs is
about 66 percent; in other words, for every additional $3 that a worker
earns, he loses about $2 in benefits.[11]

Many question whether a guaranteed income program would, in
fact, have the effect of lowering the desire to work among the poor.
Most people want the dignity and satisfaction of employment, and the
"poverty line" is, in any event, so low that most would gladly trade the
benefits they receive to sustain a meager standard of living for the
economic advantages of a full-time job. Some empirical experiments
have suggested that minimum income schemes are not really a detri-
ment to work effort.[12]

---

[10] *The example is adapted from data provided in Henry J. Aaron,* Why Is Welfare So Hard to
Reform? *(Washington: The Brookings Institution, 1973), pp. 31–6.*

[11] *For an extended discussion of this problem, see Henry J. Aaron,* Why Is Welfare So Hard to
Reform?

[12] *Harold Watts and Glen Cain,* Income Maintenance and Labor Supply: Econometric
Studies *(Chicago: Markham, 1974).*

However, the basic problem of how to design a program in which benefits do not diminish as the individual becomes increasingly self-supporting has not been solved. Always the riddle is how to reconcile work incentives with elementary justice. It does not seem fair to let the individual earning $3000 keep $2000 in benefits when he or she moves to a job paying $8000. Why should one person receive $10,000 for a job that pays $8000 to everyone who was never on welfare?

It is apparent that a guaranteed income will always be seen as unfair by the fully self-supporting whose incomes approximate those of welfare recipients. There is no way out of this problem so long as it is generally believed that income should be related directly and exclusively to work effort and performance. Only a widespread change of values would reduce this sense of injustice and resentment against the welfare recipient. For if we came to see income as a right, and not a reward, as a sort of insurance policy against disaster, our assessment of the problem would be different. The low-income worker would not view the recipient of government income payments with bitterness but conclude simply, "there but for the grace of God go I"—and if his luck ever ran out, he too would have a guarantee against destitution.

Public Choice and Welfare Policy

The position we take on welfare policy issues will depend in large measure on the criterion of justice that we apply.

1. If we conclude that people should be rewarded on the basis of desert, we might take the position that income should be exclusively related to work effort and performance. Those on welfare should be required to work except in those exceptional cases where a person is properly exempted from the general responsibility of self-support. Simply having a low income is not a good enough reason for a person to receive sustenance from the resources of others.
2. We might adopt the principle of desert, but decide that those who receive high incomes are not entitled to them. They do not result from superior effort, performance, or social contribution, but from luck, accident, or initial advantage. In that case, we might take the position that it is desirable for government to reduce income inequalities by transferring income from the better-off to the least-well-off members of the community.
3. We might adopt the criterion of need and assert that a just society would provide a decent minimum standard of living to all its citizens, and that it was the responsibility of all members of the community to assure that this basic standard was met.
4. We might view justice as a problem of *right*. Regardless of

94

*public policy: choice
on behalf of other
people*

income, all citizens are entitled to receive particular publi
services. They have a right to a good education, to police an(
fire protection, to water and electricity, to work (full employ
ment?), perhaps to adequate food, shelter, and medical care.

This is what the problem is all about. Welfare policy is a complex
technical issue. It is a controversial area of public policymaking wher(
powerful interests compete for influence. But in the final analysis
welfare is a matter of principle. How we define the problem of welfare
what stand we take, and what programs we advocate depends on how
we respond to the oldest question of political science—what is justice?

for further reading

Benn, S.I., and R.S. Peters, *Principles of Political Thought* (New York:
The Free Press, 1958). The chapter on justice contains an excellen
discussion of the rival claims of need and desert.

Budd, Edward C., (Ed.), *Inequality and Poverty* (New York: W. W.
Norton, 1967). A good collection of articles on the problems of
social justice, income distribution and welfare.

Cahn, Edmund, *The Sense of Injustice* (New York: New York University
Press, 1949). The first chapters are an excellent and sensitive
insight into our basic psychological sense of fairness and injustice.

Friedman, Milton, *Capitalism and Freedom* (Chicago: University of
Chicago Press, 1962). A classic liberal's view of the justification o
inequality. See particularly the chapters on income distribution.

Jencks, Christopher, *Inequality: A Reassessment of the Effect of Family an(
Schooling in America* (New York: Basic Books, 1972). A
sophisticated treatment in which it is argued that existing incom(
differentials cannot be justified as resulting from equality of
opportunity and merit.

Kolko, Gabriel, *Wealth and Power in America* (New York: Praeger, 1972).
On the problem of inequalities of wealth and inequalities of
political power, which is another aspect of the problem of
distributive justice.

Kristol, Irving, "Taxes, Poverty and Equality," *The Public Interest 38*
(Fall 1974), pp. 3–28. A provocative argument about the fairness o(
using taxation to reduce income inequalities.

Miller, S. M., and Pamela Roby, *The Future of Inequality* (New York
Basic Books, 1970). Another good argument on the question of
inequality and justice.

Moynihan, Daniel P., *The Politics of a Guaranteed Income* (New York: Random House, 1973). An insider's view of how the problem of welfare policy has been recast in recent years.

Okun, Arthur M., *Equality and Efficiency: The Big Trade-off* (Washington: The Brookings Institution, 1975). A short but acute analysis by an influential economist on the question of weighing distributive justice against productive efficiency.

Olafson, Frederick A., *Justice and Social Policy* (Englewood Cliffs, N.J.: Prentice-Hall, 1961). A number of essays, most more philosophical than the title suggests, on the theme of social justice. Contains Rawls' original article on "Justice as Fairness."

Rawls, John A., *A Theory of Justice* (Cambridge: Harvard University Press, 1971). A much discussed recent book on the concept of justice. Rawls' argument is extremely complex and will be hard for the beginner to follow. A better introduction to Rawls is his article "Justice as Fairness," reprinted in Olafson (above) and in Peter Laslett and W. G. Runciman (Eds.), *Philosophy, Politics and Society*, Second Series (Oxford: Basil Blackwell, 1967), pp. 132–57.

Rimlinger, Gaston, *Welfare Policy and Industrialization in Europe, America and Russia* (New York: John Wiley, 1971). A very good discussion of the evolution of the modern welfare state, in comparative perspective. Focuses on different definitions of who is *entitled* to welfare, and what problem welfare reformers thought they were trying to solve.

Tawnery, R. H., *Equality* (London: Allen and Unwin, 1964). A classic study of the problem of inequality and justice. Written in the 1920s, it is somewhat dated, but many of the fundamental concerns are still valid.

chapter
six
the choice
of measures

As stated previously, the first and most important step in political analysis is defining the problem. Thinking about basic principles can be a big help as we try to sort out the rival arguments, the conflicting facts and claims, looking for a position we can accept and defend. What is fundamentally at stake in this controversy? Is the issue one of rights, of freedom, or of fundamental fairness? These are not the only questions that have to be asked, of course. We have to think about political feasibility (which we will come to shortly), and we have to be sensitive about the patterns of conflict and coalition that are taking shape. But the classic political values—rights, freedom and justice—together with the fundamental questions of responsibility and authority, are central in coming to grips with a policy problem.

However, taking a stand on principle is not the end of political analysis. A political argument is not complete until it culminates in a recommendation for action. The most common complaint against political agitators is that "they have nothing constructive to offer." Once we have a sense of our position on an issue, we have to decide, concretely and practically, what should be done about it.

In recent years, applied policy analysis has become highly technical. High-powered economics and computer techniques have been applied in an effort to make government policy more efficient and rational. The specialists have a variety of names for their methods—PPBS (for planning-programming-budget system), cost-benefit analysis, operations research, systems analysis. It almost begins to seem that policy analysis is no longer a job for the layman but must be handled by experts.

This belief should be resisted. Technical policy analysis does not provide techniques for reaching valid and indisputable conclusions about public problems. It is rather no more than another form of political argument. The policy analyst provides reasons, backed with data, for choosing one course of action over another. Or he merely clarifies the implications of choice. In either event, his analysis has to be looked at critically, as one would any other case or claim about political action.

Even the most ardent advocates of advanced techniques of policy analysis agree that they are no substitute for political judgment. To think clearly about political issues, it is not necessary to master all the complex methods of modern policy analysis. But it is important to appreciate the common sense assumptions on which such methods rest. As Alice Rivlin says, all of modern policy analysis is based on two rather simple propositions: "It is better to have some idea of where you are going than to fly blind" and "It is better to be orderly than haphazard about decision-making."[1]

Most books on policy analysis describe the decision-making process as a series of steps, or stages:

1. Define the problem to be solved. (All agree that this is the most important.)
2. Make a list of possible alternatives for action.
3. Define the constraints within which a policy must be found.
4. Specify the costs and benefits that are relevant to deciding on a preferred course of action.
5. Within the stipulated constraints, choose the policy that has the highest ratio of benefits to costs.

This is not a method to be used slavishly. In practice, the stages do not follow neatly one after the other. All are interrelated. Furthermore, as we shall see when we come to steps four and five, it may be impossible to calculate costs and benefits in a way that is actually helpful in choosing one program over another. Nonetheless, such a procedure can be a useful guide to thinking systematically about the design of measures for public action.

what are the alternatives?

The first thing to be said about making a list of possible solutions to a problem is "be imaginative." Do not stop with the obvious possibilities. Look at the problem from a variety of angles. Walk around it slowly in your mind, taking one aspect at a time, and see where it leads

---

[1] *Alice Rivlin,* Systematic Thinking for Social Action *(Washington: The Brookings Institution, 1971), p. 2.*

98

*public policy: choice
on behalf of other
people*

you. Think about the interchangeability of means and ends. (A traffic planner might start with the problem: how to transport people to work? One thinks of the obvious alternatives: the car, the bus, railroads, subways, bicycles, walking. But it is also possible to bring work to people—by a policy of decentralizing industry and business, moving it out to integrated cluster cities.) Manipulate the problem, turn it around, as many ways as possible.

It may be that policymakers in practice consider only a limited range of alternatives, that they tend to "search for a solution in the vicinity of the problem."[2] Under the pressures of actual decision making, we are simply not going to be able, logically or practically, to consider *all* the possibilities. But that is really beside the point. We do have to think as broadly and openly as possible about the options if we do not want to make a mistake or miss opportunities that are not altogether obvious. It is too easy to stack the deck in decision making by considering only a limited number of alternatives. As Alan Enthoven says, "I can make Alternative A a sure winner if I limit the alternatives to B and C."[3]

In the give and take of politics, a lot depends on having the right idea at the right time, and being able to make a persuasive case for it. Sometimes intractible difficulties can be made to go away simply by looking at the problem from a fresh perspective.

One spur to imagination is to break the problem down by using a logically exhaustive system of categories. There are many different ways of doing this. In Chapter 4, we talked about the ways in which government can affect individual freedom: by relying on voluntary initiatives and market forces, by creating structured options, by creating biased options, and by direct regulation. Each of these possibilities suggests an array of alternatives for government action.

Let us now modify this original set of categories somewhat and apply it to the problem of developing policy options. Instead of considering simply how government affects individual freedom, let us ask what government can actually *do* to make an impact on society. There are logically, a finite number of forms of public action. An inventory of the basic tools of the trade of statecraft is given in Table 3.[4]

---

[2] *James G. March and Herbert A. Simon,* Organizations *(New York John Wiley, 1958), p. 137ff; David Braybrooke and Charles E. Lindblom,* A Strategy of Decision *(New York: The Free Press, 1963), pp. 37–110.*

[3] *Alan C. Enthoven, "Ten Practical Principles for Policy and Program Analysis," in Richard Zechauser et al.,* Benefit-Cost and Policy Analysis: 1974 *(Chicago: Aldine, 1975), p. 463.*

[4] *One of the most exhaustive inventories of the potential instruments of public policy is that compiled by E.S. Kirschen et al.,* Economic Policy in Our Time *(Chicago: Rand McNally, 1964), vol. 1, p. 148. Here the economic policy alternatives of the modern state are broken down into nearly 100 different instruments, grouped into five families and fourteen categories.*

table 3

99

an inventory of government capabilities

Political Resources

1. *Coercive power.* Government can make rules and regulations, backed by sanctions. The state, as Weber observed, is a legitimate monopoly of coercive force.

2. *Authority and guidance.* Government can create directives, set goals, standards and guidelines. It can admonish, inspire, educate and persuade. The state is not based only on coercive force. It is also a locus of legitimate authority. It is expected to make decisions on behalf of others, and citizens expect to comply, generally, with the directives of government.

Economic Resources

3. *Taxation.* The way in which government derives revenue from society can create incentives or disincentives for private action.

4. *Expenditure.* Government provides public services. It can invest directly in productive enterprise. It makes purchases and employs people. How it organizes its spending can affect the overall pattern of economic activity, and can create incentives or disincentives for individual action.

5. *Monetary policy.* Government controls the system of money and credit. While this power is mainly important for overall economic policy, it may have implications for more specific policy objectives.

Reliance on Private Action

6. Government can decide to let the outcome depend on the operation of market forces, or on the initiatives of groups or individuals. It should be noted that reliance on private action does not indicate the absence of a policy decision. This can be a deliberately chosen alternative, as when government "deregulates" an industry.

When we begin thinking about a problem like air or water pollution, our minds are immediately guided to certain kinds of remedies. We can impose regulations on industries, requiring them to take action to prevent environmental damage. But if we think about the *kinds* of things that government can do about a problem like this, we see a broader range of possibilities (Table 4). We try to fill in the blanks.

Let us now consider the problem of how to reduce fatalities on the highways. Look up from the page and try to think about what government can do to deal with the problem of traffic accidents. You will probably find that you organized your thoughts around a specific aspect of the problem. Even if you used the six categories of government action, you were probably still the victim of your own intellectual "blinders." You might have thought about what could be done to improve the performance of the driver, to encourage or require him to drive safely. Or you might have thought about how the safety of the car

100

public policy: choice
on behalf of other
people

table 4
A schedule of alternatives for industrial water pollution policies

Direct regulation

1. Criminal sanctions—fines or imprisonment
2. Civil suits, brought by the government or private citizens
3. Expropriation and nationalization of polluting industries

Authority and guidance

4. Government sets goals, guidelines, and standards for pollution abatement
5. Direct government efforts to achieve voluntary compliance
6. Government research and educational efforts in techniques of pollution abatement
7. Stimulation of private and community pressure groups against industrial pollution

Taxation

8. Permit tax deductions for installation of pollution abatement equipment
9. Impose "user charges" on polluting industries, taxes on the amount of effluent discharged into public waterways

Expenditure

10. Government subsidies to firms for installation of pollution control equipment
11. Subsidies to local governments for improved municipal waste treatment plants
12. Government underwriting or reinsurance of loans for pollution abatement equipment
13. Award government contracts or make purchases only from nonpolluting industries
14. Subsidies, or tax incentives, for firms to relocate to areas where pollution is less harmful
15. Subsidies, or tax incentives, to manufacturers of pollution abatement equipment to develop more advanced technologies or to lower costs

Rely on private action

16. Assume that community pressures, public environmental concern, and industrial interest in "goodwill" are sufficient to reduce industrial pollution to desired levels

itself could be improved. Or you might have thought about improvements in the highway system itself. But it is unlikely that you considered all three of these aspects of the transportation "system."

Furthermore, you probably did not think at all about the performance of the police, emergency medical services, fire departments, or repair and wrecker services. Perhaps the reason for this is that you were basically thinking about how accidents could be *prevented.* Here we have another question of problem definition. If the object is to reduce highway fatalities, the best way to go after the problem may not be to try to prevent accidents after a certain point, but to make it possible for drivers and passengers to *survive* accidents when they occur. Thinking about the efficiency and training of police, fire, and hospital workers might be a pertinent means to the end.

In Table 5, we classify policy options not only by the powers of government but also by the part of the system that is being acted on (the driver, the road, the vehicle, the repair and assistance facilities) and also by the *objectives* of policy—accident prevention and reduction in the damage or injury caused by accidents.

This schedule does not include all the alternatives. You should be able to think of additional possibilities for safety programs. (Or you might now want to try your hand at devising a schedule of alternatives in another policy area.) Obviously, too, the alternatives can be combined in an infinite number of "packages" reflecting different policy emphases and combinations of instruments.

Such an inventory also helps to make clear the choices we will have to make. We must decide whether to emphasize accident prevention or the reduction in damage when accidents occur. We must decide which parts of the system to act on—the human element, the road, the vehicle, the public and private services that are part of the highway system. And we have to choose the *form* of government action—whether to use direct regulatory policy or educational efforts, and standard and goal-setting measures; or whether to structure economic incentives through tax deductions or exemptions or through government subsidies, investments, subventions and purchases. We also have to decide which factors are best left alone, where government action would do little to improve the situation.

narrowing down the list of alternatives

We have tried to suspend criticism in drawing up the initial schedule of alternatives. The object was to get as comprehensive a list of possibilities as we could devise. Now we have to separate the plausible from the untenable. Where do we begin?

Policymaking takes place within a framework of stipulated *constraints.* The most obvious of these are budgetary and legal. It is worthwhile to be as explicit as possible in defining the boundaries

table 5
a schedule of alternatives for highway safety programs

Objective	Part of System Acted Upon	Government Capability	Instrument
Accident prevention	Driver (also applies to cyclists and pedestrians)	Regulation	1. Licensing requirements
			2. Rigorous enforcement of highway laws
		Authority and guidance	3. Driver education
			4. Safety campaigns
		Economic	5. Relate license fees to driving record
			6. Incentives for improvement of driving skills (adult classes)
			7. Subsidies for research into human factors in accidents, driver motivations
	Road	Regulation	8. Reduce speed limits
			9. Signs, signals markings
			10. Traffic planning and control to reduce congestion, improve flow
		Authority and guidance	11. Enforce construction and maintenance standards
			12. Set guidelines and goals for construction and maintenance—educational programs for contractors, local government personnel
		Economic incentives	13. Subsidies for construction and maintenance programs related to safety standards

	Vehicle	Regulation	14. Vehicle inspections 15. Enforce braking, visibility, control system, stability standards on manufacturers
		Authority and guidance	16. Enforce standards on garages 17. Educational programs for mechanics
		Economic incentives	18. Tax incentives or subsidies to manufacturers, mechanics to improve control characteristics of vehicle 19. Government purchases only vehicles with high standard control characteristics
	Supervisory and service system	Regulation, guidance, or incentives	20. Improve traffic court programs 21. Accident reporting and analysis 22. Training of police officers
Minimize damage from accidents	Driver	Regulation	23. Enforce use of safety equipment (seat belts)
		Guidance or incentives	24. Educational campaigns on use of safety equipment
	Road	Regulation guidance, or incentives	25. Roadside fencing, ditches, etc. 26. Accident reporting systems, communication and road surveillance
	Vehicle	Regulation, guidance, or incentives	27. Improve crash integrity, passenger protection devices, restraints through regulations on manufacturers, incentives or government purchase requirements

104

*public policy: choice
on behalf of other
people*

table 5 (continued)

Objective	Part of System Acted Upon	Government Capability	Instrument
	Supervisory and service systems	Regulation, guidance, or incentives	28. Improve medical assistance facilities, care of injured, access of ambulances, first aid training, hospital acess, etc. 29. Fire department functions 30. Removal of wrecked vehicles, traffic control at scene

Source. The above is loosely adapted from Arthur D. Little, Inc., *Cost-Effectiveness in Traffic Safety* (New York: Praeger, 1968), p. 117.

within which a solution to a policy problem must be found. As we noted earlier, the object of water pollution policy is not simply to get clean water. The problem is actually to reduce industrial pollution *without* causing widespread unemployment or a reduction of economic activity, and *without* violating basic rights—such as those of due process of law. We also do not have unlimited resources to spend on water pollution. We have to choose the most efficient and economical means for achieving the desired results.

There is an old saying that you should always "keep your options open." During the OPEC oil embargo of 1973, Secretary of State Henry Kissinger did not formally exclude the possibility that the United States might use armed force to restore the flow of oil from Arab nations. In foreign policy, it may be a good idea not to foreclose the use of extreme measures on principle. It keeps your adversary uncertain about what you might do if he presses too hard. However, we do in practice, often without really thinking about it, exclude certain options for policy on moral or ethical grounds. For example, a spectrum of alternatives for public road building and maintenance could include the following: (1) direct government expenditure through a public agency; (2) contracts with private enterprise; (3) *corvee* labor (every citizen is required to work on the roads several days a year); (4) slave labor. In evaluating alternative ways of maintaining the roads, policy analysts do not draw up a neat comparison of the costs and benefits of *corvee* or slave labor in relation to more conventional methods. In our society, these options are simply out of bounds. (Although, interestingly, convict labor is not.)

Economic analysts often miss this point. Efficiency is not the only criterion to be applied to the choice of measures. Most books on systematic policy analysis are written by economists, and they seem to suggest that the problem is entirely one of measuring the costs and benefits of various options against one another, reduced to monetary terms. In fact, we have to measure the options for public action against the full range of political values, of which efficiency is only one. Some possibilities may be excluded on the grounds that they interfere with basic rights, others because of considerations of equity. In fact, we only apply systematic comparisons of efficiency to those options that have survived scrutiny on political criteria of acceptability.

One factor we have to take into account is the relative *legitimacy* of various measures. Some types of measures are considered more acceptable and appropriate as methods of government action than others. This varies from culture to culture. For example, in Western Europe, nationalization is considered far more legitimate as a policy option than it is in the United States. This is not basically a matter of socialist ideology. Europeans are simply more accustomed than Americans to the idea that the state may directly own and operate industries. Historically, the state always played a more dominant role

106

*public policy: choice
on behalf of other
people*

in European economic life than in the United States. The largest part of the public industrial sector in most European nations—the public ownership of utilities, transportation systems, and some basic industries,—developed under conservative and not socialist governments.

The result is that, in Europe, public ownership is an alternative to be compared with other policy options—regulation, subsidies, tax incentives, and the like—in working toward solutions to basic economic problems, while in the United States, it is an alternative that is ruled out in principle in most cases. The result is that Americans often pursue the same objectives that Europeans try to achieve through nationalization by more indirect means—the regulation of "natural monopolies" and public utilities is in effect an alternative to direct government ownership. When basic industries are threatened by bankruptcy, the Europeans are far more likely to nationalize them, while the Americans tend toward complex "bailing out" operations. An interesting example of the contrast occurred in 1971, when the L-1011 transport aircraft met with financial disaster. This project resulted in the collapse of two companies—the British Rolls Royce firm, which made the engines, and the American Lockheed company, which built the airframe. The policy response of the two nations was entirely different. The British nationalized Rolls Royce, while the Americans subsidized Lockheed through a program of public spending and investment to keep the private firm afloat.

Political *feasibility* also has to be considered. Which policies will be acceptable to the legislature?[5] Which are likely to be effectively implemented? Bureaucrats may drag their feet or distort the purposes of government programs. Groups that are supposed to be regulated may be able to evade or resist the intent of policy. Where are the loopholes in the plan? We have to view policymaking as a game of chess. If we make this move, what countermoves are apt to be made?

For example, many experts believe that direct regulation is an ineffective method of controlling industrial water pollution. Under federal water pollution laws, the secretary of the interior first issues a complaint against an offending industry with recommendations for corrective measures. If the recommendations are not followed, further hearings are held and additional recommendations made. If these are also resisted, the government may bring suit in a federal court. Only if the court's decision is disobeyed may the polluter actually face fine or imprisonment, outcomes that are quite unlikely. All of this requires enormous legal paperwork, with many opportunities for delay. The industry has a greater incentive to fight the issue through the legal

---

[5] Ralph Huitt, "Political Feasibility," in Austin Ranney (Ed.), Political Science and Public Policy (Chicago: Markham, 1968), pp. 168–195.

process than to actually take pollution abatement measures. The process is so difficult that only the most flagrant cases are apt to be challenged.

For these reasons, most specialists in the field advocate effluent taxes rather than direct regulation in controlling industrial pollution. To set a charge for the use of public waterways based on the amount of waste discharged into them is a straightforward policy, uniform, relatively easy to administer, and difficult to evade. The polluter has a greater incentive to take action to clean up his manufacturing processes than to fight government orders. All that is required is that government decide how much damage is being done to a waterway by disposal of industrial waste. A fee is then set—say $10 for each ton of phosphates or other materials. Each factory along the river monitors its own operation and pays the government a tax payment on a regular basis. Spot-checks on the operations of different industries could be used to ensure that reporting was honest, the same way that we audit our self-reporting system of income tax.[6]

In narrowing down the original range of alternatives then, a variety of political judgments have to be made. Which options do we want to exclude on principle—because they encroach on important rights or interfere unnecessarily with individual freedom or raise problems of fundamental fairness? Which measures are dubious from the point of view of political acceptability or legitimacy? (We may still want to support programs that have previously been considered inappropriate, if we feel that they are best suited to our purposes, but we have to count the costs of changing peoples' minds about the acceptability of such measures.) Finally, what is apt to work out best in practice? Which measures are apt to provoke controversy and which are most likely to appear plausible to those who have the power to put them into effect? Which stand the best chance of being effectively implemented?

All these questions call for reasoned argument, not just "seat of the pants" judgment. Eventually, we have to make a case for a preferred solution to a public problem, in the face of the critical appraisal of those with different viewpoints and different stakes in the outcome. If we exclude an option on the grounds of feasibility, we have to meet the challenge of those who think it would work just fine. What is the advocate of effluent charges going to respond to those who assert that water quality in the United States has improved greatly under existing policies? Why change a policy that seems to be working? The choice of measures is not just a technical question, it is part of preparation for the political battle.

---

[6] *See A. M. Freeman and Robert M. Haveman, "Clean Rhetoric, Dirty Water,"* The Public Interest 28 *(Summer 1972), pp. 51–65; William F. Baxter,* People or Penguins: The Case for Optimal Pollution *(New York: Columbia University Press, 1974), pp. 61–83.*

108

*public policy: choice
on behalf of other
people*

efficiency as a
standard of judgment

We have talked about a variety of principles that can be applied in making political decisions. Efficiency is the criterion that applies uniquely to the choice of measures. Economy in government is always an important consideration—and a point that is sure to be raised by the critics of anything we propose to do. We have to be able to show that we have a proper regard for the public purse strings.

We do not want to spend more than is necessary to accomplish a given task. Economists talk about the "opportunity costs" of public investments or expenditures. If we use resources for one project, we cannot use them for something else—in effect, we forego the opportunity of some alternative venture. The question arises of where a given fund of resources would do the most good. The problem can be expressed in terms of the familiar axiom, "You can't have your cake and eat it too."

In evaluating alternatives, one question that has to be asked is, What works best at the least cost? Obviously, we are not looking simply for the *cheapest* alternative. What we have to find is the program that promises the best results in return for the price.

what works and
what does not?

In the field of highway safety, it is a fact that divided highways have far lower fatality and accident rates than two-lane roads. Nonetheless, we are not about to upgrade all roads to interstate highway stanards. Although it may seem repugnant to put a dollar value on human life, at some point we have to count the costs. What are our second-best alternatives? What can be done to improve the safety of conventional roads?

Finding out what works usually requires an experimental method. Different techniques of highway marking, design, and construction can be tried and evaluated. On comparable stretches of roadway, what effect do improved signs and markings, straighter stretches, or wider lanes have on the accident and fatality rates? How do barriers between lanes compare with broad median strips in reducing head-on collisions? What are the costs of each of these improvements, and what are the results in accidents and fatalities per vehicle mile traveled in comparison with divided highways? The answers to such questions cannot tell us how much to spend on highway safety, but they do give us information that is helpful in decision making. We might find out that some easy, inexpensive alternatives had as good results as the more expensive measures.

Other approaches to the problem could be evaluated in the same way. Instead of trying to prevent accidents, we might concentrate on trying to make accidents survivable. Simple and inexpensive restraining devices, like seat belts, can have a dramatic effect on the fatality rate in car crashes. Of course, we may not be doing as much to reduce property damage by increasing the safety of the vehicle as we might through improvements in the highway system, but we might be doing more, at less cost, to save lives. Obviously, we could improve vehicle safety even further, up to the point where we design cars to the basic specifications of army tanks. But more sophisticated techniques of improving vehicle integrity are costly, and at each point we have to ask whether they are worth the price, compared to alternative means of accomplishing the same thing.

Some policy experiments are fortuitous. In 1973, the United States adopted a uniform highway speed of 55 miles per hour as an energy conservation measure, in response to the OPEC oil embargo of that year. Whatever the effectiveness of this policy in gasoline consumption, it did have a marked impact on highway accidents and deaths, and the program was continued primarily for that reason. Reducing speed limits, of course, was a policy that also had costs. Truckers and professional travelers had to spend more time on the road to get the same amount of work done. Some marginal increase in shipping costs and, consequently, prices to consumer, would have to be taken into account in evaluating the policy.

In principle, at least, it would be possible to compare the relative costs and benefits of each of these approaches to highway safety. (Although, to my knowledge, this has not been done.)[7] We could make at least a rough estimate of how much we would have to pay to save more lives or reduce property damage on the highways. However, such a comparison cannot tell us which approach to choose. In the final analysis, we still have to make a judgment about how much it is worthwhile to spend to further improve highway safety. And we also have to make a decision about who should bear the costs of such improvements, for the taxpayer will bear the burden of improvements in the road system, while the automobile buyer will pay for improvements in the safety of the vehicle, and the price for lower speed limits will fall primarily on travelers and truckers.

how can we measure effectiveness?

In the case of highway safety, it is relatively easy to specify measures of accomplishment. It seems to make sense to use indices of fatalities,

---

[7] *For a study that is remarkable mainly because of the very lack of hard information on the costs and benefits of these alternatives that it reveals, see Arthur D. Little, Inc.,* Cost-Effectiveness in Traffic Safety *(New York: Praeger, 1968).*

110

*public policy: choice
on behalf of other
people*

injuries and property damage from accidents in relation to vehicle miles to compare the potential effectiveness of various policy options. However, in other policy areas, it may be more difficult to devise appropriate measures of effectiveness.

For example, let us say that we are considering alternative ways of reducing crime. What is an appropriate measure of success? Is the number of arrests a good index of effectiveness? If those arrested are not convicted, criminals will still be roaming the streets. Perhaps what we need is an index that relates arrests to convictions. This looks better on a number of counts. Such an index points up the need for thorough investigative work on the part of the police, discourages arbitrary arrest, and forces us to pay attention not only to the efficiency of the police force but also to the system of criminal justice.

There is one major drawback, however. If we adopt this index, performance will seem to be better *if crime actually increases,* for the rate of both arrests and convictions will go up in the middle of a crime wave. Other factors obviously have to be considered. An index of complaints received by the police may tell us more about "crime prevention" rather than simple "law enforcement," and will force us to look at such factors as street lighting, social services, and other possible programs that have a bearing on crime. The rate of recidivism, or repeated offenses, may be necessary to appraise the effectiveness of penal institutions. The matter begins to look very complicated. We may need a variety of measures to evaluate the potential effectiveness of various ways of reducing crime. It may prove impossible to devise a single index against which we could compare the costs and benefits of different alternatives.

Good public policy means different things to different people, and the objectives of public policy are often fuzzy and ill-defined. For example, how would we measure the effectiveness of the public schools and compare alternative ways of improving their performance? Arguments about what function schools are supposed to perform in society, and how one evaluates the quality of education, can be long, bitter, and inconclusive.

Obviously, the amount of money we spend on school buildings, or teachers salaries, or equipment tells us little about the impact of the educational system. The object of education policy is not to build buildings or employ teachers. Scores on nationally standardized tests, the number of students going on to higher education, and job placements for vocational school graduates may all be appropriate indicators of educational effectiveness, but we realize that even these are imperfect. Reading skills, mathematical proficiency, and knowledge of certain subjects can be measured by tests, but tests only indirectly reflect the acquisition of skills that are needed for effective functioning in later life, and such measures do not exhaust the many desirable

hings that we might wish education to do for the individual or for the
ociety.

In fact, we have very little idea of what works and what does not in
he field of education. Despite many sophisticated and detailed
analyses, there is little hard evidence that could help us to decide on
vhat would do the most good in improving the performance of the
chools. There are no strong relationships between the amount that is
pent on buildings, equipment, or staff and educational effectiveness.
iystematic policy analysis has given us very few clues that would
nable us to make better decisions to improve the quality of
education.[8]

The fact that it is often very hard to find fully acceptable measures
f performance is not an excuse for not trying at all. Some information
s usually better than none. Even an imperfect analysis may help clarify
he implications of policy options. We may discover unsuspected
opportunities or difficulties. And the very effort of asking, What are we
rying to accomplish and how would we know if we accomplished it?
nay lead to a clearer definition of the problem and a better understand-
ng of the criteria we want to apply in evaluating alternatives.

cost-benefit analysis

Cost-benefit analysis is increasingly prominent in decision making at
Ill levels of government. It is a technique that may be helpful in
larifying the implications of public choice. However, it is important to
ealize that cost-benefit analysis is also a mode of political argument. In
ffect, cost-benefit analysis is a way of making a case for or against a
ublic project, or for adopting one policy option instead of another.
Depending on the factors that are taken into account, how they are
veighed and measured, it is possible to come to very different conclu-
ions. Hence, a policymaker should examine such an analysis with the
ame critical eye that one would apply to any other case for publc ac-
ion. What reasons are being given for coming to a particular con-
lusion, and are those reasons convincing?

Cost-benefit analysis is an attempt to account rationally for all the
elevant direct and indirect costs and benefits that would follow from a
ublic project and to strike a balance between them. The technique
nay be used to *justify* government projects, to *compare* alternative
olicy options, or to examine the problem of how the costs and benefits
f policies would be *distributed* among various groups and interests.

Modern cost-benefit analysis was pioneered in the United States

---

For a commentary of this problem, see Alice Rivlin, Systematic Thinking for Social Action, pp. 64–85.

112

*public policy: choice
on behalf of other
people*

by the Army Corps of Engineers and other agencies engaged in large-scale water resources projects. There are many possible projects in the field of flood control, irrigation, and navigation. Which ones would it be worthwhile to undertake?

The direct costs of a large dam, of course, include the land, labor, capital, and material that go into the construction of the project, and the annual costs of operation. Indirect costs include the displacement and resettlement of people from the area where the reservoir will form and the loss of production in that area. The environmental costs of the project have to be estimated. We also have to calculate the "opportunity costs" of the project, what the money used for the dam would be worth if invested in something else. This is normally called the "discount" on invested capital, and this should have some relation to the commercial rate of interest.

The benefits of the dam might include: (1) the value of hydroelectric power generated; (2) the value of water for irrigation; (3) the flood control benefits for downstream properties; (4) the possibilities of recreation on the lake formed behind the dam; (5) new employment in prospective industries. All of these have to be estimated over the lifetime of the project.

It is hard to place a dollar value on some of these costs and benefits. At some point, cost-benefit analysis inevitably becomes controversial. How do you place a value on environmental and aesthetic factors, the loss of wildlife nesting grounds or habitats? The value of some factors may be calculated in different ways. The benefits of flood control might be based either on some estimate of increased property value in the flood plain or the cost of insurance against flood damage to downstream property owners. Depending on what standard is used, it is possible to come to very different conclusions about the balance of costs and benefits.[9] For example, some have suggested that the Corps of Engineers has often placed a very low discount rate on its proposals, making a greater number of projects seem worthwhile than would have been the case if a more realistic rate of interest were used.

Cost-benefit analysis may be used to ask the question of whether a government program is worthwhile in the first place. If we do not subsidize the symphony orchestra, there will be more money to spend for roads and schools. How do we calculate the value of each of these alternative projects? How much should the federal government be spending on cancer research in comparison to space exploration, defense, or the search for alternative energy sources? These are big

---

[9] *See J. V. Krutilla and Otto Eckstein,* Multiple Purpose River Development *(Baltimore: The Johns Hopkins University Press, 1958); and Otto Eckstein,* Water Resource Development *(Cambridge: Harvard University Press, 1961). For a critique, see Richard L. Berkman and W. Kip Viscusi,* Damming the West *(New York: Grossman, 1973).*

questions, and they are very difficult to answer. How much is a cure for cancer worth in monetary terms? Is it a convincing case to say that far more lives could be saved by campaigns to induce drivers to use seat belts than by tuberculosis control programs per dollar spent?[10] Economic analysts have tried to apply their techniques to such questions, but the results have not been very satisfactory. Nonetheless, anyone who proposes a new or expanded public program will have to try to show that the expense is justifiable. At the very least, he will have to make a case that, in some sense, the benefits to be expected from the program outweigh the costs.

Cost-benefit analysis may also be used to compare alternative methods for accomplishing a public purpose. A dam might be built at any number of points on the river system. Which would be the best location? We have already noted the possibility of using this technique to compare different means of improving highway safety.

Sometimes, estimating the relative efficiency of measures is a straightforward problem. Would it be better for a government agency to buy a fleet of cars or rent them on a long-term lease arrangement? Should the army repair vehicles in the field or send them back to a central maintenance depot? In such cases, the objectives are clear-cut, and the costs and benefits relatively easy to assess. However, most comparisons of alternative programs will involve indirect or intangible costs and benefits that are very difficult to evaluate systematically.

Finally, cost-benefit analysis can be used to ask the question of how costs and benefits should be distributed. Who will benefit from a public program, and who will bear the burden? How do we want to relate burdens and benefits? In the case of subsidizing a symphony orchestra, we noted earlier, we have to decide whether the project would be a service provided to a small part of the population or whether it would, perhaps indirectly, benefit the community as a whole. How we answer this question will determine whether we think it appropriate to finance the symphony out of general taxation or by imposing a "user charge" on those who actually do attend the symphony.

We face the same problem in deciding among alternative means of controlling water pollution. Who should pay for pollution abatement? The industries that dirty the rivers or the public that will benefit from cleaner water? We might argue for an effluent tax on the ground that industry should not receive a benefit (the free use of waterways to dispose of wastes) that imposes a social cost on the entire community. On the other hand, if we argue for government subsidy of pollution

---

[10] *U.S. Department of Health, Education and Welfare, Office of the Assistant Secretary for Program Coordination,* Disease Control Programs: Selected Disease Control Programs *(September 1966).*

114

*public policy: choice
on behalf of other
people*

abatement equipment, we might say that it is necessary to compare the value of all uses of water. Should industry bear the full burden of making the rivers more attractive to recreational users or those who own property along the waterways, or reducing the costs of water purification for municipalities?

The question of Who pays, and who benefits? can be asked about virtually every service provided by government. There are, in fact, very few pure "public goods" where costs and benefits are not assignable to specific groups in the population. In theory, at least, it would be possible to apply users fees to the financing of public parks and wilderness areas, to public libraries, to the maintenance of roads and highways. Is public support for higher education primarily a service to the individual or to society? To what extent should costs be covered by tuition charges, and to what extent by direct subsidies? Such questions have an important bearing on the problem of the choice of measures. They raise issues not only of efficiency and effectiveness but also of fundamental fairness.

Ultimately, cost-benefit analysis may be a valuable aid in decision making, but it is not a substitute for political choice and judgment. It is impossible to account for all the costs and benefits of any public program. We have to make decisions about which factors will be taken into account and which ignored, how they should be weighed against one another, and how they should be measured. There is no technical answer to the question of how burdens and benefits should be related. We can estimate the costs and benefits of different projects, but that still does not tell us whether or not a government program is worthwhile. Cost-benefit analysis may help in asking the right questions, but it is still up to the policymaker to provide the answers.

a complete political argument

It is time to pull the pieces together. At the beginning of this section, we asked what it would mean to make a political decision conscientiously, without simply following instinct, prejudice, or self-interest. Since then, we have been 'talking about what is at stake when we make choices on behalf of other people.

By now, it is apparent that taking a political position is often virtually an act of existential choice. Political enigmas have no sure solutions. Problems can be formulated in different ways; issues can be seen from a variety of perspectives.

But this does not mean that decision making is simply a shot in the dark. We have to make a choice, but we also have to justify our decisions. The policymaker has to give reasons for his or her actions; the advocate must make a case for his cause. The fundamental art of decision making is being able to make a reasonable argument for our conclusions.

To think about decision making as argument makes us self-conscious about the process of choice, about how we go about making up our minds, and why we reach a particular position. We have to think about alternative possibilities, and consider the case that can be made for them. What speaks for, and what against, different approaches to the problem?

To have "thought through" a problem means to be able to make a coherent, complete political argument. And a complete political argument will contain the following elements.

A Characterization of Reality

Political thought is always selective. We "focus" on some aspects of the situation and relegate the rest to "background." This is simply the way the mind works.

Usually, political argument begins when someone chooses to "think otherwise." In the early 1960s, Michael Harrington wrote an influential book entitled *The Other America*. [11] Harrington argued that in rich, prosperous America, the poor had become "invisible." In the late 1950s, Americans focused on issues of foreign policy and the problems of an affluent, consumer-oriented society. People were aware that many had been left out of the great prosperity of the postwar period and suffered from privation and neglect, but that fact was part of the "background" of the politics of the day. Harrington's book was important in revising America's image of itself and in raising the issue of poverty, which was to be a central issue of public policy for the next decade.

Political problems can be seen from different perspectives. A first step in political analysis is to decide on a focus. Earlier, we talked about the implications of our conception of the "community" to be taken into account in decisionmaking. Who are the "we" and who the "they"? We direct attention to the needs and interests of some people. Others will be affected by our decisions and actions, but they appear as antagonists or potential allies, or they are simply overlooked.

Once we have established a viewpoint, we have to give others grounds to endorse it. The natural response to an argument that begins "The students are discontented" is apt to be "I don't think so" or "Prove it." What evidence can be given to demonstrate the validity of our perception of "the way things are"?

Standards of Evaluation

The facts do not speak for themselves. To define a "situation" as a "problem" we have to invoke a standard of judgment. Perhaps the

---

[1] Michael Harrington, The Other America (*New York: Macmillan, 1962*).

students are discontented. So what? Simply because someone is upset or unhappy is not a sufficient reason for giving them what they want. What reasons can be given for acceding to their demands? Why would it be good public policy to do so?

Before we reach a public decision, we have to make a prior choice about the standards of judgment we will employ. We have to make decisions on *some* basis. We can use *political* criteria (What will get me reelected?), or the *interest* of some group (What is best for the poor?), or *efficiency* (What works best at least cost?), or *basic principles* (How are rights affected, or freedom, or justice?). In making up our minds about what *kind* of an issue we face, we can ask where the burden of proof should lie. Who has to give reasons, and who should have their way unless there is an overriding case to do otherwise? And we should examine the question of ideology. What system of values do I generally employ in making political judgments?

Then we have to give reasons for others to accept our evaluation of a question. Why should the question turn on this point rather than some other? (So management is angry. Somebody has to watch out for the rights of the employees.) We either have to give grounds for deciding that one standard will prevail over another, or we have to show that all relevant values point in the same direction. (The most economical course also turns out to be the most equitable course of action, will breed the least resentment, and is easiest to administer.)

A Definition of the Concrete Problem for Public Action

Simply because we have recognized that a problem exists does not mean that we know what to do about it. The next step is to ask, What are we actually trying to accomplish? We have to define the problem in such a way that concrete action can be taken to resolve it, and since a number of lines of action are always possible, we have to hit on that definition of the problem that shows the greatest promise. We can all agree that it is desirable to save lives on the highways. But should we concentrate on the objective of preventing accidents or making accidents more survivable when they occur?

Not all problems can be solved through public action. It may be true that the students are discontented, as alleged, but is there anything that university authorities can do about the situation?

We have to show that something *can* and *should* be done about a problem. In making up our minds about this, we return to the problems of authority and responsibility. What am I entitled to do about this situation? What am I expected to do about it?

In making a case for a preferred problem definition, we have to show that better concrete results are to be expected by looking at the problem one way rather than some other, and that these results will be consistent with important values.

What are the alternatives for reaching our goals? Which program would be best to adopt? We measure the options against the constraints that are part of the definition of the problem. We test the possibilities against the criteria of principle, legitimacy, feasibility, economy, and efficiency. What would be the costs and benefits of different courses of action? On whom will these costs and benefits fall? In the end, we will try to show that some program (or perhaps some limited range of programs) is particularly suited to our needs.

This model of political analysis, of political argument and public policy making, can also be used to evaluate and criticize the cases made by others. Thinking along these lines, we can ask pertinent questions of the advocates, and sort out complex and confusing issues where we are pulled at from different directions.

Political judgment is always selective. To think politically means to make choices, about conceptions of reality, about standards of evaluation, about relevant evidence, about problem definitions and alternatives for action. An obvious point of departure for examining a political argument is to ask, What has been left out? and What could be seen differently?

Asking such questions will lead us right to the heart of the matter. We will be less apt to get bogged down in details. We will be directing our attention at the fundamental assumptions on which a case is based. It is a remedy for being too easily persuaded.

When looking at a political argument, it is important to be particularly attuned to the *because* statements, those that offer grounds for assumptions, recommendations, and conclusions.

The advocate will try to persuade others that a variety of "good things," both direct and indirect, will follow from the adoption of his proposal. Especially for the more distant consequences, how strong are the reasons for expecting the result?

For example, supporters of a civic center might argue that their project will stimulate the economy *because* industries will want to locate in a city with a high level of services and a good "quality of life." The case seems plausible, but is there any evidence that industrialists, particularly those who might actually locate in the city, would make the presence or absence of a civic center a strong consideration in their decision? What evidence that this might, in fact, be the case is presented?

Also to be watched is the "parade of horribles"—all the bad direct and indirect consequences that would follow from an action. The legalization of marijuana should not occur *because* it would lead to the collapse of the family structure, the loss of American power in the world, and the decline of moral virtue as civilization degenerates in self-indulgence and debauchery.

118

*public policy: choice
on behalf of other
people*

The advocate will also give reasons for excluding certain considerations from the case. Evidence concerning the attitudes of a certain group should not be considered *because* existing studies are out of date. (Which begs the question of whether the sentiments of the group concerned are, in fact, important to making a judgment on the matter.) Prison sentences for polluters is not a viable policy *because* juries will not convict industrialists. On what grounds is the future behavior of juries predicted? Common sense? Analogies to other kinds of cases? Is *any* justification of the assertion given?

An argument does not have to be accepted or rejected as a whole. In coming to our own position on an issue, we can take up part of an advocate's case without being bound by the entirety of it. For example:

We may agree to the characterization of the situation, the relevant standards to be applied, but not the recommendation for action.

It is agreed that there is a grave urban housing shortage, and that every citizen deserves a decent home, but it is not agreed that the most efficient means to the end is low-cost housing built by government. It might be better to encourage construction for middle-income families, which would provide a larger total stock of housing, the poor inheriting the supply of used, but adequate houses.

OR

We may agree with the policy recommendation, with relevant standards, but not with the characterization of the situation.

The U.S. should have a strong defense policy to assure its security and that of its allies, and to this end a powerful nuclear deterrent is essential, but this does not entail accepting a particular estimate of the military potential or aggressive designs of any potential opponent. The conclusion need not rest on the assumption that "the Russians are bent on world domination."

OR

We may agree with the characterization of the situation, with the policy recommendation, but not with the standards proposed for its justification.

It is admitted that correctional institutions are doing a bad job, that parole should be used instead of imprisonment wherever possible, but it is *not* agreed that this policy is indicated because "society rather than the individual is responsible for crime."

There is a certain peace of mind and purposiveness that comes with taking a political stand on the basis of good reasons. This does not mean that you will not change your position in the course of the argument, that you have to stick to your guns to the bitter end. But if you have come to your position through self-conscious political analysis, the chances are good that you will change your mind also for good reasons, and not because of social pressure or intimidation. (Or if you do change your mind for these reasons, at least you will know that you are doing so—and that in itself is worth knowing.) But as we shall now see, having taken a position on a political issue is not the end of political analysis. In fact, it is only preparation for the battle.

further
ding

Baxter, William F., *People or Penguins? The Case for Optimal Pollution* (New York: Columbia University Press, 1974). An interesting, nontechnical discussion of basic options in the field of environmental policy and a good example of reasoned argument for preferred solutions.

Dahl, Robert A., and Charles E. Lindblom, *Politics, Economics and Welfare,* Revised Edition (New York: Harper and Row, 1976). A classic study that provides an excellent theoretical basis for thinking about the choice of measures. Difficult and abstract in parts, but comprehensive.

Dorfman, Robert (Ed.), *Measuring Benefits of Government Investments* (Washington: The Brookings Institution, 1965). A number of applications of cost-benefit analysis are described, including urban renewal and government research and development. Somewhat dated.

Enthoven, Alain C., and Wayne Smith, *How Much is Enough? Shaping the Defense Program 1961-1969* (New York: Harper and Row, 1971). The use of cost-benefit analysis in national security policy, one of the most important and controversial applications of the technique.

Freeman, A. Myrick III, and Robert M. Haveman, "Clean Rhetoric and Dirty Water," *The Public Interest 28* (Summer 1972), pp. 51–65. Another good example of political argument about the choice of measures.

Hanson, W. Lee, and Burton A. Weisbrod (Eds.), *Benefits, Costs and Finance of Public Higher Education* (Chicago: Markham, 1969). A good application of the problem of Who pays and who benefits? in the field of public university policy.

Mishan, E. J., *The Costs of Economic Growth* (Baltimore: Penguin Books, 1969). Some of the economics is little advanced, but this is an interesting approach to the problem of assessing the costs of environmental damage, and a critique of the use of economic growth as a prime indicator of public policy achievement.

120

*public policy: choice
on behalf of other
people*

Lampman, Robert J., *Ends and Means of Reducing Income Poverty* (Chicago: Markham, 1971). A very systematic and complete policy analysis of the problem of welfare, which also pertains to our discussion in the last chapter.

Moynihan, Daniel P., *Coping: Essays on the Practice of Government* (New York: Random House, 1972). Rambling essays on applied policy analysis by someone who has been at the scene of the action during several presidential administrations. Contains interesting chapters on the issue of automobile safety.

Rivlin, Alice, *Systematic Thinking for Social Action* (Washington: The Brookings Institution, 1971). A very readable and down-to-earth examination of systematic policy analysis applied to the field of social policy. First class as a follow-up to this chapter.

Schultze, Charles L., *The Distribution of Farm Subsidies: Who Gets the Benefits?* (Washington: The Brookings Institution, 1971). Another good example of policy analysis and policy argument.

Schultze, Charles L., *The Politics and Economics of Public Spending* (Washington: The Brookings Institution, 1968). A brief introduction to and defense of systematic policy analysis.

Vickers, Geoffrey, *The Art of Judgment* (New York: Basic Books, 1965). Very good on the role of "imagination" in the definition of problems and alternatives. The examples are British, not American, and may be hard to follow at times.

Wildavsky, Aaron, "The Political Economy of Efficiency," *The Public Interest 8* (Summer 1967), pp. 30–48. A good critique of the use of efficiency as a central criterion in policy analysis.

Zeckhauser, Richard, et al. (Eds.), *Benefit-Cost and Policy Analysis* (Chicago: Aldine, annual). Published every year since 1968, this series includes important academic articles on issues of policy analysis, decision making and program evaluation. Most are rather weighty, but some provocative essays are also included.

part two political strategy: coping with power and influence

chapter
seven
the arts
of activism

Adversaries are inevitable in politics. In any form of political action, we have to deal with opposition, hostility, and conflict. Power and influence are also important dimensions of any political situation. In any conflict some are in a better position than others to have their views prevail. Public choice, then, not only concerns what *should* be done about a public problem but also what *can* be done about it, given the intentions and capabilities of other parties to the controversy.

Political strategy is a further aspect of decision making. In political action, we have to decide how to cope with opposition and conflict, power and influence. We make an assessment of what we are up against, consider our options, and choose a course of action that will best advance our objectives.

In the following chapters, we deal with four different dimensions of political strategy. This chapter focuses on the problems of activism and advocacy, of advancing a program or a cause in the face of adverse power relationships. Then we look at the problem of strategy from the point of view of the candidate for public office. What are the crucial choices in designing a campaign and electioneering? Next, we take up the problem of revolutionary action. How does the problem of strategy appear from the point of view of those who are committed to nothing less than a sweeping change in the nature of the political order? Finally, we consider the strategies of bargaining and compromise. There is, as we shall see, an art and a logic to fashioning a workable agreement on policy where there are deep divisions of opinion or strongly divergent interests.

These are very different approaches to the problem of political action, but each has its place in the systematic study of statecraft. Taken together, they will give a fairly comprehensive overview of how the problem of strategy can be assessed and analyzed.

Political strategy has to do with how we make our way in the political arena. However, strategic decision making is part of the larger problem of politics as choice on behalf of other people. In political action, we try to mobilize people to support one cause against another. We define some groups as allies and others as enemies. We encourage others to take positions of confrontation or cooperation. We may choose strategies that sharpen conflicts or ones that build bridges between competing groups and interests. Strategic decisions may heighten conflict in a community or help to overcome it. They may encourage docility and submission to the decisions of existing elites or lead to challenges to their authority.

strategy and activism

This chapter examines the problem from the point of view of the "outsider," the activist who wants to bring about change in the program of government, but who does not hold a position of decision-making authority.

The reformer normally starts from an initial disadvantage.[1] There are always some interests that stand to benefit from the status quo, no matter how undesirable, and that would be hurt by any change. There is a tendency in any policymaking system to deal with the most pressing and urgent matters and defer or ignore problems that, for the time being at least, seem to be under control. There is normally a presumption in favor of things as they are. As John F. Kennedy said of electoral college reform while still a senator: "When it is not necessary to change, it is necessary not to change."[2] The burden of proof rests with the reformer.

The problem of building support for a new program may be faced by the citizen activist, the lobbyist for an interest group, by a legislator trying to build a coalition among his colleagues, or by an administrator seeking to call attention to a pressing problem or to win endorsement for a new idea.

What then are the first steps in designing a plan of political action? How do we analyze power and conflict and how do we define our options in dealing with these political realities?

---

[1] *Albert O. Hirschman,* Journeys Toward Progress *(New York: Twentieth Century Fund, 1963), pp. 251–2.*

[2] *Quoted in Alan P. Sindler (Ed.),* Policy and Politics in America *(Boston: Little, Brown, 1973), p. 36.*

There are many different kinds of power relationships, many different forms of political conflict. One of the first strategic decisions we have to make is how to define the political situation we are facing. Like our initial definition of the problem to be solved in policymaking, this is a crucial step, for many of our subsequent choices will be shaped by our first assumptions on this point.

When we first engage in political activity, we will be exposed to many different interpretations of power relationships and the terms of political conflict. There will be appeals to define friend and foe in different ways, to visualize some forces as the "establishment," the "power holders," and the "elite," others as "the powerless" or the "oppressed." There will be different assessments of the intentions of other actors, what they are up to, and what they would be capable of doing in a showdown.

Such assertions are also part of the political argument. Those who claim "inside knowledge" may or may not know what they are talking about. Interpretations of political relationships may be designed to influence your views and actions. Like all other aspects of political argument, assertions about power and conflict have to be approached skeptically.[3]

Those who are opposed to change will try to promote the view that reform is impractical. "The legislature would never pass such a program" they will argue, or "the voters won't stand for it." To oppose a proposal on grounds of political feasibility is a common theme in political argument. But what is the hardheaded realist trying to do? Is he pointing out a flaw in a plan he would like to see adopted? Or is he trying to undercut support for the reform?

On the other hand, the reformer has a vested interest in portraying power relationships as relatively open and flexible. Entrenched opposition may be overcome if sufficient pressure is brought to bear. Top elites may change their positions. A variety of coalitions may be formed in support of the proposal. There is room for maneuver. If the advocates work hard enough, the public may be won over to support the reform. Once again, is the reformer *telling* you something about the nature of political reality, or is he trying to win support for his approach to political action?

The revolutionary wants to promote the view that power structures are fixed and unbending. Piecemeal reforms will do no good because the elites will never permit changes that threaten their vital interests. Most reform movements merely play into the hands of the

---

[3] *One of the most interesting studies of strategic argument is Murray Edelman,* Politics as Symbolic Action: Mass Arousal and Quiescence *(Chicago: Markham, 1971).*

dominant power holders. They create greater tolerance for oppression and domination. There is no chance for peaceful change "within the system." The only remedy is to break existing structures of power and establish a government truly responsive to the "will of the people."

In recent years, there has been considerable discussion of two rival images of power relationships—the ruling elite model and the pluralist model. Each of these characterizations of power has its defenders in contemporary political argument. Each can be applied to a wide variety of political situations. Each has very different implications for political strategy.

The Ruling Elite Model

Here power is envisioned as a pyramid. At the top are the "real" power holders. In the 1960s, C. Wright Mills described the political system of the United States as a concentration of power in the hands of a small, dominant elite, primarily the leaders of the "military-industrial complex." The heads of large corporations and financial institutions, with their allies in the armed services and in government agencies, actually run the system. The formal institutions of the political order, the Congress, courts, parties, and interest groups, are a facade. Neither party actively challenges the dominance of the ruling elites. The democratic process of government actually serves merely to carry out the purposes of the ruling groups and to invest them with the trappings of legitimacy.[4]

Similar analyses have been made of the governments of major American cities. The "real" power holders are not the elected officials of government. Rather, economic elites determine policy behind the trappings of competitive politics.[5]

A wide variety of forms of political organization could be analyzed in this way. Most institutions with hierarchical organizations—the military or corporations—seem, superficially at least, to correspond to ruling elite models. The top leaders make policy and their subordinates carry it out. Those at the very top of the pyramid of power can prevent challenges to their rule.

However, on closer inspection, the structure of power in such organizations may often turn out to be far more complex than it appears at first. The corporation may not be ruled from the top down. In fact, managers may see themselves coordinating a complex coalition of forces, "responding" to the demands of various branches and sub-

---

[4] C. Wright Mills, The Power Elite *(New York: Oxford University Press, 1957).*
[5] *Floyd Hunter,* Community Power *(Chapel Hill: University of North Carolina Press, 1953).*

sidiaries, to labor unions and consumer groups. The organization may, in fact, be only imperfectly responsive to the will of the top leaders.

Plural Elite Models

Here power is envisioned as disbursed throughout the system. There are many different individuals and groups that have some influence over policy. Each has to define its actions in relation to a complex configuration of potential coalitions and power relationships. The real influentials may change from issue to issue—no elite is dominant on all matters. New groups emerge and exert political influence, new interests are expressed, the system evolves and changes over time.

Robert Dahl is perhaps the most prominent writer who has characterized American politics as a plural elite system. Power is not concentrated but divided among a variety of groups and interests. The Congress, the president, the courts, parties, and interest groups all have sgnificant power in the system, but none is preponderant. Policy outcomes depend on patterns of shifting coalitions among the critical political forces.[6]

In any organization, we might be inclined to envision power in terms of a plural elite model if it seems apparent that we cannot influence policy only by dealing with a few top leaders. Rather we will have to try to win a wide variety of groups and individuals over to our cause.

In political argument, the revolutionary who wants to persuade us that no constructive change is possible within the existing system is apt to portray power through a ruling elite model. So may the conservative, who tries to prevent change by insisting that political action would be futile. The reformer is more attracted to the plural elite model, for it promises flexibility and possibilities for action.

The model of power relationships we choose to adopt makes a great deal of difference. Ruling elite models lead to three inferences about political strategy. One must put up with conditions as they are or exert influence on the top leaders, or try to overthrow them. Plural elite models suggest that strategy focus on coalition formation, persuasion, bargaining and compromise.

sizing up the situation

Political science offers no sure methods for analyzing conflict or power relationships. Political conflict can take many different forms. Power is

[6] *Robert A. Dahl,* A Preface to Democratic Theory *(Chicago: University of Chicago Press, 1956);* Pluralist Democracy in the United States *(Chicago: Rand McNally, 1967);* Who Governs? *(New Haven: Yale University Press, 1961).*

a vague, intangible, and frequently elusive concept. Political scientists have found it difficult even to define what "power" is.[7] Hence, for the political activist this is a problem of decision making, a matter of choice and judgment. However, there are certain questions that can be asked when we begin to come to grips with the problem of political strategy.

What Game Are We Playing?

Effective political action must fit the context. Political relationships take many different forms. One way of getting an initial sense for the situation is to ask the question, How is this matter going to be settled? There are a variety of methods for resolving political disputes. Each implies a different form of analysis and action.

Problem Solving. Here there is a sense of common purpose and teamwork. The conflict is not about what ought to be done, but how to do it. Picture a committee planning a program or a candidate's supporters deciding on campaign strategy. Action takes the form of argument about means not ends, and a search for agreement.

Deliberation on the Merits. There is dispute about objectives, but positions are tentatively held and subject to revision. There is a willingness to listen to opposing views and a hope that a consensual position will emerge. Once again, argument, a search for agreement, perhaps compromise, is called for.

Voting. There is conflict over objectives, and no real expectation that a consensus will be found. Yet there is a commitment to abide by the judgment of the majority. Action takes the form of mobilizing support for a position.

Authoritative Decision. As in voting, there is conflict, but also a commitment to accept the decision of a person or persons in a position of authority. Action focuses on efforts to influence the authoritative decision makers.

Bargaining. In the face of conflict, the participants try to reach agreement by a process of give-and-take. Labor-management relationships are perhaps the best example. Action takes the form of making demands and proposing compromises.

Tests of Power. Conflict will be settled by one side forcing the other

---

[7] *On some of the problems of analyzing power, see Robert A. Dahl,* Modern Political Analysis *(Englewood Cliffs, N.J.: Prentice-Hall, 1963), pp. 38–71, and his "A Critique of the Ruling Elite Model,"* American Political Science Review 52 *(June 1958), pp. 463–9. See also Peter Bachrach and Morton Baratz, "The Two Faces of Power,"* American Political Science Review 56 *(December 1962), pp. 947–52, and their* Power and Poverty *(New York: Oxford University Press, 1970); Arnold Rose,* The Power Structure *(New York: Oxford University Press, 1967); Nelson Polsby,* Community Power and Political Theory *(New Haven: Yale University Press, 1963); William E. Connolly,* The Terms of Political Discourse *(Boston: D.C. Heath, 1974), pp. 85–138.*

to submit to its will. Action may take the form of combat, coercion, or war. Equally likely, the outcome will be determined by threat and maneuver. One side simply recognizes that the other would come out best in a showdown and acknowledges defeat.

Going it Alone. The parties decide that their dispute cannot be resolved and decide to break off relationships. Action takes the form of secession, schism, the formation of new political communities.[8]

When the outsider first enters a political arena, it is important to have a very clear idea of the kind of game that is being played there. To make a mistake can be costly. The protest leader may feel that he must mobilize power for a confrontation. The other participants may read this as a threat and present a solid front against "pressure politics" if they view the game differently. On the other hand, where a test of power is at issue, appeals for reason and moderation may be futile.

The participants define the game, and the nature of the game may shift during the course of the relationship. A test of strength may become a bargaining relationship, and those engaged in bargaining may decide to submit their differences to a vote or to arbitration. (This is, of course, a normal pattern in labor-management relations.) Or a group committed to voting may decide to go their own way.

Sometimes it can be good strategy to try to redefine the nature of the game. The activist need not accept the game that others want to play. An effort can be made to redefine the political relationship. When a student-faculty committee is set up, the student members might decide to act as though they were in a bargaining relationship. They present extreme demands, expecting the faculty to take the cue and work toward a compromise. The faculty may assume that the relationship calls for deliberation on the merits or mutual problem solving. The early meetings may be devoted to sparring by both sides. Finally, one may induce the other to accept its definition of the game, or the committee may break down completely.

If activists can convince others to accept their definition of the relationship, they can fight the battle on their own terms. For those on the receiving end, the question is whether to accept the rival's conception of the game that is to be played.

What Are the Terms of the Conflict?

Lines of coalition and conflict can be defined in different ways. In any society, there are many potential cleavages. Of all the possible lines of division—economic, racial, religious, regional, generational—we can

---

[8] *This is a loose adaptation of two typologies. One is found in Herbert March and James Simon,* Organizations *(New York: John Wiley, 1958), pp. 91–2. The other is Brian Barry,* Political Argument, *pp. 84–93.*

fight over only so many. People get to choose their enemies and allies from a long list of possibilities.

In asking this question, we return to the problem of the "we" and the "they" of politics that we discussed earlier. How have we defined friends and antagonists? Are these lines of conflict necessary and inevitable, or are there other possibilities for redefining the terms of the controversy? In the above example of the student-faculty committee, when the students make the first move of deciding whether the relationship calls for bargaining or problem solving, they are also deciding whether the faculty members will be conceived as adversaries or colleagues.

The political scientist E. E. Schattschneider once observed that in every conflict there are two elements: the antagonists and the audience. An important question is whether the audience will join the fight—and on which side. In strategic planning, we have to decide whether to try to *expand* the conflict or *localize* it. For example, a labor leader may try to win public sympathy in a strike or get government to intervene on the side of labor. Or the leader might prefer to restrict the scope of the conflict, arguing that "this is a matter between labor and management and government should stay out of it." The crucial question may be whether the balance of power would shift in your favor if third parties were brought into the conflict, or if your strategic position is better if you try to confine the conflict to the original participants.[9]

Who Has to be Accounted for and Why?

When making a plan for political action, we all, intuitively, make an estimate of power and influence. We know that some individuals and groups will be more important than others in determining the outcome. We concentrate attention on certain "key" figures. We try to gauge their probable response to our initiatives. We try to win their support or neutralize their opposition.

To draw a mental map of power relationships, we can ask the question, Who has to be accounted for and why? The "who" question states the relevant political actors. The "why" question tells us something about the critical political resources.

Politics may be seen as a process of negotiation among groups and individuals who have relevant political resources in each other's eyes. In every decision-making process there are insiders and outsiders. Many who will be affected by a policy will have little impact on its formulation. For the activist, an important problem of strategy may be simply to *appear* on the mental maps of power relationships that estab-

---

[9] E. E. *Schattschneider,* The Semi-Sovereign People *(New York: Holt, Rinehart and Winston, 1960), pp. 1–19, 62–77.*

lished contenders use in defining their strategies. To have won political influence is to be regularly and systematically accounted for by other elites and influentials. What then is the price of admission to the political arena? How does the outsider become an insider? A strategic analysis must begin with an appraisal of your own political resources in relation to those of possible allies and adversaries.

There are many different kinds of political resources, and their significance varies from situation to situation. Among the more common political resources that are brought to bear in everyday politics are the following.

Authority. Those who hold official positions are, of course, an important part of the political equation. Others expect them to make public decisions and are willing to be bound by them.

Influence. The capacity to affect the opinions and attitudes of significant groups of people is an important political resource. Some count for more than one because they have the capacity to bring others with them.

Access. Simply being in a position to get a hearing from decision makers may be important. The friends, confidantes, colleagues and advisers of policymakers may be counted among the influential.

Expert Knowledge. Those who have the ability (and the credentials) to provide a specialized, professional judgment on a complex issue may be in a position to decisively influence the outcome of a policy conflict.

Control of Economic Resources. Those who are in a position to advance or to frustrate public purposes through their economic actions are important in the web of power relationships. Corporations, banks, and trade unions may respond to public policy in cooperative or obstructive ways.

Violence, Coercion, and the Capacity for Systematic Disruption. Strikes, riots, or insurrections may lead existing power holders to "take account" of a new political force in making their strategic calculations. The threat of violence or disruption may be a tool in the hands of the disadvantaged or powerless. However, as a political resource, violence can be a two-edged sword. The response to the use of this political resource may be either accommodation or repression.

the analysis of power and conflict: an example

The strategic calculations of black protest leaders in the 1960s provide a good case study of the problem of making an assessment of power and conflict as a basis for political action.

For Martin Luther King and many of the early leaders of the civil rights movement, the game was not a test of power, but an attempt to focus public opinion on the issue of racial equality, to win allies in the white population. The conflict was not to be defined as white against black, but as a struggle against discrimination, prejudice, and the doctrine of white supremacy.

King's strategic analysis was based on the premise that blacks had virtually no political resources of their own. They were, at the outset of the struggle, virtually unorganized. Historically, they were a dependent and subservient people. They controlled little wealth. Violent resistance was unrealistic for a minority outnumbered ten to one in the nation as a whole.

Given this diagnosis of power relationships, nonviolence was the indicated strategy of action. It was not enough simply to win legislative victories or court cases. Rather, by passively refusing to comply with segregation laws, the black would not only assert his own dignity but also force the white powerholders to confront the fundamental moral and political choices—immediately and not in the remote future.

Thus, when blacks staged sit-ins at lunch counters, or sat in seats reserved for whites on public buses, or "waded-in" at segregated beaches, they posed an immediate dilemma for decision makers. Would the local segregation ordinances be upheld or would federal authorities be forced to rule that such regulations violated the "equal protection of the laws" guaranteed all citizens by the Fourteenth Amendment? King adopted a pluralistic view of power relations. There were a variety of points of authority and decision in the system. Sometimes the target of protest was action in the courts or in Congress, and sometimes pressure was brought to bear on business leaders, as in the boycotts blacks staged against department stores in Birmingham.

The key was the moral ambiguity of white America on the race issue. Gunnar Myrdal had pointed up the "American dilemma" in the 1940s. America was torn between a democratic belief in equal rights and prejudice against the black race. The problem then was to force a challenge to the beliefs and institutions that supported racial segregation. The object was to expand the scope of the conflict, to bring sympathetic white groups into the struggle for civil rights, to appeal to authoritative decision makers, and not to restrict the conflict to confrontations between black militants and southern white power holders.

Other black leaders disputed King's strategic theory. In *Black Power*, Stokely Carmichael and Charles Hamilton challenged what they called the "myths of coalition." The cause of civil rights could not be won through compromise and accommodation with dominant groups. The prior question of strategy was for blacks to establish their own independent base of power.

The powerlessness of the minority could not be resolved by appeals for the support of influential white groups. Political coalitions do not rest on sympathy and goodwill, they argued, but on mutual self-interest. When blacks form coalitions with whites, they do so essentially on the white's terms.

White support might win token or symbolic reforms. But appeals to conscience would not be enough when "gut" issues had to be faced. Northern whites could be self-righteous about segregation in the South, but integrated housing in the North was another matter. When conflicts of real interests become apparent, the only basis of coalition is recognition of the power of the other side—that each has the capacity to give or to deny what the other wants.

Carmichael and Hamilton argued that coalitions between weak and strong groups do not often serve the interest of the powerless partner. Political parties, unions, and reform groups are glad to have black support, as long as it furthers their own aims. But when there is a conflict of interest, the weak minority will lose.

The only remedy, then, was for the black community to develop its own base of power. Carmichael and Hamilton wrote, "Let black people organize themselves *first*, define their interests and goals, and then see what kinds of allies are available."[10] Blacks must take control of political, economic, and social institutions in their own communities. Once organized, aware of their own goals and purposes, they could then look for coalitions and allies, and these coalitions would be viable and lasting, for they would be based on mutual respect of the power on each side.

Carmichael's view was not that blacks had to "go it alone" (although some black separatists, the more extreme Black Muslims and the Black Panther party, called for virtual secession from the nation). Rather, he defined the game as one calling for bargaining based on recognized political resources, and not, as King did, more a process of argument, persuasion, appeals to authoritative decision makers, and mutual problem solving.

Who was right? The argument between King and Carmichael may have passed into history, but the consequences are all around us. How should minorities appraise their strategic situation at the present time? The argument well illustrates the different assumptions that can be made about power and the nature of political conflict, and the different implications for political action that follow from such assumptions.

strategies of action

Let us assume that you are an environmental activist and that you have recently become aware that the Corps of Engineers is planning to build

[10] *Stokely Carmichael and Charles V. Hamilton,* Black Power *(New York: Random House, 1967) p. 67.*

a dam that will flood a scenic stretch of river. Local interests want the dam as protection against the spring floods that occasionally do considerable damage in the area. The project has been planned for a long time. Congress has appropriated funds. The dam is part of a comprehensive design for flood control on a major river system. Many people think that the project will bring economic benefits to the area. However, the area that will be flooded to create a reservoir behind the dam is wild and beautiful. The river passes through scenic gorges and is a favorite of canoeists. The watershed is a fine area for hunters and outdoor enthusiasts.

Within a few months, work on the dam will begin. You want to oppose construction. The question is, What can you do about it?

How do we define the situation we are facing? What kind of a game will we be playing? What are the terms of the conflict? Who has to be accounted for in our strategic calculations? If we adopt the view that "powerful interests" are behind the dam, that "you can't fight the system," we are finished before we begin. So, for better or worse, we will have to adopt a pluralistic view of power relationships.

What are the options? We can consider chaining ourselves to trees and defying the bulldozers to move us. In this way we might bring about a test of power with the engineers. Some might advocate violence—threatening to blow up the dam. The conflict is portrayed as a straight fight between us and them. As cooler heads prevail, we consider possibilities for expanding the scope of the conflict. How can influence and access be mobilized in support of the cause? Where are the authoritative decision makers located who might be able to intervene on our behalf?

Sponsorship and Brokerage

It is apparent that some kind of organization will be necessary. The first object of strategy is to be taken seriously in the public debate. We have to build support, to demonstrate possession of political resources.

Every political system has its "brokers" who build their own power and influence by acting as intermediaries between the individual and the political process. Practicing politicians are on the lookout for new issues. So are journalists. Interest groups seek out causes that fit with their programs. Perhaps the most straightforward way of transforming an unrecognized issue into an acknowledged one is to have it endorsed and championed by someone with an established place in the political process.

One possible strategy then is to try to activate the network of environmental groups in the state or area, groups like the Sierra Club, Friends of the Earth, and similar organizations. We might appeal to state legislators or political leaders known for their interest in environmental problems. We might try to gain the support of sympathetic newspapers editors. Where else can we look for allies? Hunters and snowmobilers are often seen as foes of environmentalists, but in this case might they not be potential allies? Each might have an interest in the use of the natural area along the river. It seems apparent that to build a credible base of support, we will have to operate on at least a statewide level.

From the moment that we try to win support from an interest group, or to form an alliance of such groups, we will be involved in another form of politics—that of the interest organizations themselves. Every such organization has its own internal power structure and political organization. Some groups will be dynamic and active. Others will be poorly organized and ineffective. Some will be open and democratic, others led by a small group of officers. There may be factions within the organization. To win the support of interest groups one has to understand, and be able to cope with, the structure of power and conflict within the group itself.

The Choice of Arena

Citizen activism is no more and no less than a form of interest group politics. Interest groups are active at all levels of government. They include the powerful economic associations such as the National Association of Manufacturers, the AFL-CIO, the Teamsters, and the National Farmers Organization. There are groups that represent minority interests, such as the NAACP and the Urban League. There are "public service" interest organizations like Common Cause, the American Civil Liberties Union, and the Nader organization. There are special interest groups such as the National Rifle Association. Professional associations such as the American Medical Association may function as interest groups. There are at least 8000 such groups active at the national and state levels. Many have permanent offices and full-time staffs in Washington and parallel organizations in the state capitals.

Usually we associate interest group politics with legislative lobbying. But interest groups also try to influence the decisions of administrators and regulatory agencies; they are active in the courts, bringing cases that might support points of law favorable to their interests. They provide funds to political candidates and try to influence the selection of candidates by political parties. Through the media, they bring their case before public opinion.

Like any interest group, our "stop the dam" movement faces the choice of which political arenas to operate in. We might meet with the district officers of the Corps of Engineers to ascertain their commitment to the project and their rationale for it. Might the sponsors of the project have second thoughts about its desirability?

We might try to influence the congressional delegation from our state to halt appropriations for the project. Now we have to make further strategic calculations. Perhaps you should approach the congressmen directly to try to get them to vote against further appropriations for the dam. Perhaps you will try to influence state legislators, party leaders, or the governor to put pressure on the senators and congressmen. Soon you find yourself in the midst of a heated controversy. Local interests that want the dam will be active too. Newspapers and local government officials in the area begin to take sides. The politicians have to begin to calculate the support that the pro-dam and anti-dam factions have. Efforts have to be made to mobilize support, to demonstrate the political resources behind the cause.

If you do find sponsors in Congress, other strategic questions arise. Perhaps the congressman or senator who has taken up the issue is not in a position to affect rivers and harbors legislation. Perhaps the timing is wrong. There are many factors that have to do with the internal politics of Congress that have to be weighed. If it seems impossible to halt appropriations for the dam, would it be good strategy for your sponsors in Congress to introduce a bill to declare the area part of the national wild rivers system, or a national park, or natural preserve? Progress on the dam might be halted while such legislation is being considered, giving you time to develop your case and mobilize support. Hearings will be held, and you will have to develop your case further. What grounds can be given that this area is of "unique scenic beauty" or has "unusual environmental characteristics"? How will you respond to the cost-benefit analysis of the proponents of the dam, that the few hundred canoeists and hunters who enjoy the area have a far smaller stake in the project than the thousands of property owners and businessmen in the area?

The state legislature is another potential arena of action. Perhaps you can mobilize support there in opposition to the dam which will have an effect on the attitudes of the congressional delegation. In building support within the state legislature, you may want to contact administrators in the state park department or the department of natural resources. What would happen if the state proposed to create a park or natural area in the river valley? Would not such action at the state level effectively preempt the plan for the dam? What is the law on the matter? What powers do the federal government and the state government have to regulate the river and the area surrounding it?

By now, time is running short. The bulldozers are poised to begin digging. The wheels of legislative action grind slowly. You have to consider other alternatives. Every major dam project must comply with an incredibly complex set of legal requirements before it can begin. You bring in an interested attorney and begin to scrutinize the record. Perhaps a required public hearing was not held. Perhaps the cost-benefit analysis prepared by the Corps of Engineers misstated the discount rate on invested capital, making the dam appear more beneficial economically than was in fact the case. Perhaps an environmental impact statement was improperly filed or ignored significant information about the environmental characteristics of the dam.

You go to court and try to get an injunction to halt construction of the dam. You call in environmental experts from the local university to testify to the unique geological and botanical features of the river area, factors neglected in the earlier environmental impact report.

None of this is easy. Citizen activism is enormously time-consuming. It requires solid research, the careful development of political arguments, long and patient efforts at organization, coordination, persuasion, and diplomacy. In the end, you may lose. There are no sure recipes for success. The great social scientist Max Weber once likened practical politics to the act of driving nails through a hard board with your bare hands.

You might eventually be able to delay the construction of the dam, but can you halt it completely? After interest in the issue dies down and the movement loses momentum, the powerful, established interests in favor of the dam may reassert themselves. At the end, you may have to settle for what will seem a poor compromise—a dam project that takes into account some of the environmental characteristics of the river that you sought to preserve.

It should also be apparent from this example that in the American system it is often easier to prevent action than to win support for a positive program or policy. Interest groups are often most effective in vetoing measures that threaten their interests as they perceive them. There are many points of access in the system, many institutions that have partial authority over public policy. The American checks and balances system was designed to prevent a concentration of power at any point in the system. But this means that effective reform requires coordinated action by a wide variety of institutions, officials, and political forces.

Nonetheless, citizen activism is essential if the system is to work. The basic idea behind citizen politics is simply that ordinary people *use* procedures and processes that have always been open to the individual but are normally employed only by well established interest groups. Ralph Nader, for example, in his early years as a consumer advocate, had few political resources that were not available to any well-educated, forceful activist. He had virtually no organization; he acted mainly as an individual. His information on industrial practices that were unsafe or illegal, his data on suspect public policy actions, came mainly from public records and documents. He advanced his causes through appearances before congressional committees and regulatory agency hearings, through litigation and publicity. In a sense, he simply acted as an involved citizen and did so effectively at the highest levels of national politics, often with dramatic effect.

Some describe citizen activism as "alternative politics." The idea is that in the absence of direct citizen involvement, the basic processes of decision making come to be dominated by established interests. Policymakers receive the views of powerful groups, but not of the average people who will be affected by public action. The purpose of "alternative politics" is to create an argument—to identify and publicize unacknowledged problems, to measure public policy against different standards of evaluation, and to promote new solutions to problems—in effect to provide an alternative way of studying public problems and fresh approaches to the business of government.

for further reading

Alinsky, Saul, *Reveille for Radicals* (Chicago: University of Chicago Press, 1940); *Rules for Radicals* (New York: Random House, 1971). Two works on the subject of organizing communities and pressure groups.

Cavala, Bill, and Aaron Wildavsky, "The Political Feasibility of Income by Right," *Public Policy 18* (Spring 1970), pp. 321–54. An interesting strategic analysis of the political "realities" facing any minimum guaranteed income policy. An argument that such a policy would not be politically feasible.

Dahl, Robert A., *Who Governs?* (New Haven: Yale University Press, 1961). A critique of the ruling elite model, and argument for the pluralist characterization of power in an American city.

Day, Mark, *Forty Acres: Caesar Chavez and the Farm Workers* (New York: Praeger, 1971). An account of Chavez's efforts to organize migrant workers.

Edelman, Murray, *Politics as Symbolic Action* (Chicago: Markham, 1971). The language of political strategy, how different "images" of conflict may promote mass quiescence or arousal.

Hirschman, Albert O., *Exit, Voice and Loyalty* (Cambridge: Harvard University Press, 1970). Strategic alternatives for individuals faced with the declining performance of an organization.

King, Martin Luther, Jr., *Why We Can't Wait* (New York: New American Library, 1964). The best example of King's case for a nonviolent strategy of protest.

Lasswell, Harold E., *Politics: Who Gets What, When, How* (New York: Meridian Books, 1956). A classic book on political strategy, and a thorough inventory of political resources, their nature and interaction.

Lewis, David L., *King: A Critical Biography* (Baltimore: Penguin Books, 1970). An excellent interpretation both of King's conception of protest strategy and the history and development of the civil rights movement.

Lipsky, Michael, "Protest as a Political Resource," *American Political Science Review 62* (December 1968), pp. 1144–1158. The strategic calculus of the protest leaders, and the problems of demonstrating a power capability through protest activity.

McDonald, John B., *Strategy in Poker, Business and War* (New York: W. W. Norton, 1956). An informal introduction to strategic theory, including game theories.

Meyerson, Martin, and Edward C. Banfield, *Politics, Planning and the Public Interest* (New York: The Free Press, 1955). An excellent case study of strategic problems of argument, access, and influence, based on a study of public housing in Chicago.

Mills, C. Wright, *The Power Elite* (New York: Oxford University Press, 1957). The classic argument that the American political system should be characterized as a ruling elite model.

Nader, Ralph, *Working on the System: A Comprehensive Manual for Citizen Access to Federal Agencies* (New York: Basic Books, 1974). Where can the citizen go to complain or protest? This is a very detailed guide to "points of access" in federal agencies.

Nader, Ralph, and Donald Ross, *Action for a Change: A Student's Manual for Public Interest Organizing* (New York: Grossman, 1972). A how-to-do-it book for students interested in setting up a public interest research group.

Newfield, Jack, *A Prophetic Minority* (New York: New American Library, 1964). A sympathetic history of the emergence and development of the "New Left" during its formative years. The rationale and strategy of this political movement is analyzed.

Rose, Arnold, *The Power Structure* (New York: Oxford University Press, 1967). A thorough discussion of the controversy over the nature of power and the characterization of power systems. Criticizes the ruling elite model.

Schelling, Thomas C., *The Strategy of Conflict* (New York: Oxford University Press, 1963). A very interesting work on the formal theory of strategic calculation.

Truman, David B., *The Governmental Process*, Second Edition (New York: Knopf, 1971). The classic work on interest group politics.

Zeigler, L. Harmon, and G. Wayne Peak, *Interest Groups in American Society*, Second Edition (Englewood Cliffs, N.J.: Prentice-Hall, 1972). A comprehensive basic textbook on interest group politics.

chapter
eight
election
strategy

Some people think that running for office is the greatest part of politics. Others would rather submit to major surgery without benefit of anesthesia. But even the most enthusiastic politician will admit that campaigning has its bad days. Canvassing the district bears an unmistakable resemblance to selling encyclopedias or patent medicines door-to-door. Campaign funding has a lot in common with begging for charity. Discussing the issues means giving the same answers to the same boring questions. Campaign organization is like running a small business always on the brink of collapse, but you cannot easily fire the most inefficient employees, for they are all volunteers dedicated to your cause.

Nonetheless, thousands of people do run for office. There are over 524,000 elected officials in the United States. That is about one for every 400 citizens. (By comparison, there is about one doctor for every 1000 Americans.) Few of these people are full-time politicians. Most combine politics with some other job. Many readers of this book will one day be tempted to toss their hat in the ring—for the local school board, the city council, the state legislature, or perhaps the Congress of the United States.

Furthermore, in this society, running for office is an important part of the struggle for power and influence. Elections are not the only sources of power and authority in the system, to be sure, but they are important, and seeking elective office is one strategy that has to be considered by anyone who wants to have an impact on political events.

Like all other forms of political activity, running for office means making choices. You have to decide where to run, what issues to run on, how to present yourself as a cnadidate, how to organize a campaign. Many good books have been written on the art of winning elections. (Some of the best, in my opinion, are listed in the suggested readings at the end of the chapter.) The trouble with such advice is that it is necessarily very vague and general. No two elections are exactly alike. American politics is infinitely diverse. There are over 100,000 election districts in the nation, each with its special characteristics.

There are no sure-fire methods for winning elections. Candidates who hire high-priced political experts often lose, and those who break most of the rules sometimes win. But while there are few techniques of campaigning that will work in every situation, there are some basic decisions that every candidate must face.

Two of these are particularly important. First, what is your image of the electorate? How do you visualize the voters and how they make up their minds? Basic assumptions on this point have a lot to do with the business of campaign strategy. Despite massive research by political scientists and public relations specialists, there is still much about the mind of the voters, taken in the mass, that remains elusive. But you, the prospective candidate, will inevitably develop some preconceptions about the people whose support you are trying to win.

The second question goes a little deeper. What is an election supposed to prove? Are the voters deciding on the *program* of government or about *who* should do the governing? Are they voting for the best party, the best policy, or the best person? What you think about this will influence your style of campaigning. Will you emphasize your experience or your stand on the issues? More important, your whole attitude toward the democratic process of government depends to some extent on your response to these questions.

Like the decisions you make about ideology, or your conception of role and responsibility, thesé are "background" choices, overall orientations toward politics that can be pondered, discussed, and debated long before the moment of truth arrives. These are questions not just for the would-be candidate but for the voter as well. Each tells you something about decision-rules that can be applied in sizing up candidates for public office.

We will return to these questions in due course. First, however, we want to say something about the process of getting started in politics. What are the strategic problems of breaking into politics and developing a political career? We will focus on campaigning at the local rather than the national level. To be sure, presidential campaigns are the most dramatic and exciting level of American politics, but unless you happen to have liberated Europe or your father is a millionaire, running for president is not the logical place to begin a political career.

the candidate and the constituency

Sometimes political careers begin almost by accident. Without quite knowing what is happening, the well-meaning citizen gets wrapped up in a civic project, is thrust into a leadership role, and one thing leads to another. Eventually, friends and colleagues suggest running for office. In other cases, the individual simply decides to go into politics and lays a plan of action toward that end.[1] In either case, the first fateful questions quickly become apparent: What election should you run in? What experience do you have? What do you have to offer the voters? What is your base of support? How well known are you in the community? Who will form the nucleus of a campaign organization? How well does the candidate "fit" the constituency?

Do-It-Yourself Politics

For many local offices, especially where party organization is weak, it is possible for you simply to file papers and run in the primary election with some prospect of success. Campaign organization is rudimentary. With the help of a few friends, you can canvass the district, put up some signs, distribute handbills, and have meetings with voters. You are apt to get some attention from the local press and from civic organizations (like the League of Women Voters) simply by virtue of being a candidate.

If you win the primary, and have played your cards right, local influentials, party leaders, and the press may lend you their support in the general election. Even if you lose, but make a respectable showing, you have had a chance to get your name and position before the public. Simply running in a primary may be a way to break into the "political circles" of a community. Your chance may come next time, especially if you used the initial primary contest as an opportunity to build bridges to influential individuals and organizations in the constituency.

Partisan Politics

Another point of entry to political activity is through party organization. You can break into politics by attending party caucuses, running as a delegate to nominating conventions, attaching yourself to the campaigns of candidates. Especially where party organization is strong and endorsement essential to the successful candidate, such

---

[1] *Most studies seem to suggest that the ratio of "self-starters" to "recruits" is about fifty-fifty.* David A. Leuthold, Electioneering in a Democracy Campaign for Congress (*New York:* John Wiley, 1968), p. 15.

service to the partisan cause may be a vital preliminary to running for office.

The importance of party endorsement depends to some extent on electoral laws. There are still a few areas in the United States where nominations are made through party conventions rather than primaries. (Indiana, for statewide offices, is one example.) In California, Colorado, and New Mexico, the candidate endorsed by the party convention automatically appears on the ballot. In Connecticut, the convention-endorsed candidate is the party's nominee unless he is challenged, and only in this case is a primary election held. In Wisconsin, parties are only permitted to make endorsements *after* the primary election.

In some states, and for some offices, nonpartisan elections are the rule. Candidates are not identified by party label on the ballot. (Even here, however, party endorsement is still often important, for parties can provide support and resources to favored candidates.) The rules of the game vary widely, and part of electoral strategy is knowing the implications of particular nomination systems.[2]

The partisan "competitiveness" of a district is another factor to be taken into account. While we talk about the American "two-party system," in many parts of the country, one party is strongly dominant, and the second party may not even present candidates for office. In many areas, the primary is the real election, and the general election a mere formality.

However, it is not always futile to run for office as a candidate of the weaker party in a one-party area. In fact, for the self-starter in politics, it may be a positive advantage. A succession of losing elections builds a personal constituency and contacts with state or national party leaders. A shift in the mood of local or national politics may eventually bring victory.

Many prominent political leaders began their careers by presiding over the reconstruction of a debilitated party. Such Democratic leaders of the late 1960s and early 1970s as Humphrey of Minnesota, McGovern of South Dakota, Hughes of Iowa, and Proxmire and Nelson of Wisconsin built statewide electoral support, often largely through personal efforts, within weak Democratic organizations in historically strong Republican areas.

Endorsement Politics

In many parts of the country, party identification and support is on the decline. Civic groups of various kinds are playing a more active role in

[2] *Frank J. Sorauf,* Party Politics in America, *Second Edition (Boston: Little, Brown, 1972), p. 33.*

promoting candidates. In some big cities, neighborhood associations and community action organizations are taking the place of the historic party machines in selecting candidates for city offices and campaigning for them. In some areas, support by ethnic associations or labor unions may be crucial. In small towns, business organizations and service clubs, while not actually "endorsing" candidates, may form a network of influential citizens that plays a strong role in identifying and supporting candidates for local office.

Like any kind of strategic decision, running for office begins with "sizing up the situation," making an estimate of the conditions of power and influence in the particular constituency. Who has to be accounted for and why? It is helpful to study previous campaigns for the office in which you are interested. What kinds of people run for this office? How are they selected? What kinds of strategies seem to lead to success?

analyzing the constituency

Let us now turn our attention to the voters. What is the composition of the electorate? What is the occupational, financial, religious, and class structure of the district? Is it a fairly homogeneous community? Do most of the voters come from the same ethnic background and do the same kind of work? Or are there distinct groups in the district? Is it a mixture of rich and poor, Catholic and Protestant? Are there a variety of financial, educational, and occupational levels?

A good place to start is with electoral history. How do different precincts tend to vote? What proportion of registered voters actually go to the polls? How does turnout vary in primary and general elections, in years of presidential campaigns and "off-year" elections? Where are your "firm" voters likely to be located, and where is your opponent's strength concentrated? Where are the "swing" voters?

Let us assume that you are interested in running for the lower house of the state legislature in a midwestern state. You are young, a Democrat, and have some political "visibility" in the main city of the district, which has an industrial base. The district also includes a large farming area and several small towns.

The precincts in which the industrial workers live in your home city vote 60 to 70 percent Democrat. They account for about half the eligible voters. They are largely Catholic and so are you. The rural areas are predominantly Republican, and Protestant, but there is a normal 25 to 30 percent Democratic vote outside the city. Furthermore, you are virtually unknown in the farming areas and small towns. In addition you know that only a little more than half the eligible voters in the urban Democratic precincts normally vote for state legislator in off-year elections, which is when you are running. A rural Republican has held the seat for many years, and the Democrats have tended to put up merely token opposition.[3]

So the question arises. Should you try to "get out the vote" in the Democratic precincts, adopt a strong pro-union policy, emphasize your Catholicism, seek endorsement from union leaders and local Democrats, all at the risk of antagonizing rural voters and the middle class and business constituency? Or should you accept the "normal" urban Democratic vote as a firm base of support, and campaign vigorously in rural areas? It has been a bad year for farmers, and they have been known to vote to "throw the rascals out" when economic conditions are grim. The national Republican administration is not particularly popular here. There is, you sense, a groundswell of "populist" sentiment to which you can appeal. Furthermore, there is grumbling about the condition of rural roads and county taxes. Could you build on this mood of discontent, make inroads into your opponent's rural support? Or will you inevitably appear to be a "city boy," an outsider, to these people?

Your opponent has counted on winning about 70 percent of the vote (35 percent of the electorate) in the rural areas and he can break about even in the cities, due to the low turnout in the industrial wards. Since half the people live in the city, this means that the opposition picks up about 25 percent of the total vote there which, combined with the rural Republican following, makes a comfortable margin.

Your strategy might be to count on winning the predictable 25 percent of the total vote from the Democratic urban areas, add to this a possible 15 percent from rural Democratic voters, and work hard to make up the margin of difference from discontented rural voters who normally would support your opponent. Or you can try energetically to get out the vote in the urban industrial areas. A strong turnout there might tip the balance in the city in your favor. If you can carry the city by 60 percent (30 percent of the total district), pick up 15 percent from the rural Democratic vote, you can hope that rural discontent will be enough to swing the margin in your favor.[4]

Such are the questions, and the imponderables, of election strategy. You have limited resources and you have to make choices. There is only so much time and money, and you can make a strong

---

[3] *Another factor to be considered in assessing a constituency is the natural advantage of the incumbent. Voters are familiar with the present officeholders, and they have established bases of support. One study found that of U.S. congressmen seeking reelection between 1956 and 1966, almost 90 percent were reelected. Less than 2 percent lost their seats in primary elections. Charles O. Jones,* Every Second Year *(Washington: The Brookings Institution, 1972), p. 68.*

[4] *This is, of course, only a hypothetical example. To get down to cases, choose a district where you know the local conditions, and figure out how you would run for it.*

appeal to only so many groups of voters and remain a credibl
candidate.

debating the issues

Either you or your opponent will set the agenda of the campaign. Wha
issues do you want to bring before the voters? Some candidates prefe
to talk about general problems, others make specific promises anc
concrete policy recommendations. You have to decide whether to us
the campaign to promote issues that you think are important or to
emphasize problems that are on the minds of the voters. (It is interest
ing to note that in one study of legislative candidates in Wisconsin, 4
percent of the respondents said that they chose issues not for reason
of their political appeal but because of personal interest or because the
were important policy questions. The context was one, it might be
added, in which candidates were encouraged to portray themselves a
"smart" politicians.)[5]

Deciding how to present your program is often a difficult problem
One experienced politician reflects on the quandry as follows:

> How to present an issue to the public is a puzzle. Almost all
> political problems are complicated. A simple problem soon is
> solved or disappears as such. To oversimplify is to mislead, yet a
> politician has to simplify, not because the average voter cannot
> understand a clear and thorough explanation, but because he will
> not listen long enough.[6]

Many candidates believe that a basic rule of campaigning is to fight
on your own ground. Harry Truman advised Hubert Humphrey,
"Carry the battle to them. Don't let them bring it to you. Put them on
the defensive and don't apologize for anything."

When Richard Nixon ran for the Senate in California in 1950
against Helen Gahagan Douglas, his primary campaign strategy was
to accuse Mrs. Douglas of being "soft on Communism." He associated
her voting record in Congress with that of Vito Marcantonio, whom
Nixon described as "the notorious Communist party-line Congressman from New York." He accused Douglas of voting 353 times exactly
as Marcantonio. However, it was also true that in most of the instances
when Douglas and Marcantonio voted alike, so did most of the House
of Representatives. It would have been more accurate to say that both

[5] John W. Kingdom, Candidates for Office: Beliefs and Strategies (New York: Random
House, 1968), pp. 126–127.
[6] Stimson Bullitt, To Be a Politician (Garden City, N.Y.: Doubleday, 1959), p. 72.

Douglas and Marcantonio voted with the majority 85 percent of the time.

Nonetheless, in the campaign, Mrs. Douglas tried to respond to Nixon's charges. As Murray Chotiner, Nixon's campaign manager commented later, "Dick Nixon was talking about Communism . . . and what happened? Mrs. Douglas, in desperation . . . started to debate with Dick Nixon's issues . . . She made the fatal mistake of attacking our strength instead of sticking to attacking our weaknesses."[7]

political stepping-stones

Winning the first election provides a base for further political activity. To a remarkable extent, politics is a process of working up from the bottom—or somewhere near the bottom. For voters and party leaders alike, experience is an important qualification of the candidate. Most higher political leaders have held previous elective office. Only 8 percent of governors or senators elected between 1914–1958 had held no prior elective office.[8]

The way the candidate performs in his first electoral office may determine his eligibility for others. The city councilman who devotes himself to serving the voters of his ward strengthens his chances for reelection. But he may focus his attention on the problems of the city as a whole, and that may someday make him a plausible candidate for mayor. Or he may shift his attention to statewide issues and make a bid for the state assembly.

The choice of interests influences electoral prospects. The local politician who takes a strong stand on nuclear power development may be encouraged to run for a seat on the state public utility commission. The lawyer who becomes interested in criminal justice may run for prosecuting attorney. Once a base of power is established, the choice of subsequent political interests may have a lot to do with the development of a political career.

The first strategic choice is to find an "entrance point" compatible with your political resources. Once a political foothold has been won, the question is whether to strengthen your support in that constituency or to try to develop a broader political base.

There are many political arenas. The factors that make for success in one may or may not be transferable to another. The outstanding mayor may remain unknown outside his immediate community. In

---

[7] See Walt Anderson, Campaigns (Pacific Palisades, Calif: Goodyear, 1970), pp. 133–145.
[8] Joseph A. Schlesinger, Ambition and Politics: Political Careers in the United States (Chicago: Rand McNally, 1966), p. 93.

fact, it is remarkable how seldom the mayoralty of medium or large cities serves as a stepping-stone to further political office.

However, an outstanding state legislator often has the opportunity to move on to higher office. There is an opportunity for contact with those who can promote candidates for governor, the state attorney general, judgeships, or Congress.

The primary stepping-stones to higher political office (governors and the Senate) are service in the state legislature, and law enforcement experience, as a judge or prosecuting attorney for example. However, the pattern varies widely from state to state. Of all candidates for the offices of governor and senator from 1914–1958, in sixteen states, over half had previous experience in the state legislature. However, the pattern is very different in particular states. In Vermont, 78 percent had legislative experience, but only 11 percent had such a background in Michigan. Law enforcement backgrounds ranged from 68 percent in Kentucky to 14 percent in Massachusetts. Administrative experience is less common as a stepping-stone to higher office, but in Michigan, 56 percent of the political leaders came from this background. And while purely local elective experience (city councils, county governments) is rare as the background for a candidate for governor or the Senate, in Maine, 40 percent had such experience.[9]

The career of Harold Hughes of Iowa is an interesting case study of a largely self-made politician, of an outsider who came to political prominence by building successive constituencies. Hughes returned as a veteran of World War II with little formal education, few contacts, and fewer prospects. He drifted from job to job, ending up as a truck driver. He became a field representative for the Iowa Motor Truck Association. Eventually, he broke with this group and formed an independent truckers organization. Dissatisfied with state regulatory policy, he ran for a seat on the Iowa Commerce Commission, which regulates the trucking industry. From this base in state politics, he strengthened his ties with the Democratic party and in 1960 tried for the gubernatorial nomination. He lost but ran again in 1962 and was successful. A visible, popular, and controversial governor, he subsequently ran for and was elected to the U.S. Senate. In 1972, he was considered as a Democratic presidential possibility.[10]

the image of the electorate

It was suggested earlier that it is important for the candidate to be self-conscious about what he sees in the mind's eye when envisioning

---

[9] *Schlesinger*, Ambition and Politics, *p. 74.*

[10] *Herbert M. Baus and William R. Ross,* Politics Battle Plan *(New York: MacMillan, 1968), pp. 27–28.*

'the voters." Since the candidate cannot know what is going on in every individual's mind, some general assumptions have to be made about the electorate. They may be seen as tough-minded, informed citizens who can be reasoned with. Or the candidate may think that they tend to vote in their own self-interest. The "political realist" may picture the voters as a mass that can be manipulated by calculated psychological appeals. The candidate may feel that voters decide mainly on the basis of the personality and style of the candidate, or on the basis of the issues, or conclude that the party label is the most important factor in electoral choice.

Some images of the electorate focus on a picture of the "typical" voter. One influential book written prior to the 1968 elections described the average voter as "a forty-seven year-old housewife from the outskirts of Dayton, Ohio whose husband is a machinist."[11] To the authors, the key issues of American politics in the late 1960s and early 1970s were not those that attracted the attention of the young, the minorities, or the highly educated and articulate. The average voter is unyoung, unblack, and unpoor. The winning strategy would appeal to the "middle voter" whose predominant concerns were crime, drugs, racial pressure, and disruption. The electorate is personified as a composite individual.

In contrast, many politicians work with an image of the electorate as a complex kaleidoscope of groups and factions. Politics is a matter of "building with blocs," of forming coalitions on the basis of appeals to various occupational, ethnic, and other groups.

Practicing politicians seem to differ greatly in their images of the voters. In one study of Wisconsin legislative candidates, 44 percent reported that they made no appeal to different groups while 55 percent said that they did. A large proportion did not seem to conceive of the electorate at all in group terms. John Kingdon, the author of the study, reports on his experience:

> Would you tell me first what groups of people supported your candidacy in the last election? It is interesting to note that at this point, one-fifth of the sample rejected the whole group concept. Some of them asked, "What do you mean?" Others refused to deal with groups, saying "I don't categorize people like that," or as another respondent put it, "I don't suppose I could be called a groupist. I felt I represented all the people."[12]

[11] *Richard M. Scammon and Ben J. Wattenberg,* The Real Majority *(New York: Berkeley Medallion Books, 1970), pp. 71–72.*

[12] *John W. Kingdon, Candidates for Office: A Study of Political Cognitions (Unpublished Ph.D. dissertation, University of Wisconsin, 1965). See also his A Study of Political Cognitions, pp. 116–121.*

Other pictures of the electorate have been created by political science research. One classic study, *The American Voter*, singled out party identification as the critical factor in electoral choice. At the time this investigation was done in the late 1950s, a sizable majority of the American people associated themselves with one of the major parties. Party identification was a relatively stable factor in American politics, a better guide to how people would vote than the characteristics of the candidates or the nature of the issues. In addition, this study portrayed the voters as rather poorly informed about political issues. One-fourth of the voters were familiar with less than half of the major issues in the campaign, and only a third could be said to be informed about the issues by the most modest of standards of what "being informed" implied. Of sixteen issues presented, 18 percent had no opinion, and another 20 percent had opinions but no idea of what government was presently doing about the problem at issue.[13]

More recent investigations have questioned this image of the electorate. Some political scientists, like Stanley Kelley,[14] feel that voters decide primarily on the basis of impressions of the candidates and only when they have mixed feelings about them do they fall back on party identification in making voting choices. Others have found that issues are far more important to the voters than they seemed in early studies of electoral behavior. Political science research has not settled the question of how the voters decide, of what image of the electorate it is best for the candidate to hold in mind when he develops his campaign strategy. There is general agreement that the three crucial factors in electoral choice are perceptions of the candidates, party identification, and positions on the issues, but how these factors are mixed in the minds of the voters probably varies greatly from election to election and office to office.

Different strategies are suggested by different images of the electorate. Many political scientists feel that in normal American politics it is rational for the candidate to enforse a moderate position, to appeal to the "average" or "middle" voter. The theory is that the more committed partisans and the voters with the more extreme stands are not apt to desert to the other side of the political spectrum. The strong liberal Democrat is not about to join the Republicans nor will the right-wing Republican join the Democrats. The candidate can count on the support of those who are closest to his ideological position. They have no place else to go and still retain a chance of winning power. The contest is for the votes of the uncommitted, those in the middle of the spec-

[13] *Angus Campbell, Philip E. Converse, Warren Miller, and Donald E. Stokes,* The American Voter *(New York: John Wiley, 1960), pp. 100–101.*

[14] *Stanley Kelley, Jr., and Thad W. Mirer, "The Simple Act of Voting,"* American Political Science Review *68 (June 1974), pp. 572–591.*

rum, who could provide the margin of victory to either side. According to this theory, two-party competition will move both candidates to endorse similar, moderate positions, and it is rational that each should do so, lest the opponent dominate the crucial middle ground.[15]

Why would not the more committed voters, feeling betrayed by their increasingly bland and compromising candidate, turn to a more extremist party in protest? The answer, in this theory, is that to do so would split the vote and assure the election of the opposition. All of this presumes, however, that voters are rational about trying to win power for their cause. In fact, as the nominations of Barry Goldwater in 1964 and George McGovern in 1972 suggest and as the sizable vote won by candidates like George Wallace indicates, ideological integrity is often more important than winning the support of the "middle voter" to the most committed in the political process. Hence the candidate who concentrates on the middle voter cannot really take the support of the more passionate partisans for granted. Yet the more the candidate tries to reassure those with the more extreme views, the greater the risk of appearing as a "dangerous radical" to the middle voters. The candidate who can walk this tightrope successfully is doing very well indeed.

In defining your image of the electorate, perhaps the most important choice is whether you think of the voter as basically rational or irrational. Two basic positions on this question can be outlined. We can call them the "realist's" and the "rationalist's" point of view. Perhaps these are polar positions, with the truth lying somewhere in between. Nonetheless, the important question is which you would be more likely to adopt if you were to be a candidate for public office.

The Realist's View

The average voter cares little about politics. He or she is apt to be uninterested and uninformed. Only about two in five people know the name of their congressman, and only one in five can say how he voted on any major bill.[16] Voting is hardly an act of carefully calculated choice. Most people vote according to inherited party loyalties. Beyond this, voters are apt to make up their minds on the basis of simplified conceptions of the issues or the "images" presented by candidates. They vote for someone they think is "sincere" or "one of us."

Images of candidates have to be manufactured. The candidate must be made to appear as a trusted "father figure," a vigorous hero,

[15] Anthony Downs, An Economic Theory of Democracy (New York: Harper and Bros., 1957).

[16] Fred I. Greenstein, The American Party System and the American People, Second Edition (Englewood Cliffs, N.J.: Prentice-Hall, 1970), p. 14.

or a sober and distinguished statesman. People have to "identify" with the candidate. Consequently, he (or she) will be shown with a large and happy family (presumably his own) or on his way to church (which may be a novel experience for him). He is associated with positive symbols and images. As in beer or cigarette advertising, the consumer is not buying the beer, but the great outdoors, or the life of adventure with which it is associated. In the same way, it is not the candidate the people are buying, but peace, the American dream, or happy children playing in the park.

Complex issues have to be reduced to simplified appeals, slogans, and symbols. In campaigning, political argument becomes advertising and public relations. Simple repetition of a meaningless slogan will eventually seem to be an important message. Saturation exposure is important so that even the most indifferent will eventually hear your name. As professional public relations experts sometimes say, it is impossible to underestimate the intelligence of the mass.[17]

The Rationalist's View

The alternative position is that the voters are not fools. One of the strongest spokesmen for this position, the late V.O. Key, Jr., wrote:

> In American presidential campaigns of recent decades the portrait of the American electorate that develops from the data is not one of an electorate straightjacketed by social determinants or moved by subconscious urges triggered by devilishly skillful propagandists. It is rather one of an electorate moved by concern about central and relevant questions of public policy, of governmental performance, and of executive personality.[18]

The voter is capable of making a shrewd estimate of self-interest and how this is related to public policy questions. From this point of view, the task of the candidate, as Adlai Stevenson insisted, is to "talk sense to the people." The job of the candidate is to find the issues that concern constituents, respond to them with practical proposals, and present a program in terms that appeal to the common sense of the voters.

The factors that influence the voter's choice are not irrational. Party identification usually rests on plausible assumptions about personal and group interests. To identify with a party is a standard of

---

[17] *There is a large literature on public relations techniques in politics. Two quite different examples are: Stanley Kelley,* Professional Public Relations and Political Power *(Baltimore: The Johns Hopkins University Press, 1956); and Joe McGinnis,* The Selling of the President *(New York: Trident Press, 1969).*

[18] *V. O. Key, Jr.,* The Responsible Majority *(Cambridge: Harvard University Press, 1966), pp. 7–8.*

political evaluation, a kind of decision-rule. One will vote for a Democrat or a Republican unless good reasons can be given to do otherwise.

The ideas that voters have about the characteristics of candidates reflect assumptions about desirable qualities in leaders. It may not be true that the voter "responds" to simplified appeals and slogans, but simply that this is all he is given. The American public is, after all, highly skeptical of the press, political rhetoric, and public relations appeals. It is possible that the "political experts" have been more successful in selling their wares to the candidates than to the voters themselves. In any event, the voters are not undiscerning, and the candidate who sells them short may make a fatal error.

As previously stated, these are polar positions. The political expert would respond to the rationalist's attack by saying that the job is not one of deceit but getting the candidate's message across to the voters. And those who have the most faith in the good sense of the voters must recognize the importance of apathy, indifference and emotion in political campaigns. Political science can offer no sure guidance about what goes on in the minds of the voters. Yet the assumptions the candidate makes about this question are an all important part of campaign strategy.

the function of the election

In making an electoral choice, the voter must decide whether to vote primarily for the party, the program, or the candidate. In the same way, the candidate must choose to run basically in terms of a stand on issues, on personal qualities, or as a member of a partisan team, a potential alternative government. The choice is reciprocal, both the candidates and the voters making assumptions about the role that elections play in the political process.

What is an election supposed to prove? What kind of a political decision is the citizen being asked to make? This is another crucial question that the would-be candidate (or the voter) must face. Again, how it is answered will have a great bearing on the design of a campaign strategy.

Elections as Policy Decisions

This approach to the question might be outlined as follows. In a democracy, the court of last resort is the will of the people. Political arguments over concrete policy options should be settled by the voters. Therefore, it is the responsibility of candidates to put forward definite programs of action. If government is to represent "the will of the people," the voters must be presented with alternative proposals for action.

An election is a mandate to carry out a particular program, and the electorate should be able to make a judgment in the next election on whether a government has, in fact, made good on its promises.

Campaigns, then, should be devoted to debate on the issues. Vague and meaningless appeals, irresponsible promises to do something for everybody mindless of the costs, and the need for making hard choices among priorities simply defraud the voter and deny him effective choice.

This approach is subject to the following criticism. A large number of issues arise in a campaign, and a choice between candidates cannot indicate the preference of voters on any particular issue. A majority may support a candidate on a number of issues but be definitely opposed to his stand on others. How then is the winner to interpret his mandate? The winner can hardly claim that his election proves that the voters want each program he endorsed.

Furthermore, elections occur at particular times and cannot reflect the ongoing process of policymaking. The issues that seemed important in a campaign may be displaced by new policy problems a year or two later. Is the candidate tied to his election promises if conditions change, or if new insight or information indicates that proposals made during the campaign were not as sound as they seemed at the time?

Elections as Choice of Decision-Rules

In light of such criticisms, it might be argued that elections are not choices between specific policy proposals, but should be regarded as an opportunity for voters to select from among alternative decision-rules. If candidates make clear their philosophies, operating assumptions, and criteria of choice, the voters have a reasonable basis for predicting how a given candidate is apt to approach the task of policymaking.

Elections then establish where the burden of proof should lie —that unless there are overriding reasons to do otherwise, government should play a less interventionist role in economy and the private lives of individuals, or that active programs should be adopted to solve pressing problems. The winner is held responsible in that he or she is called upon to explain and to justify deviations from the norms endorsed.

The criticism of course, is that campaigns based on first principles are apt to degenerate into "glittering generalities," and that the higher abstractions of politics are hard to communicate and are often unconvincing unless connected with concrete programs of action. Issues are complex and the application of decision-rules often ambiguous and open to interpretation. The official cannot be held directly accountable for his accomplishments—or lack of same—during the term of office.

Elections as Personnel Decisions

Here it is argued that the essential function of an election is to provide a government. The people are not expected to *make* policy decisions but to select their own leaders. Governance is a specialized function in every society, and direct participation of every citizen in policymaking is an impossibility. The distinctive characteristic of democracy is that rulers are selected not by heredity, class, or armed struggle, but by consent. The voters select those who win their confidence and to whose authority they will assent. The voter is very much like a personnel manager, choosing among candidates to do a job for him. Personal characteristics, trust, the qualities of leadership, overall competence, and experience are quite as important as concrete proposals and promises or the statement of a philosophy of government.

The criticism of this view is that it totally removes the people from policy choice. The electors select trustees who govern in their stead. The voters are presumed less capable than leaders in decision making.

Elections as Providing Alternative Governments

From this point of view, the primary task of the voter is to evaluate the quality of government received in the last period. The decision is between the "ins" and the "outs." If generally satisfied, the voter elects to retain the incumbents. If not, the choice is to "throw the rascals out." In a two-party system, there is always an alternative government available. The task of the opposition is to oppose. Criticism of the party in power is the expected role of the minority, far more than maintaining a consistent ideology or philosophy. (This conception of party competition seems to be far more generally accepted in Britain than in the United States. In Britain, the party out of power creates a "shadow cabinet" prepared to take over the reins of government at any time that new elections are held.)

Against this position, it might be argued that a simple "thumbs up" or "thumbs down" decision is not sufficient. The elector is restricted to only two possibilities, while politics admits of a wide range of options. The idea that the essential electoral choice is between alternative *governments* tends to downgrade the voter's role in choosing among specific candidates or policy proposals.

Conceptions of Elections and Political Strategy. There does not seem to be a clear consensus in American politics on the function that elections are supposed to perform in the political process. In each election, appeals are made to support the party, the program, and the candidate, and as we have seen, voters may be inclined to base their electoral choice on any of these criteria.

Nevertheless, how you envision the function of an election will have a profound effect on how you play your role either as candidate or voter. In designing a campaign strategy, your answer to this question will lead you to stress your program, your philosophy, your experience and personal attributes, or your partisan affiliation.

In many cases, of course, the context will provide the appropriate conception of the electoral test. In many local elections, as in clubs, associations, and organizations, elections are basically personnel decisions. There are no real issues or party formations. Candidates run mainly on their records and experience. Only where there is a strong two-party system can elections be viewed as a choice between alternative governments. And only when there are clear-cut issues in the community are elections apt to be used for policy decisions.

It is probably to the strategic advantage of challengers to run on the issues and for incumbents to stress experience and qualifications for holding office. Reformers are more apt to stress programs and conservatives, philosophy or personal qualifications.

At one level, the two basic questions of campaign strategy—your image of the electorate and your conception of the purpose of the election—are closely related. The successful candidate gives the people what they want. If your analysis of the constituency leads you to the conclusion that the voters will decide primarily on the basis of the party, the program, the philosophy, or the personal qualifications of the candidate, then you will fashion your appeal accordingly.

However, there is also a deeper issue. The candidates set the stage in an election. Campaign strategy poses a basic problem of political action—of choice on behalf of other people. The voters only get to choose between the alternatives that candidates present. As V. O. Key, Jr., once said, if voters are only able to choose between two rogues, they will inevitably select a rogue.[19] By the same token, if candidates only run on their personal qualifications, voters inevitably will be making a personnel decision. If they run on programs, voters will be making a policy choice. The candidate who accepts the first rule of strategy, to fight the campaign on his own terms, is also making a decision about what the election is supposed to prove. Hence, the decision the would-be candidate makes about the function of the election is a question not only of strategy but also of political leadership.

campaign organization

Professional politics is often a lot less calculated and efficient than it is sometimes made to appear. Even at the highest levels, campaigns are

---

[19] *V. O. Key, Jr., The Responsible Majority, p. 9.*

often poorly organized and haphazardly thrown together. The candidate may be at the mercy of his or her more willing and aggressive supporters and have no choice but to accept techniques that may not seem fully sensible or desirable. There are so many imponderables and uncertainties in electoral politics that it is hard to calculate a rational or economical strategy. As a consequence, most candidates adopt fairly traditional approaches. They make standard appeals to the party faithful and to recognizable groups, issue press releases, rent billboards, radio and television time, print posters, leaflets, and buttons, meet as many voters as possible, and organize volunteers to canvas the constituency, provide rides to the polls, and so on. How much of this is useful and how much wasted effort is often an open question. The rituals of campaigning serve their own purposes. They provide excitement, involvement, and reassurance for those who want and need them. But they are also perpetuated because no one is really sure about what works and what does not.

A campaign requires people and organization. Parties can provide a network of activists, but increasingly individual candidates build their personal teams of managers and organizations of workers. Winning the support of the voters is one thing, but it is becoming increasingly important for the candidate to appeal to those people in the community who have the time, interest, and dedication to carry out the routine jobs of politics. The "independent reform" candidate may be able to attract the enthusiastic support of students, and "avocational civic activists" in the community. This kind of voluntary participation is something of a new political resource in American politics, but it is one that is probably available only to a certain kind of candidate. However, in some places, it strengthens the prospects of the self-starter against those with close ties to party organizations or major interest groups.

campaign finance

Campaigns, even at the lowest levels, cost money, and the question of campaign funding poses serious problems for the candidate. The candidate needs resources, but contributions may imply obligations or seem to tie the candidate to special interests in the eyes of the voters. Increasingly, the sources of campaign funding are becoming a major political issue.

Campaign costs vary widely. A candidate for the state assembly in California may spend as much as $50,000, but in Wisconsin, the cost is often below $1000, and in Kentucky, the average is about $500. Between 1966–1968, campaigns for the House of Representatives averaged $29,600 for Republicans and $17,900 for Democrats in Wisconsin,

$23,300 for Republicans and $12,300 for Democrats in Massachusetts, and around $53,000 for both parties in Connecticut.[20]

Abraham Ribicoff spent $350,000 in his 1968 Connecticut senatorial campaign and Charles Percy $1 million in his race for the Senate in Illinois in the same year. Nelson Rockefeller's campaign for governor of New York cost $5 million in 1966. In the 1972 presidential campaign, Richard Nixon received $37.6 million in gifts and $1.6 million in loans, while George McGovern got $13 million in gifts and $8.2 million in loans.

In recent years, campaign funding has been a controversial public issue. Proponents of public regulation of campaign finance argue that wealthy individuals have a great advantage in politics and that powerful contributors exercise undue influence over candidates and consequently government policy. Limits on campaign spending and a system of public financing of election campaigns at all levels of government would go far, they claim, to making elections more competitive, politics more responsive to popular will, and would help reduce the prevailing mood of cycnicism about politics.

On the other hand, many claim that outright limits on the rights of individuals and groups to support candidates constitutes an abridgement of constitutional rights of free speech and political participation.

In 1974, Congress passed legislation limiting campaign spending by candidates for national office. At the same time, it created a system of public financing for presidential elections based on matching grants. Up to a specified limit (for presidential candidates, $10 million for nomination contests and $20 million for general elections), the government would "match" funds raised by individual candidates. A basic rule was adopted that no individual could give more than $1000 to a single candidate in any election and "political committees" were limited to $5000 contributions.[21]

In 1976, the Supreme Court ruled that absolute limits on campaign expenditures were unconstitutional. However, if candidates accept public financing, they still must abide by the congressionally imposed limitations. In effect, a rich candidate who accepted no public money for his campaign could spend as much as he liked. While the Supreme Court upheld the low limits on individual and group contributions that could be made directly to candidates, they said that no restrictions could be placed on "indirect" expenditures on behalf of

---

[20] *David W. Adamany,* Campaign Finance in America *(North Scituate, Mass.: Duxbury Press, 1972), pp. 39, 42.*

[21] *David Adamany and George Agree, "Election Campaign Financing: The 1974 Reforms,"* Political Science Quarterly 90 *(Summer 1975), pp. 201–220.*

political candidates. This means that if a wealthy contributor decided to purchase an advertisement in a newspaper or rent a billboard to support his favorite candidate without the express knowledge or consent of the candidate, he was free to do so.

The problem of finding a system that will reconcile effective public regulation of campaign financing with individual rights of political participation will no doubt be a public issue both at the federal and state levels for many years to come.

How are campaign funds spent? By far, the largest proportion go for advertising and the mass media. The budgets of gubernatorial and senatorial campaign committees in Wisconsin in 1964 break down as follows:[22]

Candidate expenses	2.8%
Headquarters	6.1
Party organization	18.4
Fund raising	6.9
Public relations costs	1.8
Campaign materials	10.3
Mass media	52.6
Opinion polls	1.0
	99.9%

investing political resources

The three critical political resources in campaigning are people, money, and time. The problem of strategy is to invest them efficiently. Some politicians argue that the three functions of a campaign are *reinforcement* of the faithful, *conversion* of the undecided or opponents, and *activation* of the indifferent. A workable campaign strategy must apportion resources among these objectives.[23] Although those already solidly in your camp cannot be totally neglected, the basic strategic question is how to cut into potential support for your opponent. It is interesting to note that Carl Stokes, the first black mayor of Cleveland, in his primary race for that office, made *no* appearances in Negro areas and devoted his entire personal effort to winning support in white neighborhoods. In the primary election of 1967, 96 percent of black voters supported Stokes, but he also received 20 percent of the white vote.[24]

[2] *David W. Adamany,* Financing Politics: Recent Wisconsin Elections *(Madison: University of Wisconsin Press, 1969), p. 71.*

[3] *Paul F. Lazarsfeld, Bernard R. Berelson, and Hazal Gaudet,* The People's Choice, *Second Edition (New York: Columbia University Press, 1948), p. 103.*

[4] *Anderson,* Campaigns, *p. 221.*

A major battleground may be that of the support of the undecided or indifferent. The margin of victory in competitive elections may lie with those who are least interested or involved. The "slack" in the system is the difference between those eligible to vote and those who actually go to the polls. But will a campaign to "get out the vote" work in your favor or benefit your opponent? If surveys and historic voting trends seem to indicate a safe majority from the more regular, predictable voters, a low-key campaign is probably the best strategy. Only if it seems that defeat could be turned to victory by higher turnouts would a large-scale effort to activate the apathetic be in order, for such campaigns are costly, both in money and personnel. Generally, although there are more Democratic registered voters than Republicans in the nation as a whole, Republicans have the higher turnout rates, and appeals to the less active are normally of greater benefit to Democrats.

Of the vital campaign resources, the one that is most frequently squandered is the candidate's time. Campaign workers, the press, interest groups, and party leaders all seem to have license to make unlimited demands on it. Exhaustion leads to impaired judgment and loss of effective performance. The candidate needs time away from public exposure to plan, to think through issues, to prepare key speeches, to relax. Campaigning at the higher levels requires unusual vigor and endurance in the best of circumstances, but it should be possible to avoid the kind of situations that George McGovern, for example, found himself ensnarled in during the 1972 presidential campaign, as recorded by Theodore White:

> Albuquerque, New Mexico, has been scheduled by the McGovern planners as a weekend of semi-rest, one more attempt to let the candidate catch his breath and think a bit. But the rising pressure from the press is too great, and he must rise early on Saturday morning to prepare for a press conference to appease the writing reporters. Thus, he must review once more, in complex detail, his version of the Salinger affair; must be available for several exclusive television interviews, including one with a Dutch television crew that has been following him for days because of someone's promise that it would get a visual exclusive alone with him; must receive a deputation of twelve Pueblo Indian chiefs, who want to talk land and education policy with him, and who are received only because the New Mexico McGovern leaders insist the Indian vote is critical there.[25]

[25] *Theodore H. White, The Making of the President: 1972 (New York: Atheneum, 1973), p. 310.*

As a form of political argument, campaigning means giving reasons to an electorate sufficient for them to choose you over rivals for public office. Campaign strategy involves the mobilization and organization of people, money and time. It means making an accurate assessment of the strengths and weaknesses of self and opposition. But ultimately, it is a matter of discerning the decision-rules that the voters will apply in making their electoral judgment. Studies of election behavior, polls and surveys may assist the politician in understanding the mind of the voter, but basically, this is a matter of sensitivity and instinct, an awareness of the concerns of people in different situations and positions, and a sense for their conception of the significance and implications of the electoral act.

further
ding

Bullitt, Stimson, *To Be a Politician* (Garden City, N.Y.: Doubleday, 1959). Observations of a reflective practising politician on the problems and dilemmas of political judgment faced in running for public office.

Campbell, Angus, Philip E. Converse, Warren Miller, and Donald E. Stokes, *The American Voter* (New York: John Wiley, 1960). The classic social science study of voting behavior in the United States.

Greenstein, Fred I., *The American Party System and the American People,* Second Edition (Englewood Cliffs, N.J.: Prentice-Hall, 1970). A short, comprehensive study of the place of elections and parties in the political system as a whole.

Key, V. O., Jr., *The Responsible Majority* (Cambridge: Harvard University Press, 1966). Argues that voters generally make intelligent, rational choices and that electoral behavior is not primarily a matter of image management and public relations.

Murphy, William T., Jr., and Edward Schniedger, *Vote Power* (Garden City, N.Y.: Anchor Books, 1974). Another practical guide to electoral strategy. Stresses citizen activism.

Polsby, Nelson, and Aaron Wildavsky, *Presidential Elections: Strategies of American Electoral Politics,* Second Edition (New York: Charles Scribner's Sons, 1968). Discusses strategic considerations in national elections.

Schlesinger, Joseph *Ambition and Politics* (Chicago: Rand, McNally, 1966). A study of career patterns in American political life and/or strategies of political mobility.

Schwartzman, Edward, *Campaign Craftsmanship* (New York: University Books, 1972). A useful how-to-do-it book on campaign strategy.

Shadegg, Stephen C., *How to Win an Election* (New York: Taplinger, 1972). Similar to Schwartzman in theme and content.

Sorauf, Frank, *Political Parties in the American System,* Second Edition (Boston: Little, Brown, 1972). Surveys nominations, elections, parties with special attention to the rules of the game and variations between states.

White, Theodore H., *The Making of the President* (Separate volumes discuss the 1960, 1964, 1968, and 1972 elections.) Well-written, engrossing treatment of the practice of American politics.

chapter nine
the revolutionary's dilemmas

It may seem strange to discuss the decision-making problems of the revolutionary alongside those of the political activist and the candidate for public office. The idea of revolution seems remote from the problems of everyday, normal politics that we have been considering so far. Yet logically, revolutionary action is an alternative strategy for coping with power and influence. In every society there are movements committed to the overthrow of the existing political order. The decision of whether to rebel against established authority is one that has been faced by people in politics throughout history. The Virginia House of Burgesses faced the same crucial questions as the National Liberation Fronts of the present day.

This chapter does not deal with the question of when revolution is justified. That is a big question and is better handled in a book on political theory. We are rather concerned with the problems of choice and action faced by those who have committed themselves to the revolutionary position.

It is not inappropriate for a treatise on the arts of politics to consider revolution as a form of political action or to take up the problems of the revolutionary on his own terms. Revolutionary doctrine is part of the science of politics. The study of the practice of politics need not be confined to those who act within the system. The essential questions of public choice apply to the revolutionary as well as to everyone else who decides to act in the political realm.

There are many kinds of revolutionaries in the world. Some who advocate revolution would accomplish their ends through violence, others by peaceful means. Revolution is a broad and ambiguous term.

There have been democratic revolutions, Communist revolutions, and revolutions that led to military governments. Sometimes the term "revolution" is applied to a general social process, as when we talk about the Industrial Revolution. Those who describe themselves as revolutionaries share no single ideology or set of political purposes.[1]

However, of all the major world ideologies, only Marxism possesses a self-conscious and well-developed theory of revolutionary action. For the rigorous Marxist, revolution is a technical problem, a matter of applied science. Marxism postulates a system of laws of political dynamics and change that are believed to be scientifically valid. Like the engineer, the work of the Marxist revolutionary is to find the correct solution to the problem of how these laws apply in a concrete situation.

This chapter focuses on the way the committed Marxist understands and analyzes the problem of revolutionary action. The broad ideological framework of Marxism is the point of departure for much contemporary revolutionary thought. Most modern revolutionary ideologies are either explicity based on Marxism or have been influenced by its conceptions, categories and approach.

Marx's science of revolution

The scientific basis of Marx's thought is a theory of evolution, not totally unlike Darwinian biology. The survival and success of the human species is due to the human being's special capacity as a toolmaker and his ability to organize for productive purposes. The purposes of society are essentially economic, and economic and technological relationships define social and political structures and determine the patterns of change. The dominant class in any society is that which controls the means of production. The rest of the population is dependent on the controlling group for survival and, as such, can be organized, manipulated, and exploited by them. The relationship of slave owner and slave, lord and serf, capitalist and worker are all of the same type.

Yet, all such systems are inherently unstable. Conflict and tension between the ruling and exploited class is inevitable. Each system suffers internal "contradictions," and it is the task of the revolutionary theorist to analyze these and to seek out the form of change that will resolve fundamental class contradictions. The dialectic of rival class interests is the critical political phenomenon and the motor of human history.

[1] *Charles W. Anderson, Fred R. von der Mehden, and Crawford Young,* Issues of Political Development, *Second Edition (Englewood Cliffs, N.J.: Prentice-Hall, 1974), pp. 169–197.*

Sometimes the tension is resolved, or at least shifted to a new plane, by the creation of new means of production and new technologies. The transformation of Europe in the eighteenth and nineteenth centuries came with the rise of industry, machines, and factories. The new capitalists wrested political power from the land-owning class, economically dominant in the medieval age. A new underclass was formed as industrialists brought peasants and handicraft workers together in factories. The dominant historic tension was now between the capitalist class and the industrial workers—the proletariat.

However, the new capitalist order is itself unstable. Although it has been amazingly successful in transforming nature to human benefit, it bears within itself the seeds of its own destruction. Its internal logic requires ever-increasing production and persistent capital accumulation. Eventually, the system collapses of its own weight, as overproduction gluts markets. Unemployment, depression, and war follow. The dominant class loses control of the resources that kept the underclass dependent and subservient.

Furthermore, the complex organization of modern society, its ever more specialized division of labor, alienates the individual, turning him into a specialized cog in a machine that he cannot comprehend and is helpless to control. Eventually, humans become conscious of their misery and estrangement and turn against the absurdity of the system. The proletariat, which has borne the brunt of oppression and dehumanization, will be the first class capable of detaching themselves from the "false consciousness" on which support for the system is based. They become the mass force, the lever of power, which can bring the exploitative system down.[2]

argument among revolutionaries

From the beginning, there have always been disputes over the nature of revolutionary strategy within Marxism. There were significant ambiguities in Marx's thought. The collapse of capitalism was inevitable, a matter of historical necessity, but Marx also endorsed calculated action to bring about revolution.

The early theorists of Marxism disagreed vigorously about the strategy of revolution. Lenin felt that the revolution could be forced,

---

[2] *The literature on Marx and Marxism is of course vast. Some good introductory sources include: Alfred G. Meyer,* Marxism: The Unity of Theory and Practice *(Cambridge: Harvard University Press, 1954); Bertram Wolff,* Marxism *(New York: Delta Press, 1967); Lewis A. Feuer,* Marx and Engels: Basic Writings on Politics and Philosophy *(Garden City, N.Y.: Anchor Books, 1959).*

decisive action by a dedicated minority who understood the nature of "objective reality" was possible before the masses were mobilized, conscious of their historic role, and ready for rebellion. The Menshevik faction in the Russian socialist party objected that the capitalist phase of history had to work itself out, that the crisis had to become apparent and the masses achieve full self-consciousness before revolutionary action could take place. Lenin's impulsiveness they saw as "adventurism."

Eduard Bernstein denied that the capitalist crisis was becoming more acute. The proletariat was not being driven toward desperate action. With other "revisionists," he argued that social democrats should work through electoral processes and existing political systems to bring practical reforms in living standards and working conditions. Leon Trotsky argued that the socialist revolution did not necessarily have to take place only in "ripe" capitalist societies where agrarian feudalism had been obliterated by the forces of industrialism. The peasantry, in a preindustrial society, could act as a revolutionary class alongside the incipient proletariat, and the two revolutions—the capitalist and the socialist—could be collapsed into one.[3]

There are arguments among Marxist revolutionaries, and Marxism rests on a process of reasoned argument quite as much as Western democratic political thought. The standards of judgment, the terms of reference, are alien to most Americans, but there is as much technique and system to this form of political analysis as there is to the kinds of political questions we have been discussing throughout this book.

Maoists, Castroites, Trotskyites, and Leninists all have their distinctive conceptions of revolutionary purpose and different answers to the questions of strategy. Although all Marxist revolutionary movements share a common hostility to Western capitalism, each tends to see itself as the unique custodian of valid political analysis. Dispute over goals and tactics, mutual criticism and denunciation, is characteristic of the Marxist revolutionary style.

Marxist revolutionary theorists do agree that the strategy of revolution must be adapted to the level of political and economic development reached by a particular nation. A different approach is called for in an underdeveloped, peasant society and in an industrial nation with an advanced capitalist system. In the "Third World," the critical mass force is more apt to be the peasantry than the industrial working class. "Economic imperialism" is a particular problem for revolutionary action in Africa, Asia, and Latin America. These nations have become dependent on the world capitalist system. Capitalist powers may intervene politically or militarily in the affairs of these nations to protect their foreign investments. These problems call for a

---

[3] *Alfred G. Meyer,* Leninism *(New York: Praeger, 1957).*

special interpretation of Marxism, and pose special problems of revolutionary strategy.

The question of revolutionary strategy is even more controversial for Marxists in the advanced capitalist societies of Western Europe and North America. The revolutionary cause has not been very successful in these nations. The capitalist system has increased its power, and the industrial workers have lost class consciousness with increasing prosperity. It is possible that these systems have developed beyond the kind of capitalism that Marx analyzed. Perhaps orthodox Marxism is no longer adequate to diagnose the "revolutionary situation" in advanced capitalist societies. There are contradictions and crises that make for instability in these societies, but perhaps a new theory of revolution will have to be devised to understand and exploit them.

Some Marxist theorists continue to believe that the industrial working class is the critical agent of revolution in advanced capitalist systems. Others argue that the situation has changed radically. Western Europe and North America are now "postindustrial" societies. Factory labor is no longer the representative mass occupation. Perhaps the revolutionary should now appeal to the shared class interest of professional, service, and industrial workers, all "dependent" on monopoly capitalism. No one who works for a giant corporation really controls his own "means of production." The exploited "workers of the world" now include not only manual workers but also white collar employees and even middle management. Still another group of Marxist theorists simply feel that the stage of revolutionary action has shifted. The fundamental contradictions do not occur *within* capitalist societies, but between the major capitalist nations and the Third World. The industrial worker has become part of the capitalist class, and his prosperity rests on the expoitation of cheap labor in the less-developed nations.

All revolutionaries are not Marxists, and all Marxists are not revolutionaries. Many Communist parties today, particularly in Western Europe, seek power by electoral means. Nonetheless, in the contemporary period, the general style and rhetoric of Marxist thought has been a major influence on revolutionary thought of all kinds. Consider the following excerpt from the writings of Huey P. Newton, one of the leaders of the Black Panther party in the 1960s. "We knew, as a revolutionary vanguard, repression would be the reaction of our oppressors. . . . We expected the repression to come from outside forces which have long held our communities in subjection. However, the ideology of dialectical materialism helped us to understand that the contradictions surrounding the party would create a force that would move us toward our goals."[4]

---

[4] *Huey P. Newton,* To Die for the People *(New York: Random House, 1972), p. 54.*

For most Americans, viewing the world from the standpoint of the revolutionary requires an act of imagination. To get inside this frame of reference, one must feel both estrangement from the existing political order—and defiance. Hence the first problem is to begin to see politics as the revolutionary sees it.

For the committed revolutionary, the established order is no more than a system for the domination and oppression of the population. Constitutional processes are a mere facade. The ruling elites will accept no challenge to their rule. The people are held in bondage; they are no more than instruments of the will of the powerful.

Peaceful reform will not work. Those who win influence through the political process merely become the victimizers rather than the victims. To the committed revolutionary, the greatest hatred is reserved for the "careerists," the willing bureaucrats and servants of the establishment, and for those who make their way by appeasing the ruling class. The problem of strategy for the revolutionary, then, is not how to win influence, but how to destroy the power of the ruling elites and lay the foundations for a new political order.

The professional revolutionary is not apt to understate the magnitude of the problem he faces. In the first phase of revolution, almost by definition, the ruling class is all-powerful, and the revolutionary forces virtually powerless. The government maintains a monopoly of coercive force and, in league with the capitalist class, controls the means of production. What is more, the powerful, on the whole, receive the support of the broad masses. The masses have come to accept their condition as inevitable, if not desirable, and the authority of the rulers as legitimate. A "superstructure" of ideology has been created and widely accepted, affirming the right of the rulers to rule. The people believe that the authority of the rulers comes from law, or consent, or timeless tradition. The economic order is an integral part of the political system providing livelihood, abundance, even comfort. The workers realize that defiance could mean deprivation. They have become dependent on the rulers. What is more, they are normally grateful for the benefits they receive from the system.

Hence the revolutionary does not see oppressive governments as resting only on coercive force. Oppression is a condition that relies on beliefs, and on dependency. It is not the police and the army alone that maintain the system. Oppressive governments are sustained by passive support.

Given this estimate of the situation, what is the revolutionary to do? Where is the point of leverage for action against a well-entrenched system? The serious revolutionary has witnessed many uprisings that have failed, and he has studied and diagnosed their mistakes. He faces a peculiarly difficult problem of strategic decision.

For the revolutionary, the first problem is to make an accurate, "scientific" analysis of the situation of power he confronts. Political argument concerns a search for the proper definition of "reality," stripped of myth, false hope, or ideology, attuned to the operation of historical forces.

Central to this search is a valid conception of the "objective" and the "subjective" conditions of revolution. The objective conditions concern the strengths and weaknesses of the established order. Revolutionary action is futile when the system possesses overwhelming coercive force, when the economy is operating at full efficiency, when morale is high and support for the regime solid. However, after defeat in a war (as in Russia in 1917), the government may lose effective control of the population, its armies and police may be debilitated and demoralized, and chaos may ensue as basic public services are disrupted. During a period of economic crisis, unemployment, scarcity, and disruption of production may lead to political ineffectiveness, divisions among elites, and disaffection in the population. The revolutionary must make an accurate diagnosis of the strengths and weaknesses of the regime in calculating the appropriate course of action.

The "subjective conditions" of revolution concern the state of mass consciousness. Government may have been objectively weakened, but direct action will still be ineffective if the masses will rally to the support of the old order at the moment of confrontation. Unless the people fully comprehend their exploitation and see a pertinent and effective course of action open to them at the moment of struggle, they will remain disengaged, and the government will easily put down the small cadres of revolutionary militants.

When the objective and subjective conditions for revolution coincide, the task of the revolutionary is clear. The old order has lost its authority, and its effectiveness is in question. The moment has come to act quickly, decisively, surgically, to activate the maximum plan and seize power. On the other hand, when government effectiveness is at its peak and political awareness low, it is a time for quiet agitation and education, for planning and keeping the revolutionary movement alive in the face of the government's efforts to suppress it. When signs of weakness appear, and consciousness begins to grow in isolated sectors of the population, first efforts at mobilization and organization are in order, together with action—strikes, demonstrations, terrorism—to accentuate the crisis of the regime.

Obviously, constructing an accurate assessment of the objective and subjective conditions of revolution and prescribing the strategy that precisely fits those conditions is a formidable task of political judgment and political argument. To the professional revolutionary, it is a deadly serious problem. To make a mistake means to commit people to a struggle in which they will be destroyed. Not to be prepared for the decisive moment means that the oppressive system may be able to rally its forces, to endure and persist indefinitely. The essential problem of assuming responsibility for the destiny of other people, the heart of the problem of political choice, is one the serious revolutionary appreciates fully. The professional spares no scorn for the naive and the romantic. The disdain of the toughminded revolutionary for those who refuse the discipline of hard analysis and merely "play" at revolution is suggested by the title of one of Lenin's pamphlets, *"Left Wing" Communism: An Infantile Disorder.*

In the wake of the failure of student "revolutionary" movements in the 1960s, many elder theorists branded these efforts as "childish," "stupid," and "irresponsible." Those who believed that the revolutionary moment had arrived were totally wrong in their assessment. What they had done was to impute their own frustrations to the community as a whole. They became so caught up in the enthusiasm and ideology of the movement that they simply assumed that everybody else felt the same way. They had made a fundamental and an elementary error.

Along with the question of assessment of the "revolutionary situation," the critical issues are organization, planning, and relevant action when the decisive moment has not yet arrived. The sort of argument that revolutionaries engage in when debating such issues is illustrated by the following excerpt from a work of the contemporary Marxist theorist, Andre Gorz:

> First of all, *when* is the organization to be built? If its existence is decided by some leadership group, who first define a doctrine and program and then coopt people who agree with it, the organization will never belong to the masses . . . The cornerstone of further bureaucracy, dogmatism and sectarianism will thereby have been laid. A genuinely revolutionary organization can be built only *after* the need to organize has been experienced by people engaged in mass struggles. The role of the initial leadership group is not to organize people so as to get them struggling later, but first to spark them into action and help them self-organize so as to expand and coordinate their actions. The proper moment for building and organization is when mass action is developing."

The concern for *timing* is apparent in Gorz's analysis, and it is easy to see that his argument rests on a conception of the subjective conditions in the revolutionary situation. Gorz continues:

> The choice of the proper moment is important also in regard to the question of *who* is to build the organization. Ideally, the answer should be: the masses themselves; all those who are submitted to daily oppression, exploitation, violence, arbitrariness and therefore can liberate themselves only by resorting to collective

counter-violence. In practice, however, those who are aware of their oppression and want to fight are initially a minority. They do not know each other, are isolated by institutionalized repression, cannot communicate or get together and evaluate their strength. Therefore, an initial vanguard group is needed that could communicate or get together.[5]

Before the decisive moment is at hand, there are still forms of direct action open to the revolutionary. During the past ten to fifteen years, militants have debated the merits and disadvantages of the following approaches.

Rural Guerrilla Warfare

The successes of Mao Tse-tung in China and Fidel Castro in Cuba inspired many rebel leaders, particularly in Latin America and some other parts of the Third World, during the 1960s.

Che Guevara's effort to re-create the Cuban revolution in Bolivia in 1967 illustrates the tactical rationale of one approach to guerrilla warfare, as well as its limitations. Where dominant elites are well entrenched and supported militarily by imperialist powers in traditional agrarian societies where political consciousness is low, even a small armed band—perhaps no more than thirty or forty strong—can plant the seeds of revolution. The indicated strategy is to establish a base in the "backlands." From here, the guerrillas harass the forces of the government, attack isolated garrisons and outposts when their military superiority is great, and disrupt communication and transport systems, retreating to rugged and sparsely settled terrain when the military begins to hunt them down.

The object is to pin down the conventional forces of the regime and to demonstrate the limits of its power. Guerrilla actions dramatize and keep alive the message of revolution, inspiring other small groups in both urban and rural areas. The initial focus is expanded by recruitment and conversion of the local peasantry. The guerrillas become dominant in a limited area and win the sympathies of the local population. Gradually, they link up with other forces in the nation. Should urban unrest topple the existing government, they are prepared to enter the capital and seize the reins of power—as Castro did in Cuba in 1959. Otherwise, their support gradually increases until the balance of power tips in their direction.[6]

---

[5] *Andre Gorz*, Socialism and Revolution (*New York: Anchor Books, 1973*), *p. 65. This book is an interesting "handbook" on revolutionary strategy.*

[6] *Regis Debray*, Revolution in the Revolution (*New York: Monthly Review Press, 1967*); *John Gerassi*, Venceremos! The Speeches and Writings of Che Guevara (*New York: Monthly Review Press, 1967*).

In revolutionary self-criticism, many guerrilla movements were admitted failures. In Bolivia, Che Guevara was defeated. He failed to win over a peasantry that, secure in land received in an agrarian reform of the early 1950s, remained loyal to the government. Counterinsurgency forces, trained and equipped by the United States, were capable of tracking down and defeating the guerrilla bands. Traditional power structures proved too strong and "revolutionary consciousness" among the peasantry too weak for most movements of rural rebellion to achieve their objectives.[7]

Terrorism

Bombings, kidnappings, and hijackings of aircraft and ships are other tactics used by contemporary revolutionaries. Although much of this activity is unrelated to any overall philosophy of revolutionary action, in some cases terrorism is a carefully chosen means to revolutionary ends. Acts of terrorism may be a way of attracting attention to a cause. Or hostages may be taken to gain tactical objectives, such as the freeing of political prisoners. The terrorist seeks out the most vulnerable points in modern complex society, where the force of government can be nullified.

Sometimes terrorist activities are linked to an explicit theory of revolution. Assuming that mass uprisings do not occur in oppressive societies because of fear of the power of the state, the purpose of the terrorist is to demonstrate that insurgency can be committed with impunity. The bomber or kidnapper can attack, escape, and attack once more. The viability of revolutionary action is dramatized by press coverage, and ransom for hostages provides needed financial resources to the movement. As in the guerrilla strategy, the effort is to keep the message of rebellion alive, to inspire other small movements, gradually to link up with them and expand the power base. However, many revolutionaries argue that such tactics are simple "adventurism," that terrorism only strengthens the hand of the existing regime, and neither promotes constructive mass consciousness or organization.

Alliance Politics

Another strategy that is sometimes endorsed by contemporary revolutionaries when the prospects for overturning the established order seem remote is to work for reform in concert with labor, minorities, and other disadvantaged groups. With the failure of the "revolutionary moment" in the 1960s, many who remain faithful to the more

---

[7] *See John D. Martz, "Doctrine and Dilemmas of the Latin American 'New Left'," World Politics 22 (January 1970), pp. 171–196.*

radical goals of that period have endorsed what they call "alliance politics." They diagnose their failure to gain mass support in advanced industrial society in recent years as a product of the isolation of the revolutionary movement. The "real" revolutionaries of that period failed to gain the support of the masses. The groups that might have been mobilized for the revolutionary cause turned to protest leaders or remained committed to the trade union movement or reformist factions in the established political parties.

Hence, many of those who remain committed to the most radical forms of politics in the United States and some Western European countries argue that the revolutionaries must not isolate themselves from reformist groups but affiliate with them. Serving on the picket lines, working with minority groups, the revolutionary can show identification with the causes of the exploited and attempt to win them over. He can raise the consciousness of the dispossessed and undercut the followings of leaders interested in mere protest or reform.

Of course, the cooperation of the revolutionary with working class and minority movements is tactical rather than real. Those who endorse "alliances" with existing reform movements see their goal as one of creating revolutionary awareness among the members of such groups. This is the most effective alternative, they will argue, where the forces of revolution are particularly weak, as in the United States.

Critics of this strategy argue that "alliance politics" tends to dilute the revolutionary message and weaken the cohesion of the revolutionary forces. The most dissatisfied wage earners, the ethnic and racial minorities, may be satisfied with short-run material victories. The revolutionary is in effect "co-opted" by the reform movement.

Guerrilla warfare, terrorism, and alliance politics are all strategies endorsed by revolutionaries who feel that the objective and subjective conditions for revolution are far from ripe. This seems to be the diagnosis of most serious revolutionaries in advanced industrial societies. The problem is to raise mass consciousness wherever possible and to keep the revolutionary movement alive. In the long run, they are convinced the "crisis" of capitalism is inevitable. Increasingly, strains and conflicts are becoming apparent in the system. They must remain attentive to developing trends in these societies, for new political "realities" will call for different tactics and strategies.

clusion

This chapter examines revolutionary strategy as a technical problem and in particular, deals with the way this problem is understood by the most orthodox revolutionary theorists, especially those closest to traditional Marxist ideology, in nations where revolutionary movements are weak. This is not to suggest that this is the way leaders of nations as Russia, China, or Cuba, where Marxism is the established philosophy of government, understand their long-range plans. Nor does this logic necessarily apply to the outlook of leaders of established Marxist parties, as in France or Italy. The strategic calculations made by such leaders are much different, and the study of the policy arguments that take place in such movements really belongs to the study of comparative politics, which is beyond the scope of this book.

There are many different kinds of revolutionaries, and people engage in revolutionary action for all kinds of reasons. Here we have only dealt with those who see revolution as a form of political action calling for a highly developed level of political analysis.

To "get inside" the logic of the revolutionary is to begin to understand another approach to thinking about politics, and making political decisions, one that is quite different from the rest of this book. This is another form of political reasoning and public choice, but for many people in the world, this is what politics itself is all about.

for further reading

Berger, Peter, and Richard J. Neuhaus, *Movement and Revolution* (New York: Vintage Books, 1970). A contemporary study of revolutionary tactics and strategy.

Brinton, Crane, *The Anatomy of Revolution* (Englewood Cliffs, N.J.: Prentice-Hall, 1938). A classic study of the nature and causes of revolutions.

Debray, Regis, *Revolution in the Revolution* (New York: Monthly Review Press, 1967). The case for a strategy of guerrilla revolution.

Feuer, Lewis A., *Marx and Engels: Basic Writings on Politics and Philosophy* (Garden City, N.Y.: Anchor Books, 1959). A good collection on basic Marxist philosophy.

Gorz, Andre, *Socialism and Revolution* (New York: Anchor Books, 1973). An analysis of the problem of revolutionary strategy in advanced industrial societies.

Gurr, Ted Robert, *Why Men Rebel* (Princeton: Princeton University Press, 1971). A sociological and psychological treatment of the causes of revolution.

Meyer, Alfred G., *Marxism: The Unity of Theory and Practice* (Cambridge: Harvard University Press, 1954). A good source for background on the Marxist theory of revolution, but does not include contemporary developments.

Newton, Huey P., *Revolutionary Suicide* (New York: Ballantine Books, 1974). An autobiographical account by the leader of the Black Panther movement of aims and strategic considerations.

Shub, David, *Lenin* (New York: American Library, 1948). The biography of the classic revolutionary theorist.

Vo Nguyen Giap, *People's War: People's Army* (New York: Praeger, 1962). The problem of revolution analyzed by the military theorist of North Vietnam.

Wolf, Eric R., *Peasant Wars of the Twentieth Century* (New York: Harper and Row, 1969). A very interesting discussion of the nature of peasant revolution.

Wolff, Bertram, *Marxism* (New York: Delta Press, 1967). A good source of Marxist theory.

chapter ten
the creation of agreement

Compromise and conciliation are fundamental to the practice of politics. Sometimes policy decision is a clear-cut choice between rival points of view. Equally often, the task of the policymaker is to contrive a solution that reconciles differences, one that at least partially accommodates the positions of different parties to the controversy.

From the standpoint of the advocate, the question of compromise arises when it becomes apparent that it is better to settle for half a loaf than to get nothing at all. The problem of strategy is that of promoting an agreement that preserves at least the advocate's most essential objectives. The advocate tries to engineer an accord *in the direction* of a preferred policy position.

Conflict resolution can also be approached from the standpoint of the conciliator. Sometimes the conciliator is a neutral third party brought in by the deadlocked factions to try to arrange a settlement.[1] However, in the everyday work of politics, in committees, legislative bodies and organizations, different members may assume the role of peacemaker, trying to find a way out of conflict and indecision, seeking a formula for policy that the community can accept with a minimum of dissent and injured feelings.

---

[1] *In the terminology of conflict resolution, a* mediator *tries to bring together parties in conflict but does not propose a solution. A* conciliator *may propose a solution, but the parties are not obligated to accept it. An* arbitrator *proposes a solution, and the parties are bound by his decision.*

Three processes are central to the art of conflict resolution: bargaining, coalition formation, and compromise. This chapter discusses each in turn.

bargaining and conflict resolution

Bargaining and compromise are possible only when the parties to a controversy are willing to settle for a second-best position rather than face the consequences of achieving no solution at all.

The degree to which any party is willing to depart from his preferred policy position is a rather precise measure of how much he values his relationship with his adversaries. At each stage in the bargaining process, each individual must calculate the costs of accepting less than he wants against the costs of going it alone, breaking off existing relationships, and perhaps engaging in outright hostilities.[2]

Not all conflicts can be settled by negotiation. When one party would just as soon sever all contact or go to war, compromise short of giving in completely is not possible—as those who tried to reach an accommodation with Hitler were to learn. However, as long as debate continues, there is some presumption that the parties involved have an interest in finding their way out of their dilemma.

In the classic bargaining situation, each side knows what it wants to achieve, and is engaged in a strategic game of move and countermove, trying to arrive at the solution that is most favorable to its "real" expectations. Each side is trying to steer a course that avoids two totally undesirable outcomes. The first of these would be giving in completely to the interests of the other side. The second would be for the other side to break off negotiations and exercise its maximum "threat." In labor relations, management calculates how little it must concede to prevent a strike. Labor estimates how little it must give in to prevent a lockout. In international relations, each side may be calculating how small a concession the other will accept rather than resort to war.

In classic bargaining strategy, each party begins with a larger demand than it reasonably expects to achieve. Both parties know this. But if there is a mutual assumption at the outset that the other side is making exaggerated claims, why does bargaining not begin from positions that are close to real expectations? The fact seems to be that the original "excessive" demands are a ritual that defines and identifies the game. Neither wants to be placed, or to place the other, in a take-it-or-leave-it situation. To make a large demand signals that there is "room for negotiation." It is insurance against the possibility that

---

[2] *See William and Joyce Mitchell,* Political Analysis and Public Policy *(Chicago: Rand McNally, 1969), p. 502.*

both parties will arrive at such clear-cut commitments that they will fail to reach an agreement.[3]

It is sometimes argued that the party that makes the more outrageous initial demands is more likely to force the opponent to move more than halfway to achieve a settlement. As give-and-take proceeds, the side with the larger "shopping list" has the most left over at the end of mutual concessions. This may work, but only when the other party is quite ignorant of the other's intentions and capabilities, or when the respective bargaining power of the two parties is unequal. When one side has far more to lose than the other by the failure to reach agreement, the stronger can either present an ultimatum or make a very large demand and bargain back to the take-it-or-leave-it position for the sake of form or because unexpected benefits may arise from the bargaining process itself.

However, when the parties know the capabilities and expectations of each other rather well, the excessive original demand may weaken the position of the party making it. It may suggest ignorance of the stakes and possibilities or be taken as a sign of lack of willingness to bargain in good faith. The other party may become mistrustful or fixed in an unyielding position.

When there is real mistrust or hostility in the bargaining relationship, it is sometimes helpful to give more than expected initially simply as a token of willingness and eagerness for cooperation. The "peace offering" symbolized by the accommodative first move may bring the other side to quicker concessions in the interest of agreement than would have been possible through "classic" bargaining. Henry Kissinger is said to have used this approach in the initial stages of his efforts to negotiate a settlement of the Arab-Israeli controversy. He surprised Anwar Sadat of Egypt and other Arab leaders by generous concessions. This may have helped to allay suspicions of America's role as mediator, given its historic friendship for Israel.

This approach may be particularly effective when one party perceives the other as starting from a relatively extreme position. Legislative leaders sometimes win reputations as gifted compromisers in this way. For example, when Gerald Ford was Republican leader in the House of Representatives, he was known as an effective engineer of compromises. In part, this may have resulted from the fact that given his well-known conservative views, any willingness to endorse some liberal measures was seen as a gesture of conciliation and cooperation.

There is another alternative to the classic opening of the large demand in bargaining relationships. It is possible to start with a carefully reasoned proposal, one that is designed to appear fair and equita-

---

[3] *Carl M. Stevens,* Strategy and Collective Bargaining Negotiation *(New York: McGraw-Hill, 1963), p. 76.*

ble by any reasonable standards, and then simply stick to your guns. The negotiator responds to counterproposals with arguments supporting his initial position.

Here political argument to some extent takes the place of bargaining. One negotiator tries to shift the nature of the game. The emphasis is placed on the search for a justifiable policy position, rather than maneuver and countermaneuver alone. And it is true that in pure bargaining relationships, narrowly focused on reducing the differences between two strong contending parties, general public interests, and the rights and interests of parties outside the immediate conflict are frequently neglected.[4]

What role does political argument, in fact, play in bargaining? We know that when parties negotiate, they give reasons in support of their proposals and counterproposals and seem to be trying to persuade the other side to change its preferences, perspective, and position. However, in a pure bargaining encounter, it seems unlikely that one side can persuade the other to accept its view of the situation. Many claim that argument in bargaining relationships is no more than "window dressing," rationalizations used for public relations effects. It is not to be presumed that the contestants are really in quest of good public policy or the solution that best serves the interests of the community as a whole.

However, political argument may play an important role in bargaining. Many political situations are not clear-cut bargaining relationships. In many policymaking arenas, such as legislatures, planning commissions, city councils, and the like, bargaining may only be an aspect of a far more complex decision-making process. Some give-and-take occurs among partisans of rival policies, but it is a subordinate process used to facilitate agreement within the context of a broader process of considering public policy.

However, it is probably true that the most important function of argument in bargaining is as an appeal for the support of third parties. Thus, in labor management relationships, the employer who tries to show that a wage offer is fair and reasonable is probably not speaking directly to the union negotiators, but beyond them to the community, to public officials, perhaps even to the employees themselves. The union must then estimate how the employer's appeal is apt to be received by these other groups. The respective power of the parties to the bargaining relationship will be affected by the support that their positions receive from other forces in the community. The party that will have to move more than halfway will be the one that cannot justify its position in terms of a broad coalition of support.

Argument has other functions in pure bargaining relationships. In

---

[4] *Ibid.,* *pp. 34–35.*

giving reasons in support of proposals and counterproposals, each party may be providing information to the other on the "zone" in which agreement may be possible. For example, in a city council dispute, the advocate of a very elaborate civic center complex may call attention to the relative success of a neighboring city in attracting convention business with a much simpler facility, but note that if their city is to compete successfully with the rival, it will have to offer something more attractive. In this way, he may signal his intention to compromise somewhere between his orginal plan and a project on the scale of the rival city.

As we noted earlier, argument also provides the bargainer with the opportunity to commit himself to a stand on principle that cannot be abandoned without embarrassment. If he backs down, he will appear to be hypocritical or to have "sold out" to the opposition. In this way, he makes his threat to stand by his position more credible.

Argument may also provide each side with information about the background and rationale for the demands that the other is making, thus making it possible to identify specific areas of agreement and disagreement. Finally, argument may provide the bargainer with a justification for retreat should that become necessary.

coalition formation

Political conflict is often unlike pure bargaining because of the number of parties and interests involved. There are not two sides, but many. The dispute cannot be reduced to a single dimension. Rather, bargaining in the political arena often involves complex trade-offs with a variety of parties. Compromises come in complex packages. There has to be something for everybody to win agreement. Any arrangement with any particular party may affect the bargaining power of any other. The conservative legislator who comes to terms with a trade union or militant reform movement then has to "mend his fences" with his more reactionary supporters. Their bargaining power is now enhanced, and they may be able to bring demands to bear on the legislator which narrow his room for negotiation with other necessary allies. The politician's situation becomes like that of the juggler who must keep a dozen balls simultaneously in the air and is apt to be hit on the head by the one he misses.

Given the complexities of political bargaining, it seems to some that the rational politician should try for no more than the minimum winning coalition.[5] Since every bargain requires some weakening of

[5] William Riker, The Theory of Political Coalitions (New Haven: Yale University Press, 1962).

the desired goal, under conditions of majority rule, all support over 51 percent is wasted effort. It is unnecessary to win over any more supporters to achieve victory.

Under certain very restricted conditions, this may be good advice, but it is more often too neat and mathematical to serve as a working strategic principle. It is usually impossible for the politician to calculate his base of support with enough accuracy to achieve the minimum margin necessary for victory. To assure success, he must overcompensate, and thus find a position more widely acceptable than the one that might be closest to his initial aspirations.[6]

In any event, in politics, unlike football, winning is neither the most important thing nor the only thing. To pass a bill on a slender majority in a divided community is apt to result in ineffective policy and may create unnecessary problems and further divisions that will have to be faced in the future. Payment for the tough-nosed strategy that forces the issue in the short run may well be exacted in the long run. The goal of politics is to set the program and define the course of a community, and that requires assent and willing collaboration far beyond that which might suffice for simple legislative victory.

the art of creating agreement

Conflict resolution is an aspect of any kind of political leadership. The executive has to resolve differences among his staff or subordinates. The committee chairman tries to find an acceptable policy when the group seems deadlocked. The chief of an engineering section has to bring a group of experts together on a single recommendation on a technical proposal. The leader of a political movement has to keep peace between various factions. Anyone who participates in any kind of political activity will face the problem of bringing a divided group together to work for a common purpose.

Sometimes, as we noted earlier, the conciliator plays a specialized role. This person may be a "professional" as in the case of a mediator in a labor dispute or in an international conflict. Like policymaking and interest advocacy, conciliation is one of the techniques of politics, and a particular form of political analysis, decision making, and political action.

Conflict resolution can never be reduced entirely to a matter of analysis and reason. The personal attributes of the conciliator are always important. In conflict, a variety of human emotions are unleashed—of fear and aggression, of anger and anxiety. Conflict is

---

[6] *Anthony Downs,* An Economic Theory of Democracy *(New York: Harper and Row, 1957).*

often a bruising experience for the human ego. The conciliator must have prestige in the eyes of the group, and must seem to be disinterested and impartial. But it is also vital to exercise tact and diplomacy. Humor, warmth, openness, and sympathy may all be important in defusing tensions. In contriving compromise, everyone is going to lose something. However, it is important that psychological losses be kept to a minimum. Building an atmosphere that encourages mutual respect and that moves the plane of the controversy from personal antagonisms to deliberation of issues may be the most important contribution of the conciliator.

The engineering of agreement is one of the most subtle skills of political craftsmanship. To unravel the threads of a controversy and reweave them into a formula for reconciliation is a real accomplishment.

As a form of political argument, conciliation means *making a case* for a policy designed to reconcile divergent views and interests. The parties in conflict have to be given reasons for modifying their initial positions and reaching a working agreement with their adversaries. The grounds that can be appealed to include the following: that collective purpose and common interests are more important than partial interests; that the proposed solution represents a fair accommodation of divergent interests; or that particularistic interests can best be realized through collective action.

Sizing Up the Situation

The first task for the conciliator is to understand the complexity of the dispute. All conflicts exist at a variety of levels and have a number of dimensions. Probably, to reach accord, it is going to be necessary to redefine the conflict in some significant respect, to shift the ground from emphasis on the most antagonistic points to those on which the parties may be able to reach agreement. Again, as long as debate continues, it may be assumed that the parties have *some* interest in restoring a working relationship. Often, conciliators work by trying first to reach accord on relatively minor and nonantagonistic points, postponing consideration of the most conflictual issues until some rapport and willingness to reach accommodations has been established. Therefore, in sizing up a conflict, one of the first tasks for the conciliator is to factor out and distinguish the elements of the controversy.

Except for the most straightforward bargaining relationships, political conflict is normally contradictory and confusing. It is hard for the would-be conciliator to get a sure grip on the nature of the controversy. But to keep asking the question, What *is* at issue here? will suggest a number of alternative possibilities. From this array of options, a pattern of consistency and a formula for reconciliation may eventually emerge.

Compromise can take a wide variety of forms. Whereas the patterns that accommodation can take are really only limited by the possibilities of insight and ingenuity, there are certain fundamental types of compromise, here presented in order from the simplest to the more complex.

The Simple Compromise, or "Splitting the Difference"

Each party moves toward the position of the other in the interest of agreement. The classic form is the trader's bargain. The seller quotes a price of $1000. The buyer offers $800. They settle for $900. Such compromises are most practical when the controversy is one-dimensional and there is a divisible commodity at stake—money, time (as in setting deadlines), or territory (as in defining boundaries).

When the parties cannot strike a bargain by simply "splitting the difference," the problem for the conciliator may be to define a justify a fair settlement, which may not be precisely a fifty-fifty division. "Compensation" may be due one party or the other for risk, loss, or sacrifice in coming to a settlement that is not shared by the other side. For example, if one party has no staff or organization, it may feel that it should be compensated for the cost of researching and developing its case. Such supplemental agreements on minor, related matters are sometimes called "side payments" in bargaining strategy.

It might seem that this simple form of compromise is inapplicable to either-or situations. However, "split the difference" compromises where the unit involved is not readily divisible may only take a little more imagination. For example, where a union wants a closed shop (all employees must be union members) to eliminate the "free rider" problem (workers who take advantage of higher wages and better working conditions won through union bargaining power without assuming the costs and obligations of union membership) and management is dead set against the closed shop, it may be possible to contrive an agreement whereby management agrees to give union members priority in case of layoffs and both agree that union membership should not decline during the life of the contract.

The "both and" compromise is closely related to the "split the difference" compromise, and is also potentially useful where differences are categorical rather than matters of degree. At the American Constitutional Convention of 1787, the smaller states wanted equal representation in the legislature, while the larger ones argued for representation according to population. The compromise adopted called for a bicameral legislature, the House of Representatives elected directly by the people according to population, the Senate elected by the state legislatures and including two members from each state. (Senators have been directly elected only since 1913, with the passage of the Seventeenth Amendment.)

Compromises by Expanding Time

Some of you may have seen the puzzle in which the object is to connect nine dots with not more than four consecutive lines (without lifting pencil from paper).

```
*   *   *

*   *   *

*   *   *
```

The solution, reproduced below,[7] requires that we step outside the *apparent* boundaries of the problem. The same is true of the art of compromise. When parties are in deadlock, the task of the conciliator may be to shift perspective on the problem and bring new resources to bear on the situation.

The most elementary way of doing this is to expand the time dimensions of the controversy. One party gets its way this time in exchange for the promise that the other side will win the next. In a university department, the compromise is to hire a theorist this year and a methodologist the next time there is an opening. In legislatures, agreements of the form "if you vote for my bill, I'll vote for yours next time" are frequent and can often lead to the accumulation of influence in the hands of certain members, who can "call in their IOU" when an issue arises that is vital to them.

Compromises by Expanding the Number of Issues

In case of a deadlock, another approach to compromise is to expand the agenda of action and attempt to arrange a "package settlement" of a bundle of issues at one time. In international affairs, for example, instead of a major power trying to mediate a specific two-nation dispute, a high-level diplomatic conference is called to consider all interests and problems of a region—the Middle East, for example. Although such an approach violates the principle of "letting sleeping dogs lie," to open the controversy when hard and rigid positions separate the parties may create new possibilities for alliances and bring the initial deadlock into new perspective. It is assumed that the parties

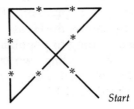

in controversy are not equally divided on all issues and that trade-offs may be possible between votes on different issues when they have to deal with the total configuration of problems.

In legislative parlance, a related process is "logrolling." A dam in Colorado may seem an outrageous extravagance to the congressman from Maine, and the dredging of a Maine fishing harbor totally unnecessary to the Coloradan, but in an ombibus rivers and harbors bill, each agrees to the project of the other as a condition of getting support for his own.

Shifting the Ground of Controversy

As we have noted, any public problem can be formulated in a variety of ways. Where hostilities have festered, and the opposing camps have had time to build antagonistic images of the intentions and interests of the other, it is likely that the problem, as stated by the rival advocates, will seem far more intractable than it, in fact, is. In bargaining relationships, too, it is to the interest of rivals to construct arguments that emphasize the differences between the sides, rather than their shared interests. In such cases, it is often wise for the conciliator not to accept the terms of the controversy as defined by the adversaries but to look through and beyond the apparent controversy, to some other formulation of the public problem as a whole.[8]

It is often worthwhile for the conciliator to try to shift the ground of controversy. One approach that can be tried in breaking a deadlock is to change the *level* of the controversy.

One can attempt to *lower* the level of argument by breaking the apparent dispute down into its component parts, or "disaggregating" it. Especially when the debate seems vague and indeterminate, it is worthwhile to ask what concretely could be done about it, what actual decisions or projects are really at stake. It may be desirable to reduce a conflict on "fundamental principles" to the actual interests of the opposing sides, to make these manifest, which may perhaps suggest "split the difference" compromises.

A relatively simple policy choice often becomes volatile when it comes to symbolize larger antagonisms. A simple curriculum change in the schools, for example, can become the focus of racial, class, or group antagonisms. The problem then becomes one of separating out the concrete issue of decision making on educational programs from the overtones that it has taken on and trying to deal with the "larger" issues separately.

To *raise* the level of debate is, in effect, an attempt to move from a situation of bargaining to one of policymaking. This may mean to move from a position where concrete interests are perceived to be at stake to

[8] *Kenneth I. Boulding,* Conflict and Defense *(New York: Harper and Brothers, 1962), p. 316.*

one of principle, where the effort is to get the adversaries to agree to a decision-rule that is perceived as legitimate and fair in deciding the controversy. The conciliator may invite the contestants to take into account third party rights, or to consider the impact of their success or failure in reaching agreement on the community as a whole. In some sense, this appeal to overridding public interests is a "threat" by the conciliator to define a position that will appear reasonable and fair to the general public and thus bring pressure to bear on the parties to the dispute.

In reformulating a problem the task of the conciliator is to provide *saliency*, to make a case for selecting an aspect of the problem as particularly significant, one around which agreement can crystallize. If the deadlocked argument has focused on the norm of *equality*, with one side demanding rewards identical to the other, the conciliator might try to shift the decision-rule to one of "fairness," and to cause the argument to be reformulated around what each side is *entitled* to, and on what grounds. If the issue is phrased as one of *entitlement* to an extravagant claim, the ground might be shifted to the question of what can be appropriately expected of government policy, given the limits of the public budget and public powers, and the ongoing commitments of the system.

Separating Symbolic and Tangible Interests

One approach to the reformulation of a problem by breaking it into component elements is to divide matters of principle from the material consequences of a solution. When it becomes apparent that one side is going to have to relinquish most of its initial aspirations, it may be very important to create the appearance that it has not lost at all but has, in fact, been successful. For example, it is possible to enact sweeping social reform legislation while providing a budget that would not permit its effective implementation.

This may seem a mere exercise in face-saving when capitulation is inevitable and not a compromise or accommodation at all. The realist will say that verbiage is cheap and that what counts are concrete pay-offs. However, to award the symbolic rewards to one side and the tangible results to the other may not be a bad bargain under some circumstances. Agreement on principle sets precedents and decision-rules for future policy issues. The long-run advantage may lie with the party who has accepted the symbolic payoffs.

The conservative may stick to his guns in a fight on welfare policy and get his way on the concrete point that no payment should be made without a "means test," only to discover to his astonishment that he has gone along with a large-scale, long-term expansion of public welfare commitment on principle. The Latin American landowner may win exemption of his cattle-raising interests from an agrarian reform law and discover that, in the process, he has assented to the principle of agrarian reform itself. Often, in fact, when the momentum of change has been established, the weaker party is the one that seeks to exempt its particular interests from the impact of reform, and recognition and acceptance of such tangible interests is, in fact, a concession that the strong make to the weak to win wider support and endorsement for an overall pattern of change.

political procedures and conflict resolution

The most common and important technique of creating agreement remains to be considered. As we have seen, in any political conflict, there are various levels of agreement and disagreement. Conflict resolution is possible because there are *some* shared principles, some common interests. When there are acute disagreements on the substance of policy, the contestants may still be able to come to a conclusion *because they accept a particular procedure as binding on them.* They agree to take a vote and adhere to the will of the majority or to accept the verdict of a court of law or to defer to the judgment of a person in a position of authority.

The success of any political order depends on its capacity to create legitimate procedures for resolving conflict. The critical test of the legitimacy of any political system is that even those who lose, those who are seriously disadvantaged by the outcome of a decision, accept the *way* in which the decision was reached. Political instability and breakdown occur when divisions on *issues* come to be seen as more important than agreement on the *means* for resolving them.

The design of institutions and procedures for conflict resolution is part of the art of statecraft and poses further problems of political choice and judgment. In effect, political order and constitutional structure emerge out of the problem of finding means for the contrivance of agreement. And that is the subject of the third part of this book.

R
RTHER
ADING

Boulding, Kenneth I., *Conflict and Defense* (New York: Harper and Bros., 1962). A basic theoretical treatment of conflict and conflict resolution, with emphasis on the importance of images and perception in antagonism and cooperation.

Buchanan, James, and Gordon Tulloch, *The Calculus of Consent* (Ann Arbor: University of Michigan Press, 1962). A sophisticated treatment of rational choice in conflict resolution. When is it rational for an individual to come to terms, to prefer collective over individual action, to agree to be bound by a decision-rule such as the majority principle?

Hirschman, Albert O., *Journeys Toward Progress* (New York: Twentieth Century Fund, 1963). The last chapters are a fascinating consideration of the art of "reform-mongering," of contriving change and assent to change in a perverse political context—in this case, Latin America.

Jackson, Elmore, *Meeting of Minds: A Way to Peace through Negotiation* (New York: McGraw-Hill, 1952). Somewhat dated, but still useful as a discussion of the problems of the conciliator, particularly in international relations.

Karass, Chester L., *The Negotiating Game* (Cleveland: World, 1970). Some useful practical and theoretical pointers on the problems of negotiation.

Kerr, Clark *Labor and Management in Industrial Society* (Garden City, N.Y.: Anchor Books, 1964). The processes of bargaining and conflict resolution with particular reference to industrial relations. However, much of the analysis is applicable to politics generally.

Stevens, Carl M., *Strategy and Collective Bargaining Negotiation* (New York: McGraw-Hill, 1963). Again the emphasis is on industrial relations, but the analysis of bargaining strategy and especially the function of argument in bargaining is fascinating and has many applications to politics if interpreted with a little common sense.

part three political structure: the design of institutions

chapter
eleven
political
architecture

When facing a policy decision, some of the first questions we have to ask are these: What do we have the authority to do? Whose approval do we have to get? What rules and procedures have to be followed? Political structure is one of the primary determinants of choice and action. We make decisions according to the rules of the game of a particular political system.

But political structure is also the object of choice. In politics, we decide not only what government should do but also how it should be organized. This is not just a task for the "founding fathers." In fact, it is an everyday aspect of politics. Every time we adopt a new policy, we have to create procedures for carrying it out; whenever a new committee is established, it has to decide how it is going to go about its business. In most organizations, rules and procedures are constantly being revised and interpreted. We are always tinkering with the design of our political institutions.

The problems that have to be faced in creating a new organization or reforming an old one are, in fact, very much the same. In either case, questions and controversies will arise about what government has the power to do, about the authority of various officers and officials, about the participation of individual members in the affairs of the organization, about the process to be used in making decisions, implementing them, and interpreting rules in specific cases.

What questions should be asked when we come up against problems of this kind? Once again, we have to cut through the particular details of concrete situations to underlying principles that can be used to organize our thoughts on controversies of this kind and to arrive at policy conclusions. On what grounds can we argue that an organization should be made more democratic—or less so? What reasons can be given for granting government the power to carry out a certain activity—or for denying government that power?

fundamentals of institution-building

A constitution, a charter, or a set of bylaws, whether for a club or for a country, will normally contain the following elements:

1. A statement of the purposes and powers of the organization.
2. A definition of the principal authority roles: how officials are to be selected, their powers and responsibilities.
3. A decision-making procedure: how the organization will arrive at binding commitments on common purposes.

The first point raises the issue of the rights *of* the organization and of individuals *within* the organization. The second and third require that we decide how democratic the organization will be. This chapter discusses these basic questions of political architecture and the design of institutions.

What Functions and Powers?

Most statements of purpose begin grandiloquently and a little vaguely. "The purpose of this organization is to advance the study of politics." So far so good. Our real problems begin when we start to decide what follows from *that*.

How precisely is our hypothetical political science association going to advance the study of politics? By "taxing" all members and giving research grants to some of them? May grants also be given to nonmembers? By publishing the research of the members? Or of nonmembers as well? By making expert judgments on the controversial issues of the day in the name of the members of the organization? Will the organization have the power to judge the professional conduct of the members, can it expose and expel them for "malpractice," for not *properly* advancing the study of politics?

The point should be apparent. A statement of purposes empowers an organization, but it states the limits of its authority as well. It is an important aspect of the structure of rights within the organization. Where the organization has the power, and the decision has been properly made, the member is obligated to abide by the policy of the group. But where the power is not stated, the individual is not so obligated. He has a right to do as he pleases. The organization has "no right" to compel him to abide by its decisions.

Thus, in thinking about a statement of purposes, we are really considering an aspect of the total system of rights, and everything that was said on this subject in Chapter Three becomes pertinent once again. What rights should the organization have over the conduct of individual members? What rights should individuals have against the authority of the organization?

Liberalism and Limited Government

Most of our ideas about constitutional government come down to us from the classic tradition of liberal thought. For John Locke, as for James Madison, the central problem of political architecture was to prevent the concentration of power in government from being used arbitrarily or tyrannically. Government should only do those things that individuals cannot do for themselves. The power of the state should be limited by a constitution, which is a form of law binding on government itself. The appropriate functions of government, then, are specified in advance. All public actions must be justified as consistent with the fundamental law. The burden of proof is always on the state to demonstrate that its actions are lawful.

For the classic liberals, checking the power of government over the individual was seen as virtually the entire problem of political design. This tradition is so much ingrained in the American mind that most of us would accept as a matter of course that the principal problem of institution-building is the limitation of government power. As Samuel P. Huntington writes,

> When an American thinks about the problem of government-building, he directs himself not to the creation of authority and the accumulation of power but rather to the limitation of authority and the division of power. Asked to design a government, he comes up with a written constitution, bill of rights, separation of powers, checks and balances, federalism, regular elections, competitive parties—all excellent devices for limiting government. The Lockean American is so fundamentally anti-government that he idéntifies government with restrictions on government. [1]

Government must be limited, but it must also be effective. The liberal way of looking at the problem of political design may not give enough emphasis to the point that private power may be abused as well as public power. Individual rights apply not only against government but against other individuals and private organizations as well. But to be effective, the individual cannot be asked to defend his own

---

[1] *Samuel P. Huntington,* Political Order in Changing Societies *(New Haven: Yale University Press, 1968) p. 7.*

rights against those more powerful than himself. He must be able to call upon the assistance of government to counterbalance the power of forces in society that are stronger than he is.

Some would argue that in America we have worked so hard to protect the individual against government that we have left him vulnerable to many forms of private arbitrariness and outrage. In large cities, for example, many crimes go unreported, both because people think the police are unlikely to catch the criminal, and because they suspect that those brought to trial are unlikely to be convicted. Many womens' groups argue that in rape cases the victim is as much on trial as the assailant, and that the process of bringing charges can be as humiliating and degrading as the crime itself when defense attorneys attempt to prove that the victim provoked the assault.

Others feel that our reluctance to use government authority exposes us to the arbitrary power of giant organizations. In the absence of effective government regulation and planning, corporations and trade unions may in fact be the planners of the economic life of the society. Furthermore, they may exercise extensive arbitrary power over the individual. Managers of large firms can transfer employees from job to job, city to city, honor and enrich them, disgrace and demote them, often with very little regard for what we generally understand as due process of law. The employee, it is argued, can always quit. But if he does, he will have to find work somewhere else, and normally it will be with another large organization that will claim a similar authority over his life and purposes.[2]

Obviously, we need to strike a balance between the principles of limited government and political effectiveness. But how we define that balance often depends very much on personal preconceptions and political ideology. We tend to identify either with the "insiders" or the "outsiders," with the purposes of the organization or the individuals who are subject to its control. Either we are trying to "get something done" or we want to go about our business without interference from "busybodies" or "bureaucrats." In our society, ideologies of the left—what we normally call the liberal position—are generally more enthusiastic about the exercise of government authority and take a dimmer view of unrestrained private power. Ideologies of the right —the conservative position—are more apt to regard government as potentially dangerous and private activity as generally benign.

If we ask the right questions, it may be possible to cut through such preconceptions when we face particular choices about the functions and powers of a political organization. If we look at a political structure as a system of rights, we may be able to strike a balance

---

[2] Anthony Jay, Management and Machiavelli *(New York: Holt, Rinehart and Winston, 1967), p. 178.*

between the principles of limited government and political effectiveness.

political organization
as a system of rights

The problem of political design—the question of the powers and functions of an organization—can be represented in the form of a triangle.

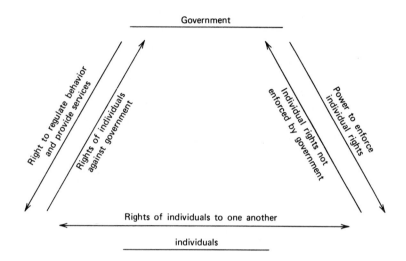

In assessing the functions and powers of any organization, our attention is now directed to the following questions.

What Functions Shall the Organization Be Entitled to Perform? What Rights Shall It Have to Compel Members to Comply with Its Decisions?

The right of a government in this sense is the same thing as its authority. When a government has the authority to provide a service or to regulate conduct, the citizen is obligated to comply with decisions properly made. One classic right of local governments is to "protect the health and safety of the community." To this end, they may license restaurants, motels, and other public accommodations; inspect them to ensure that they meet certain standards of sanitation, cleanliness, and so on; and administer fines or other forms of punishment to those who do not comply with regulations.

What Rights Do Individuals Have to Expect Specific Services or Forms of Regulation from Government?

If a government has the right to exercise authority, does it also have the obligation to do so? If government has the right to regulate the cleanliness of restaurants, does this mean that it may do so or not, at its own discretion? Or does the citizen have the right to expect that governments will adopt appropriate statutes and ordinances concerning sanitary standards in public places and see that they are enforced? Does the right of government to "protect the health and safety of the community" *imply* a responsibility to look after the healthfulness of eating establishments? Returning to our example of the political science association, is the power of the organization to be that it "may" publish the research of members or that it "shall" do so? In the former case, this is a service that the organization may provide if it sees fit to do so. In the latter case, the member is *entitled* to receive a journal or something like it, and the organization has the responsibility for providing such a service.

Many foreign constitutions, unlike America's, stipulate particular public services that the individual is entitled to receive as a matter of right—the right to security in old age and sickness, to education, and the like. A question that should arise in designing any set of political institutions is whether the members are entitled to receive certain services as a result of membership. The government of the organization then becomes obligated to adopt policies that provide these benefits to all members, and such policies have a privileged claim to the resources of the organization.

What Rights Do Individuals Have Against the Organization?

What actions and policies will government *not* be entitled to undertake? Does the power of government to "protect health and safety" imply that it might ban smoking or drinking, both of which are injurious to health, or for that matter, that it might require all citizens to assemble for mass calisthenics at five in the morning in the interest of *promoting* health?

In working out the design for any political institution, we have to answer the question of the limits of public authority. There are two specific kinds of rights of individuals against governmental action that should be considered.

Personal Rights. Where should individuals be free to do as they please without being subject to any regulation, guidance, or direction from government? In creating a political science association, is it important to spell out in advance whether the organization will have the right to judge and censure the professional conduct of members or whether each individual will have the right to study and write about politics as he or she pleases, at least so far as membership in the organization is concerned? Do we want the organization to have the right to take stands on public issues, or is it important to reserve that right to individuals, to specify that members can advance their own opinions without committing the association and without the association committing them?

The line of absolute personal freedom is a very difficult one to draw. Some argue that government regulation should only be used to prevent individual actions that potentially do harm to others or the community. There is a right of privacy developing in American constitutional law which seems to exclude from regulation those actions that have no conceivable serious effect on anyone else or that involve fully free and consensual relationships between mature adults—the right to read pornographic literature in the privacy of one's own room and the right to sexual activities between consenting adults are examples.

In defining the limits of personal rights, the crucial question, as we noted in Chapter Three, is to decide what will count as an injury. Almost everything we do has some impact on others. But when is the impact so significant that it requires regulation to prevent abuses?

One way of looking at this problem is to assume that human conduct is always somehow regulated, and then compare the advantages and disadvantages of different forms of regulation. If public authority does not provide a formal system of rights and duties, human relationships may be regulated by social pressure, custom, conformity, or the informal power of the dominant members of a group.

This is a problem that applies not only in the realm of government but also to private organizations. For example, should university authorities have the right to enforce a code of conduct in student dormitories? It can be argued that this is an unwarranted intrusion into the private lives of students. Most students are legally adults, and the university has no right to stand *in loco parentis,* in the place of parents.

Now what, in fact, is supposed to happen when a student comes home from the library exhausted, with no thought but getting to bed as soon as possible, and discovers that his roommate has decided to dedicate the evening to holding a wild party in the room? Does he protest politely? Does he call the police and bring charges of disturbing the peace? Does he get together with the biggest friends he can find and physically eject the offending parties? And what happens to the rights of the partymakers in the last instance? Is the roommate to be left lying in the bushes protesting that his side of the story has not been heard? Perhaps these remedies are preferable to a system of enforced regulation, but it is not altogether obvious that an intervening layer of regulation between the individual and civil authority might not be a good idea. The important question is what individual rights have to be protected against any abuse of power, whether by government or other individuals, and what individuals can do to protect their rights against those more powerful than themselves.

Political Rights. Another important category of rights of individuals against governments are those of political activity and organization. Policymakers have to structure the process of government. Decisions have to be made about the qualifications of voters and elections, the timing and administration of elections, and so on. The problem is how to prevent the incumbent leaders from rigging the process so as to perpetuate their own power.

In any democratic organization, the rights of free speech and assembly, the ability to oppose the existing leadership, to present candidates and run for office, to campaign on equal terms with the incumbents, to have the outcome decided in a free election, are all essential safeguards against abuses of power.

Once again, important questions inevitably arise about how such rights should be defined. For example, "freedom of speech" is not a *personal* right but a *political* right. You have no right to libel or slander another individual, to willfully injure that person's reputation. This involves the rights and duties of individuals to one another, not a right of political action. Similarly, as Justice Holmes noted, freedom of speech does not entitle you to shout "Fire" falsely in a crowded theater.

Freedom of speech is fundamentally intended to ensure that those out of power will have the opportunity to mobilize dissent against those presently in power. But this does not mean that government is helpless to defend itself against incitement to riot or revolution. The right is fundamentally one of persuasion, advocacy, and argument. Thus, in American constitutional law, freedom of speech covers the advocacy of revolution in the abstract but not the use of speech to actually organize an insurrection. (The distinction is clear enough. It is one thing to say, "When government no longer rests on the consent of the people it must be overthrown" and another to announce, "The guns will be in the first building and the ammunition in the second. We attack at dawn.")

In designing any political organization, it is important to stipulate decisions that policymakers *cannot make* concerning such matters as: who is entitled to participate, how arguments between existing leaders and opponents will be presented and resolved, and how new leaders will be selected.

How Will Conflicts of Rights be Decided?

The constitution of any political organization is a complex system of rights and duties. The exact limits and boundaries of rights may not be clear in any particular case. What happens, then, when conflicts arise over rights of the organization and those of the individual?

It will not do simply to let the leaders make the final decision. They will always win. The power of the organization will, in fact, be unlimited. The constitution will impose no limits on the authority of those in power. What we need is some appeal *against* the authority of those at the top.

This is why the principle of judicial independence has been so important in Anglo-American law. The courts must be insulated, so far as possible, from political pressures, for it is their obligation to adjudicate in cases of conflicts of rights, including claims of rights against the authority of government. In the United States, the principle of judicial review rests on the logic of a constitution as a system of rights. The Supreme Court is entitled to judge whether the acts of Congress or the president are in conformity with rights guaranteed to individuals in the Constitution, or to the states.

This is an aspect of political design that is frequently neglected in private organization. One of the basic rules of justice is that no person should be a judge in a case in which he has an interest. Yet there is seldom an independent judiciary in a private body. If a person questions whether a particular policy conforms to the powers of the organization, the appeal is often only to the officers, who are hardly disinterested parties.

Setting up an impartial tribunal in a private organization is often a tricky business. Who is truly independent when all have some stake in the policies of the organization?

Often the best that can be done is to set up a special procedure and rules for adjudicating fundamental disputes over the powers of the organization. For example, in university disciplinary or tenure cases, a special board of senior professors may be constituted, who are obliged to follow special rules of procedure. An open hearing must be held, both sides must have a right to present testimony, the decision and the rationale for it must be made public, and so forth. The board is itself protected by tenure against reprisals from the university authorities.

In designing a political system, care must be given to these rights of "due process of law": to appeal beyond immediate supervisors; to a hearing; to a structured adversary process in which both sides can make their case in the presence of the other, can respond to the testimony of the other side, and can have the case decided by known rules and procedures.

argument and political architecture

Issues of political design do not come up only when an organization is being founded. They are part of every policy decision, for we always have to ask whether we have legitimate authority to take action and which of the alternatives before us are compatible with the total system of rights and powers. In making decisions, we have to interpret the basic charter on which the organization is founded, and in doing so, we change the nature of the system itself. Every government evolves through interpretation of its basic operating rules.

Many exercises of public authority are arguable. And a principal form that this dilemma of decision making takes is a division between "strict constructionists"—those who want to read the constitutional documents literally—and "loose constructionists"—those who want to be flexible in interpreting the power and authority of the organization.

Sometimes those who want to restrain the exercise of public authority will call for a literal reading of constitutional provisions to block change. Other times, those who want fundamental reform will insist that the organization live up to the absolute "letter of the law." Those who want to expand the scope of public action may urge that formal statements of power and rights be read flexibly, insisting that the organization adapt to changing needs and conditions. Or those who want to inhibit change may argue that "one has to be pragmatic" and not take "mere formalities" too seriously.

In ongoing policy debate, we often face the problem of whether a close reading or an open reading of constitutional provisions, of basic rules and procedures, is called for. Two hypothetical problems illustrate the kind of choice that has to be made when such a controversy arises.

The first example is one that could come up in any organization. The charter specifies a schedule of dues to be charged all members to support the "purposes of the organization." A project is proposed that is consistent with the statement of purposes but requires large additional funding. It is proposed that a special fee be charged and a special fund established to provide this service. The strict constructionists argue that the charter makes no provision for special assessments and therefore the proposal cannot be adopted. The loose constructionists respond that if the organization has the power to adopt a program, it obviously must also have the power to raise resources to put it into effect. What is your appraisal of this problem?

Now let us examine a slightly more complicated issue. A government that has experimented with prohibition and failed decides to adopt a high tax on alcoholic beverages instead, in the belief that it is easier to enforce a tax than a total ban on liquor consumption. The opponents argue that the purpose of taxation is to raise revenue, not regulate human conduct. Since the proposed tax on liquor is almost prohibitively high, the obvious purpose is not to raise money—it is designed to keep people from drinking. If the taxation power is interpreted so broadly that it can be applied to anything, what limits are there to the powers of government? Government has no stated power to regulate the sale of alcoholic beverages, they observe. The previous prohibition law required a constitutional amendment which was subsequently repealed.

The proponents of the tax, in their turn, argue first that health and safety are legitimate public concerns. Drinking is injurious to health and a major cause of traffic accidents. The only question is the most efficient means to the end. Furthermore, governments have always used taxes as a means of regulation. No tax has an absolutely neutral effect. Tariffs affect imports, corporation taxes affect investment, and sales taxes affect consumption. A perfectly equal tax—everyone pays the same—tends to favor the rich over the poor. Hence the power to tax always involves a related policy decision. Policymakers have the inherent power not only to raise revenue but also to determine what the incidence of a tax should be. Therefore, the liquor tax is a perfectly legitimate exercise of public authority. How are you inclined to evaluate this dilemma?

Obviously, the statement of powers and purposes of any organization has to be interpreted. Not all contingencies and problems can be foreseen. For the organization to survive, it must adapt and change. The problem is where to draw the line. Beyond a certain point, fundamental or constitutional law ceases to be a limit on the power of government. Authority becomes so broad and sweeping that the individual can claim no right against the demand for his compliance.

Implied Powers

When we face a problem not anticipated in the statement of purposes of an organization, the most natural place to begin looking for a solution is by thinking about the logical implications of stated powers, what is necessarily entailed or can be rationally deduced from them. This is what is happening in the above examples. The loose constructionists are arguing that the power to regulate conduct through taxation is a logical implication of any taxation decision itself. The strict constructionists remain dubious about this interpretation, for to them it seems that the implication is that the taxation power becomes unlimited, and nullifies any other stipulated limits on government powers.

In the early years of the American republic, an issue of this kind arose. The Hamiltonians, advocates of a strong federal government, wanted to establish a national bank. The followers of Jefferson, wary of centralized power, argued that the Constitution, in enumerating the powers of the federal government, contained no provision for a bank. Those who favored the project insisted that the necessary authority could be deduced from the power to regulate currency and borrow money, as well as the power to "make all laws necessary and proper for carrying into execution the foregoing powers. . . ."[3] The strict constructionists, in turn, replied that any measures not specified in the Constitution had to be demonstrated to be *indispensable* to achieving

[3] *Art. I. Sec. 7.*

the purposes of government, and they did not feel a bank was one c
them. The Supreme Court, in the case of *McCulloch* v. *Maryland*[4] rule
for the loose constructionists and set the key precedent for the flexibl
interpretation of the Constitution.

The process of expanding the power of the federal governmen
through a broad interpretation of constitutional provisions has been
constant theme in the American political experience. Thus the powe
of government to manage the economy, which today reaches int
almost every aspect of production, rests in large measure on interpre
tation of the clause that grants Congress the power to "regulate com
merce among the states." A narrow reading of this power would seen
to limit Congress to regulating the actual passage of goods across stat
lines. But does "commerce" only mean "transport" or all the activitie
that go into buying and selling goods and services? By 1824, th
Supreme Court had ruled that commerce meant intercourse, no
merely traffic.[5] To the Supreme Court, it seemed logical to infer tha
Congress had the power to regulate all aspects of business that had a
"substantial effect" on interstate commerce. For example, if the rate
charged by grain elevator operators in Chicago affected the price o
wheat in New York, should regulation of elevator rates be left to th
Illinois legislature? Was not the intention of the Constitution, in de
priving the states of the power to set tariffs, for example, to create a
national common market? Did not the power to regulate commerc
then apply to all the forces that go into the distribution of goods an
services across the nation?

While this power was steadily expanded, it was only in the 1930
that the principle was established by the Supreme Court that th
production and distribution of goods was an intricate network o
transactions, all dependent on one another, each aspect of which ir
some sense had an impact on the economy of the nation as a whole.
The stage was set for the very broad economic powers of contemporar
government, which range from the regulation of transport and com
munications, to prices, wages, labor relations, the stock exchange
business organization, advertising—virtually all the factors that ente
into the economic life of the nation.

The Intentions of the Framers

Another ground of argument in interpreting statements of powers is t
examine the intentions of those who drafted the basic charter. Fo
example, in the impeachment proceedings against Richard Nixon ir
1974, the House of Representatives had to decide, in drafting a bill o

[4] *4 Wheaton 316.*

[5] Gibbons *v.* Ogden *9 Wheaton 1.*

[6] National Labor Relations Board *v.* Jones and Laughlin Steel Corp. *301 US 1.*

impeachment, whether the president's actions constituted "high crimes and misdemeanors" within the meaning of the Constitution. In debating this, they went back not only to the meaning of these terms in the law at the time the Constitution was written but also to the records and documents that surrounded the writing of the Constitution—Madison's notes on the Constitutional Convention, the *Federalist Papers*, the records of the ratifying conventions in the various states—to determine if the debates and deliberations of that age could clarify the implications of the bare words of the Constitution.

The Problem of Decision

It might seem that whether one takes a strict constructionist or a loose constructionist position simply depends on the situation. If we see an urgent problem that needs solution, we will find an interpretation that fits intended action to the powers of the organization. If we oppose a policy, we will be as nitpicking as possible. To a certain extent this is true. However, if we change positions frequently on purely opportunistic grounds, our arguments from constitutional authority will eventually lose persuasive force. If we are going to appeal to the structure of rights and powers of an organization in support of our position, we have to be relatively consistent. And this means a prior, general decision on the issue.

Once again, where we decide to place the presumption will largely depend on our attitudes toward public authority in general. If we tend to favor public solutions to problems, if we prefer active to passive government, we will be apt to adopt a loose and flexible attitude toward the power of public authority. If, on the other hand, we believe that government should be strictly limited, that on the whole people should work out solutions to their own problems, we will tend to place the burden on government of proving that its actions are justified.

what positions of authority?
what decision-making processes?

After the statement of purpose, the next basic problems of political organization are those of creating a structure of authority and designing a decision-making procedure. What officers will the organization have? How will they be selected? What will be their roles and responsibilities? What will be the division of labor among them? If there is to be a bureaucracy, how will personnel be appointed and how will they be organized?

And, then, through what process will we make policy? How will proposals and problems be brought forward, analyzed, and debated? How will the agenda for action be created? Finally, how will we make decisions? Who will have the authority to commit the group to a course of action, one which will be binding on the members?

Every organization has its own unique characteristics, and how we go about answering these questions will depend on the kind of body we are dealing with, its particular traditions, precedents, purposes, and functions. Any rules of political organization that would cover the diverse circumstances of clubs, associations, churches, corporations, and governments would have to be so general as to be virtually meaningless. However, whenever the structure of authority or the decision-making process actually becomes a controversial issue in a group, certain kinds of fundamental interests and principles are apt to be at stake. It is around these that we can begin to organize our thoughts about the decision-rules that should be applied in creating or reforming a political structure.

First, no system of authority or decision-making procedure is ever perfectly neutral. Structure is always one of the aspects of power in an organization. Established institutions always work to the advantage of some interests and to the disadvantage of others. Hence, disputes over political design are part of the struggle for power and influence. Arguments over change in institutions may be a part of political strategy. Those who feel thwarted by entrenched power holders are likely to be the ones who will demand that decision making be made more participatory and democratic. Those who are trying to ward off threats to their position are apt to insist that "it is essential to follow normal procedures."

In analyzing problems of political design, it is worthwhile to ask whether any important interest in the group is being systematically privileged or ignored because of the characteristics of the political system. An ideal political system would be one in which all parties regarded the procedure for making policy as fair and acceptable. But in that case, there would be small likelihood that the design of institutions would become an issue. Usually, political institutions represent an accommodation among competing interests as they existed at an earlier period in the organization's life. But patterns of cleavage and conflict change over time, and the established order may not be able to cope successfully with the new situation.

Protest may raise the issue of reform, but it does not resolve it. Simply because some faction is not getting its way is not a sufficient reason for change. Many people criticize a political system because it fails to generate the kind of policies in which they are interested. The argument, "Congress is ineffective" may often be translated as, "Congress does not pass the laws that I think ought to be passed." On the other side, of course, are those who think the Congress is indeed an excellent body, whose institutions and procedures were wisely contrived to prevent the passage of rash, hasty, and ill-considered legislation.

Once again, the assertion that a decision-making body systematically works to the advantage of some interests and not of others *may* be a good argument for reform. But the fact that it does not generate particular kinds of policies, in itself, is not. Policy is by nature controversial, and the test of a decision-making system is not that we get what we want, but that the system is able to successfully resolve controversies, to generate policies acceptable to the community.

What standards of judgment should be applied in making decisions about the design of political institutions? Just as such principles as rights, freedom, and justice can be helpful in thinking about the *substance* of public policy, the idea of democracy is widely accepted in our culture in judging the *procedure* through which decisions are made. We start with the presumption that governments ought to be organized on a democratic basis and ask for reasons to do otherwise.

how much democracy?

In our society, democracy is a word with almost totally positive connotations. We believe that a political system is legitimate to the extent that it is democratic. To argue that a decision was made "through democratic process" is almost a conclusive case that it ought to be accepted and obeyed.

To be sure, democracy is a hard term to define, for it is broad and vague in meaning and has been applied to many different types of political arrangements. Nonetheless, we are still aware of its basic meaning of "rule by the people" or "government by those who are governed." We also acknowledge that many of the systems we label as democratic are not such in the pure sense of the term.

We are so accustomed to thinking that democracy is always desirable that we seldom realize how often we argue against it in practice. To be sure, we never say we are against democracy, but in designing political institutions we often do conclude that it is desirable to strengthen authority structures and reduce the amount of participation in policymaking. Furthermore, many of the organizations that are part of our political life—corporations, churches, universities, and the like—are far from democratic in political structure, but we do not necessarily conclude that they should be reconstituted along totally democratic lines.

In considering change in any political system, the problem we really face is the extent to which it should be democratic. In designing political structures, we have to decide when, where, and how the "will of the people" will be expressed and channeled, and in doing so, we are making a series of choices about whether there will be more or less democracy.[7]

---

[7] *Douglas W. Rae, "Political Democracy as a Property of Political Institutions,"* American Political Science Review 65 *(March 1971), pp. 111–120.*

the argument for increasing democracy

What grounds can be given for increasing participation in policymaking in any organization? On what basis can we advocate making government more responsive to the will of individual citizens? Historically, four kinds of arguments have been particularly important in the justification and extension of democratic rule.

Democracy and Equality

The classic case for democracy is simply that all people ought to have the same right to participate in political decisions. All will be affected by decisions made on public purposes, and all should therefore play a similar role in determining what those purposes will be. To argue against democracy, it would seem, we would have to be able to say that some people have a right to determine how others will conduct their lives. On what basis could we justify the establishment of such a ruling class? Are the most intelligent entitled to rule? What does intelligence have to do with deciding on the final purposes of human life? Are those who claim insight into God's will entitled to rule? Who judges the validity of their claims to divine insight? Should those who know "the laws of historical development" be the rulers? How do we test whether their "scientific knowledge" is correct—and who makes the decision? If we argue against democracy, are we not saying that it is appropriate that the largest part of the population serve as the instruments of the will of a ruling class?

Democracy, Human Development and the Health of the Community

A second basis for arguing for democracy is that political participation is essential to human dignity and personal development. An individual who plays no part in the decisions that affect him becomes inhibited and servile. Participation is psychologically important in bringing about a sense of self-esteem and self-confidence. The person who plays a role in political life earns to take initiative and to exercise responsibility in his conduct toward others. He becomes more unselfish as he takes part in making decisions on behalf of other people and does not act entirely for himself.

Furthermore, participation strengthens feelings of loyalty and solidarity in the community. Taking part in decision making engenders support for the political order. Where authority is remote and impersonal, as is so often the case in the modern world, individuals frequently do not understand the reasons behind policies. Decision makers and citizens inhabit entirely different worlds. The reasons of public life are not the reasons of everyday life. The individual becomes skeptical of authority whose motives he cannot understand. At the xtreme, he retreats into cynicism, resistance, and alienation. Only if he individual becomes a part of the policymaking process itself is he pt to comprehend the objectives and the problems of public choice nd willingly cooperate in decisions made for the community as a vhole.[8]

ncreasing Democracy Results in Better Decisions

The purpose of democracy is not to make decision making simpler, but o make it more adequate. Obviously, policymakers do not want to encourage criticism of their performance. The presentation of unusual or unexpected demands and problems, the clash of interests and diverse points of view, complicates a task that they would prefer to keep simple and straightforward. Like anyone else, those in authority would prefer to let sleeping dogs lie.

The purpose of democracy then is to structure the environment of decision making so that policymakers have to deal with problems at a more complex level than would be their natural inclination. By increasing participation, we attempt to structure a situation in which the policymakers are required to consider the implications of choice for various groups and affected interests. Any constraints we impose on participation will have the effect of encouraging some options and foreclosing others. The committed democrat argues that only through open, participatory process can policymakers really know the alternatives that are available to them and obtain information sufficient for intelligent choice among these alternatives. To restrict participation is to define in advance what problems will be dealt with, what interests considered, which options given privileged status in making policy.

Democracy Is Essential to Assure Control of Rulers by the Ruled

Reduced to its bare essentials, the premise underlying the democratic position is that no individual should become merely an instrument of the will of another. The problem that democratic theory tries to resolve is how to prevent tyranny, despotism, slavery, and suppression. Democracy is necessary to preserve limited government, to protect the rights of individuals against the state.[9]

It is inevitable that people will disagree over public purposes. There are many forms of conflict resolution, but the barest requirement of civil society is that conflicts not be settled by the capacity of the stronger party to impose its will on the weaker. Force alone cannot justify political authority. And the inference drawn in democratic

---

[8] *Terrence E. Cook and Patrick M. Morgan (Eds.),* Participatory Democracy *(San Francisco: Chandler Press, 1971), pp. 6–11.*
[9] *Robert A. Dahl,* A Preface to Democratic Theory, *pp. 3, 4.*

theory is that no exercise of authority is legitimate and binding unless i "derives from the consent of the governed."

A fourth ground for arguing for an increase in democracy in an organization, then, is that procedures ought to be adopted by whic ordinary citizens can exert a relatively high degree of control over th actions of leaders, that authority is only justified when it serves to carr forward the purposes of ordinary citizens, and that leaders have n right to use political order as a means of imposing their wishes on th members of the community.

the case for pure democracy

Taken absolutely literally, and carried relentlessly to its full logic implications, the case for democracy results in a demanding politic prescription.

1. If no individual or group can demonstrate possession of abso lute knowledge concerning the nature and ends of life an therefore of public purpose,
2. Then *each* person must have equal opportunity to advocat potential public purposes,
3. And *each* person must have equal weight in judging amon alternatives that might be made binding on the community a a whole,
4. And since *no* person should be an instrument of another will, no decisions will be taken that are not acceptable to a members.

Such pure "participatory democracy" is rarely found in practice When it does occur, it is often a transitory rather than a stable form c political order. Perhaps the business meeting of a traditional Quake church is the best example of a pure democracy that has endured ove time. The Quakers, sharing a belief in the importance of eac individual's personal religious convictions and spiritual insight an dedicated to peaceful persuasion and nonviolence in political action have often been able to sustain a very simple and unstructured politic system.

Each adult member has an equal voice and responsibility in arriv ing at public decisions in the Quaker church. In the meeting, eac speaks to his "concerns" for the common activity of the body as he c she feels "called upon" to do so. These issues are deliberated by th other members of the group. No votes are taken. No rule of th majority is applied. The discussion continues until a "sense of th meeting," recognized commonly, is achieved. What if there is an acut division of opinion? As one authority describes it, "In cases where th meeting seems almost equally divided, a pause for prayer is frequentl called for. After this some way out of the difficulty is sometimes found; if not, the matter in question is dropped or deferred."[10]

Patience, persuasion, the reformulation of questions so that they are acceptable to all, and a common conviction of the importance of a political system in which all are actually free and equal because no decisions are taken against anyone's will, these are the beliefs and values that make such a policymaking process possible.

case for increasing authority

Since the time of Jean-Jacques Rousseau, social critics have used the theory of pure democracy to argue for radical reconstruction of society. Much of the New Left protest of the 1960s, particularly in the United States, was far from Marxist in orientation. Such statements as the Port Huron Manifesto of 1962, for example, essentially argued that America had failed to live up to its democratic ideals.[11]

However, we do not often conclude in practice that the imperatives of pure democracy are the only criteria that should be applied in designing political institutions. In fact, we do measure the case for democracy against other principles of political organization.

The Argument from Efficiency

Certain doubts come immediately to mind when we consider the case for pure democracy. The first reservation is a purely pragmatic one—it will not work, except perhaps in only the smallest and most intimate groups and associations.

Any workable political system must somehow reconcile participation with efficiency in coming to conclusions. Debate cannot become interminable. Political order should provide means for conflict resolution rather than sustaining divisiveness in a community. Political institutions should be designed so that people have incentives to arrive at agreements on common purposes.

The idea that no person should be bound by any decision that has not personally been consented to seems to lead to the rule of unanimous consent. Yet, we normally believe that majority rule is a principle compatible with democracy.[12] Normally, we consider majority consent necessary on grounds of expediency. It is simply easier to get a majority vote than to continue debate until a position satisfactory to

---

[10] *Edward Grubb,* What is Quakerism? *(London: Allen and Unwin, 1940), p. 94; William Comfort,* Just Among Friends *(New York: MacMillan, 1941), p. 92.*

[11] *Students for a Democratic Society, "The Port Huron Statement," in Robert A. Goldwin (Ed.),* How Democratic Is America? *(Chicago: Rand, McNally, 1972), pp. 1–16.*

everyone is found. However, majority rule can also be shown to be consistent with democratic principles. It may be true that those who voted with the minority have not consented to a decision that is binding on them, but we argue that in establishing majority rule, all members have tacitly consented to accept decisions favored by the greater number.

Further, it would seem that majority rule is consistent with the principle of equality—that no person should count for more than one in making decisions. In a system of unanimity, by what right can one individual frustrate an action desired by the rest? Does this not make the opponent infinitely more powerful than all the other members? To justify a "veto" power of a minority, it would seem that we would have to establish a separate rule that does not necessarily follow from the logic of democracy—that no collective action will be taken that hurts anyone in their own estimation.

However, majority rule poses further dilemmas. Is it not possible that a "permanent majority" will exploit and suppress small and powerless minorities? Is not majority tyranny as threatening as the power of a single individual to dominate others? This is a very real problem—as in such areas as discrimination against racial minorities. Many feel that it is a basic flaw in democratic theory. It has perplexed political theorists through the ages.[13]

Is the majority entitled to do anything it pleases? Can it expel those it does not like from the organization, or more seriously in the case of nations, can it subjugate the weaker members of the population or decide on a policy of genocide against a minority group? A fuller account of the idea of democracy has to include the structure of rights in the organization, the idea of limited government, and the principle of majority rule. These are complementary principles. The majority may only bind all members to purposes that are consistent with the constitutional powers of the organization.

At the very least, for majority rule to be consistent with democratic theory, we have to stipulate other rules and institutions, for our effec-

---

[12] *There are in fact some cases where we do think unanimity is appropriate. For example:*

   A. Trial by jury. *Here we want to "stack the deck" against a particular decision (conviction) by requiring unanimous consent. The same principle applies when we require "qualified majorities" (two-thirds, three-quarters) for important decisions or constitutional amendments.*

   B. Where the group is very homogeneous. *As in the Quaker meeting, where there is a strong consensus on basic values and the group is tightly integrated, the rule of unanimity may be a real possibility. In fact, many political organizations take few votes in making policies. In many committees, governing boards, and the more peaceful university departments, the effective rule of procedure is consensus.*

[13] *For example, see James Madison's consideration of the problem in* Federal Paper No. 10. Alexander Hamilton, James Madison, and John Jay, The Federalist, Or the New Constitution *(New York: E. P. Dutton, 1911), pp. 41–48.*

tive principle must be *majority rule with the ability of any minority to become a majority at some future time.* At a minimum, this would require:

1. Periodic, competitive elections.
2. Guarantees of freedom of expression and political organiza tion.
3. Procedures so that any individual can advocate a policy proposal and have it voted on as an alternative for public action. (The agenda of problems and possibilities is not restricted to that favored by the majority.)[14]

Efficiency and Authority We frequently endorse political systems that are less than fully democratic simply on the grounds of efficiency. Fully democratic procedure frequently seems wasteful, frustrating, and time-consuming. Too much participation and debate may heighten conflicts rather than resolve them. We want to get the public business transacted and go on to other things. It may be that political participation is good for the individual and the community, but none of us wants to spend all of our time—or frankly, very much of it—in political activity.[15]

If in a community of 30,000 people, each individual was given ten minutes speaking time, it would take at least 220 days, day and night, to resolve any issue. Either everybody would *not* be an equal participant, or the community would engage in very few collective decisions. Hence, in any group, we simplify and structure the process of decision making, so that we can get the public business done. We give the presiding officer power to control the agenda and direct debate. We insist—sometimes with considerable impatience—that routine items be disposed of by officials and that the full assembly not waste their time on them. We appoint committees with the authority to study a problem and report back their findings to the body as a whole.

To a large extent, reducing democracy in an organization is a sign of growing trust in it and in its political system. As organizations mature, there is a tendency to put more authority in the hands of officials, to "routinize" the conduct of business. Participation becomes reduced to electing these officials, hearing their reports and adopting them, usually after only limited debate. It is only when there is a crisis of confidence in the leadership that reform in the direction of restoring the vitality of democratic procedures is sought.

The Argument from Competence

One of the most challenging arguments against majority rule is found in Henrik Ibsen's play, *An Enemy of the People.* In this play, the central

---

[14] *Robert A. Dahl,* A Preface to Democratic Theory, *pp. 63–84.*
[15] *Robert A. Dahl,* After the Revolution? *(New Haven: Yale University Press, 1970), p. 44*

character, Dr. Stockmann, discovers that the mineral springs, around which his town's tourist industry has been built, are polluted and insists that they be closed, for he fears an outbreak of epidemic disease. However, the community insists that the local economy depends on the tourists who come to swim and bathe in the waters and that it is the will of the majority that they remain open. Extreme pressure is put on Dr. Stockmann not to publish his findings and jeopardize the future of the town. But he remains adamant and, in the end, is declared an "enemy of the people" by unanimous vote of the town meeting and is driven from the community. Ibsen's point is obvious; democracy does not always result in "better" political decisions.[16]

We do not always conclude that all members have equal ability to make public decisions. Some kinds of policymaking require specialized, expert knowledge. The problem is to determine when expert standards, rather than the expressed will of the people, should be binding on the community. Consider the following. In which cases do you think that expert judgment is better than democratic decision?

A. The safety of atomic power plants should be decided by scientists rather than popular vote.

B. Legal insanity should be decided by psychiatrists rather than juries.

C. "Good design" criteria for buildings, advertising signs, and downtown areas should be decided by architects and city planners rather than by popular consent (or by "politicians").

D. Military affairs should be left to generals rather than politicians.

A central problem of political design, then, is to decide when expert judgment should prevail over popular consent. We face this problem whenever we have reason to believe that there are clear-cut criteria that ought to be applied in making a decision, and that how those criteria ought to be applied is not a matter in which one person's judgment is as good as any other. We do, after all, believe that some issues ought to be settled by a court of law rather than by majority consent, and that the advice of medical doctors ought to weigh decisively in making decisions on public health issues.

To opt for expert competence over popular consent need not imply that we believe that specialists have "all the right answers" or are somehow in possession of absolute truth about what ought to be done. Experts seldom agree entirely on any policy question. But this is no cause for disillusionment. What we are in effect saying when we opt for competence over popular consent is that the argument ought to be

---

[16] *This play, which is an excellent study of politics at a number of levels, is found in Henrik Ibsen,* Four Major Plays, *vol. II (New York: New American Library, 1969).*

settled according to the rules and standards of a particular profession and that the views of those who know these rules and standards ought to carry greater weight in decision making than the views of those who do not. Thus, we acknowledge that economists have very different views on economic policy, but we may nonetheless believe that economic policy issues ought to be resolved in terms of the criteria of judgment applied by professional economists. Similarly, we know that the Supreme Court often divides on the interpretation of the law, but we do not therefore conclude that any citizen's judgment on the law is as good as that of any justice of the Supreme Court.

However, if we do decide that competence is to be preferred over consent in a specific field of policymaking, we have to satisfy ourselves that professional criteria are *relevant* to the issue at hand. The views of a public health doctor, such as Ibsen's Dr. Stockmann, might be the right ones to apply to epidemic control. But while nuclear scientists might be the right ones to decide whether a new type of bomb *can* be built, their professional standards might not be appropriate to deciding *if* it should be built. Of the aggressive Air Force general who created the Strategic Air Command, John F. Kennedy once said, "It's good to have men like Curt LeMay commanding troops once you decide to go in, but these men aren't the only ones you should listen to when you decide whether to go in or not."[17]

The Argument from Responsibility

A position closely related to the argument from competence is that better decisions will result if authority is vested in a specialized group of decisionmakers, whether they have expert training and knowledge or not. In the mass, people are apt to be uninformed and apathetic. The individual citizen is not apt to take the process of public choice very seriously. His role in the outcome is very small and he knows it. As Joseph Schumpeter said, the citizen realizes that "he is a member of an unworkable committee, the committee of the whole nation, and this is why he expends less disciplined effort on mastering a political problem than he expends on a game of bridge."[18] The citizen realizes that he is not really responsible for the fate of society, and this diminished sense of responsibility leads him to devote little effort to public problems.

The advantage of specialized policymakers is that they can and must devote concentrated attention to public affairs. Decisionmaking becomes a full-time, professional job. And they know that their responsibility is direct and immediate. Consequences can be traced

[17] *Arthur Schlesinger, Jr.,* A Thousand Days: John F. Kennedy in the White House, *pp. 832–833.*

[18] *Joseph A. Schumpeter,* Capitalism, Socialism and Democracy, *Third Edition (New York: Harper and Bros., 1962), p. 261.*

directly to the decisions they take. Furthermore, the view of the individual citizen is partial and incomplete. He tends to evaluate policies according to their impact on him—in his own particular situation in society. Only the specialized policymaker is in a position to consider the welfare of society as a whole. (Of course, it could be that he is actually considering how to perpetuate himself in power!) But for democratic theorists like Schumpeter, the role of the people should be limited to selecting a *government*—to voting on leaders who are vested with authority to make decisions on their behalf.

summary

In considering how democratic a particular political system should be, we have to weigh the importance of the following factors.

1. The classic argument that all have an equal right to political participation—that a permanent ruling class cannot be justified.
2. The value of direct participation to the personal development of the individual and the morale of the community.
3. The "completeness" of the decision-making process—the assurance that the final decision will reflect the full implications of public choice as they are perceived and experienced by various sectors of the community.
4. The ability of the community to control the power vested in policymakers.
5. The question of efficiency—how much time people can reasonably be expected to devote to public affairs, and the capacity of the system to make policy without unnecessary delay.
6. The question of whether "expert judgment" is more appropriate than the individual judgments of citizens for the particular *kind* of policy at issue.
7. Whether a specialized group of decision makers or direct participation will result in more responsible, conscientiously considered and informed decisions.

These are the issues of political design and democracy that we would face either in a new organization or an existing one—whenever the question of basic structure and operating rules arises. They tell us something about what is at stake when we decide on questions of political form. But a consideration of these principles does not complete our study of political architecture. Now we have to consider the fundamentals of political form itself—what processes and functions

have to be provided for in any type of government. The question of
how these principles can be applied to the actual design of any political
system is the subject of the next chapter.

*further
ling*

Buchanan, James M., and Gordon Tullock, *The Calculus of Consent*
(Ann Arbor: University of Michigan Press, 1962). The creation of
political institutions is here treated as a problem of rational
calculation by self-interested individuals. A difficult, challenging
book.

Dahl, Robert A., *After the Revolution?: Authority in a Good Society* (New
Haven: Yale University Press, 1970). A very useful discussion of
the question, "how much democracy?" in the design of political
institutions.

Friedrich, Carl F., *Man and His Government* (New York: McGraw-Hill,
1963). A monumental study, which goes far beyond this chapter in
dealing with the problem of political architecture.

Huntington, Samuel P., *Political Order in Changing Societies* (New
Haven: Yale University Press, 1968). This book is central to
understanding the total process of political development and the
creation of political order. A broad, comparative treatment.

Mayo, Henry B., *An Introduction to Democratic Theory* (New York:
Oxford University Press, 1960). A standard work on the major
issues of democratic theory. A bit dated, and I find it dull, but
others think it is basic.

Madison, James, Alexander Hamilton, and John Jay, *The Federalist*,
Max Beloff (Ed.) (New York: Oxford University Press, 1948). Many
other editions are available. Still a crucial work for anyone who
would understand the arts of political architecture and the nature
of political argument.

Schumpeter, Joseph A., *Capitalism, Socialism and Democracy*, Third
Edition (New York: Harper and Bros., 1962). Especially good as a
skeptical view of the classic democratic ideal.

Thorson, Thomas L., *The Logic of Democracy* (New York: Holt, Rinehart
and Winston, 1962). A very clearly reasoned defense of democracy
and a philosophic justification of a particular conception of
democratic government.

chapter
twelve
designing
for decision

Aristotle, who might be called the first political scientist, thought that neither pure democracy nor rule by the few could provide the ideal basis for political order. The best government would be a mixed system, a balancing of the principles of participation and authority.

The significance of this idea becomes apparent when we consider the choices we actually do make in designing political institutions. When a relatively simple political system like a committee is first created, the members usually act quickly to impose some form and structure on their activities. An order of business and a procedure for debate and voting are established. A chairman may be selected. Perhaps this person will be empowered only to preside and direct debate, but perhaps the chairman will be expected to be an active leader, to give overall direction to the affairs of the body, and to see that decisions are carried out. As the committee develops, subcommittees may be appointed; a staff of employees may be created.

Most political systems are complex combinations of democratic and hierarchic principles. There are some almost pure authority systems—the army might be an example—and we have noted the Quaker meeting as an almost pure participatory democracy. But most political systems are more intricate. Complex organizations like corporations, universities, and governments involve very elaborate combinations of authority and participation structures.[1] Any national

[1] On the mixture of participation and authority in the corporate structure of General Motors, see Peter F. Drucker, The Concept of the Corporation (New York: New American Library, 1964).

political system, whether formally classified as a dictatorship or a democracy, will in fact contain elements both of participation and centralized power, often in intricate and seemingly contradictory combinations.

In making choices about the design of organizations, we have to decide when, where, and for what purposes we want to create authority structures and when, where, and for what purposes we want popular participation. To get at this problem, it is useful to look at a political system as a decision-making mechanism. A prime purpose of political design is to systematize the process of decision making for a community. The problem of political architecture becomes that of creating institutions and processes that will predictably generate workable and acceptable decisions and put them into effect.

A stable political system must meet new challenges over time. A government, as Karl Deutsch has noted, is a self-steering mechanism.[2] At its best, it enables a community to cope with an unknown and unforeseeable future. The basic issue is to reconcile the fullest consideration of alternatives with efficiency in coming to conclusions. The extremes to be avoided are the "debating society," which is still arguing about what to do long after the time for action has passed, and the dictatorship, which can be quick, effective, decisive, and also dead wrong.

the fundamentals of a decision-making system

In evaluating a political system, and in formulating a case for continuity or change in its institutions, it is useful to focus on the functions that must be performed in arriving at and carrying out public decisions. One way to do this is to break down the process of decision making into its component parts.

1. *Initiation.* How is the political process to be set in motion? How do policymakers become aware of problems and proposals for public action? At any time, in any community, there is a virtually unlimited supply of potential public issues. Almost every citizen occasionally feels that "there ought to be a law." How are the interests and ideas of ordinary members to be channeled so that they can become the subject of policymaking?
2. *Agenda-setting.* No political system can cope simultaneously with every problem and interest in the community. How then to select some issues for concentrated attention, establish an

---

[2] *Karl W. Deutsch,* The Nerves of Government *(New York: The Free Press, 1966), pp. 182–199.*

order of priorities, and relegate the rest to the background?

3. *Formulating alternatives.* How to move from inchoate problems and ideas to concrete proposals for action? Some system must be created for planning, for gathering information, assessing alternative lines of action, estimating the relative efficiency and effectiveness of various possibilities, examining potential consequences and side effects, and so forth.

4. *Deliberation.* How to structure the public debate? What kinds of forums should be created for the confrontation of rival advocates? How to devise institutions that maximize the chances for the "creation of agreement," bargaining, compromise, and persuasion? How to appraise policymakers of the implications of choice as seen from the point of view of various interests, and various perspectives on the principles and stakes involved?

5. *Enactment.* How will debate culminate in a public decision, binding on the community as a whole? Who will be entitled to make the final decision?[3]

6. *Implementation.* How is a decision to be put into effect? How do we organize to carry out a project? How is compliance with rules to be enforced? How will we decide on the application of rules in specific cases?

A political system does not always have to operate precisely in this order. The stages in the process become intertwined and frequently fold back into one another. In the course of implementation, we may identify new problems that require the reconsideration of policy. Or administrators may have to decide between alternative ways of carrying out a project, and they will then establish a subsystem of the entire process to deliberate various possibilities and decide among them. No matter how neat and logical our formal design for decision, it will become complex and convoluted with usage. In analyzing a policymaking system, we have to look not only at the formal structure but also at all the informal processes and understandings that have grown up around it. These too, of course, are the products of choices made about the design of institutions. When we implicitly agree to turn routine matters over to the chairman, though the charter says that the board of directors has the power to act on them, we are changing the structure of the organization every bit as much as if we had formally amended the charter.

---

[3] *It should be noted that there may be a distinction between* enactment *and* ratification, *between those institutions actually used to make decisions and those more ceremonial forms that signal that a community is committed to a course of action. For example, in Great Britain, Parliament makes laws, but they only come into force officially when the queen signs them. Yet the queen plays no real role in policymaking. Her consent is a formality.*

n deciding how democratic a political system ought to be, we have to
ask what it is we are trying to accomplish through participation and
through concentrated power and authority in the hands of officials.
Why do we want ordinary members to become involved at some points
in the process, and *why* do we want them excluded, or their participation limited, at others?

In societies with a strong commitment to democratic principles,
there is usually a presumption that the process of initiation ought to be
as open as possible. Everyone ought to have a chance to "speak their
mind." There should be effective channels of communication between
citizens and policymakers. This does not mean, we note, that every
voice ought to be heeded, only that it should be heard. In dictatorships, the problem is otherwise. Then the question of political design is
one of how to *prevent* certain ideas or groups from being heard at all. In
a country like the Soviet Union the issue is how to prevent alien ideas
like liberalism from "corrupting" the society. The single-party system
assures that the interests that are heard are the "right" ones, those
sympathetic to the system. Repression and persecution are used
against those who choose to think otherwise. Of course, formally
democratic systems are not immune from such practices. In the United
States, as in every Western society, a great deal of thought and care has
often been given by those in power to the problem of how certain
groups can be effectively excluded from the political process.

However, if we are committed to the view that, at the point of
initiation, the democratic principle ought to apply as fully as possible,
the problem becomes one of how to achieve involvement and participation. The largely negative guarantees of political rights—freedom of
speech, assembly, and the press—really only assure that the most
interested and active and the best organized will be heard.

The problem may be one of identifying those groups that are not
getting a fair hearing and creating corrective measures. Through political structure, we might try to reduce the imbalance in the flow of
information from the most articulate and the least articulate sectors of
the population.

In recent years, a number of government programs have been
designed to encourage political participation by the poor and minority
groups. The Community Action Programs of the late 1960s are one of
the best examples. In these projects, control of a specific government
program was vested in a board representing the residents of a neighborhood rather than being administered directly by federal, state, or
city government agencies. The idea was that the citizens of a community in an inner city or ghetto area knew their own needs in such fields as
urban renewal, public health, job training, or education better than
remote policymakers or administrators. An effort was made to secure

the "maximum feasible participation" of the poor. Congress, in the law that created the program in 1967, specified that one-third of the representatives on the Community Action Program boards must be chosen from the poor and minority groups. Although it was often difficult to overcome suspicion and apathy, the system did in fact stimulate participation among groups that had previously been almost entirely outside the political process. Nonetheless, questions can be asked about how democratic such participation was in fact. Daniel P. Moynihan notes that very small proportions of eligible voters —sometimes less than 5 percent—actually voted in elections for Community Action Program boards. Perhaps the effect was as much as anything to develop leadership groups, new elites among the minorities and the poor.[4]

If we do decide on an active policy of representing the unrepresented, we face a second important problem. If we structure participation according to some conception of the interests that exist in the community, are we not predetermining who has a right to be heard? We may decide that minorities, or the young, or the elderly, or any other group, is not sufficiently active in the organization, and that their interests are being ignored. But if we consciously attempt to organize them, or, failing that, if we appoint a representative to speak for them, how can we be sure that the spokesman thus created actually represents the interests and ideas of the group? Perhaps people do not see their interests in terms of youth or age or ethnicity, but occupation or social class. Any system of representation will bias the information that policymakers receive. The structure of participation we adopt at this level will affect the substance of policy, for it will determine which issues and problems get attention and which do not. Nonetheless, despite the risks and the difficulties, it is sometimes desirable to structure channels of communication for the least organized and articulate members of the organization, lest they be ignored altogether.

agenda setting

At some point, the problem of designing a policymaking system becomes not that of increasing participation, but of channeling, codifying, and simplifying it. We cannot deal with everything at once. Decisions have to be made on priority problems and on an order of business.

In simple bodies like committees, the chairman may be empow-

[4] Daniel P. Moynihan, Maximum Feasible Misunderstanding (New York: The Free Press, 1969); Ralph M. Kramer, Participation of the Poor (Englewood Cliffs, N.J.: Prentice-Hall, 1969); John Strange, "Citizen Participation in Community Action Programs," Public Administration Review 32 (October 1972), pp. 276–280.

red to set the agenda. Old business is considered first. New issues are introduced at the end of the meeting. *Robert's Rules of Order* provides a minimum system for setting priorities. A motion, made and seconded, focuses debate on a single item. No further issues may be considered until that problem is settled.

In complex, bureaucratic organizations, the agenda-setting function is normally performed by top officials or the board of directors. In legislative bodies, committees often do this job. In the United States Congress, the 10,000 to 15,000 bills introduced each session are assigned to committees, which study them, sometimes revise them, and decide which to report for consideration by the House as a whole. In the House of Representatives, the bills reported by committees then pass through a rules committee which establishes the order of debate. In the Senate, this is normally decided by the leadership of the two parties.

In this phase of policymaking, we normally opt for some measure of authority over democratic principle. Each individual obviously thinks that his own ideas and problems are the most urgent, but someone has to determine which interests and issues are more significant for the community as a whole. Yet there are dangers here. The ability to set the agenda provides a formidable base of power. Those who have this authority can advance the issues they endorse and ignore others. This power can be used to build a personal base of support; it can be used to reward friends and punish enemies.

The chairmen of congressional committees have the authority to call committee meetings, determine the order of consideration of bills, and refer them to subcommittees for study. This is a power that can be wielded in an autocratic manner. Chairmen can advance the particular interests of their constituents by making sure that bills favorable to them get privileged attention. Thus, a chairman of the House Committee on Agriculture, who normally will come from a rural area, can make sure that policies favorable to farmers from his section of the country get quick action. A chairman of a committee dealing with defense appropriations may make sure that military installations in his own district are not affected by an economy drive. Chairmen of strategic committees, such as Ways and Means in the House, have extraordinary influence over the tax policies of government as a whole. To be sure, a majority of the committee can overrule the chairman's decisions on priorities. But this is a power to be used guardedly. Rebellion on one issue may lead to retaliation later, as the chairman decides to "pigeonhole" a bill much desired by the recalcitrant junior member. All congressmen are not created equal.

While the system has long been criticized, there is little consensus on an alternative. There has to be some process of deciding on priorities. Committee chairmen are formally elected by the caucus of the majority party in Congress, though the rule of seniority is normally applied—the member with the longest consecutive service on the committee becomes the chairman, all other considerations being equal. From time to time, as new generations of younger congressmen with ideas and priorities that differ from those of the elder politicians are elected, there are attacks on the system, and some senior chairmen are displaced, but there has never been a complete overhaul of the system. The rule of seniority itself may seem indefensible. It seems to give crucial power simply to those who have managed to get reelected time after time. Yet many fear that the alternatives would be worse. The agenda-setting power is so strategic that an open struggle for power over committee chairmenships could tear the party in Congress apart. It would necessarily lead to complex compromises and trade-offs that might not improve the quality of leadership in the legislature or make it more representative.

In any organization, the system of setting priorities will eventually become controversial. Those who feel that the power is being used to frustrate their interests will urge that the system be democratized, made more responsive to the will of the members. The issue is apt to be recurrent, for any agenda-setting decision will seem arbitrary to some.

What checks can be placed on the power of the agenda setters? Competitive election is the obvious answer, perhaps coupled with some procedure for submitting disputes to the determination of the legislative body or the membership as a whole. But there are limits beyond which the process of democratization becomes ineffective. In any complex body, where there are real differences and cleavages, the membership as a whole is seldom capable of doing an effective or fair job of setting priorities. Most of us have at one time or another participated in a meeting ostensibly run by rules of parliamentary procedure, which eventually became so confused and convoluted after various motions, amendments, and points of order that the only way to get the business done was to remove the problem of structuring the debate and the order of business from the control of the body as a whole and placing it in the hands of authoritative decision makers.

formulating alternatives and planning

When an assembly is faced with a problem, debate on what to do about it often becomes desultory, confused, and inconclusive. The matter requires "further study," detailed consideration in a more systematic way than is possible in a large body. Once again, we retreat from the democratic principle of full and equal participation in the name of efficiency and competence. We appoint a subcommittee, or we refer the matter to a staff of professionals.

Planning and policy formulation are tasks that seem to require expert analysis. The top officials, the legislators or the individual members cannot be expected to be conversant with the detailed implications of every subject of public decision. Evaluating the impact of a taxation system requires the skills of the trained economist. In appraising the efficiency of a transportation system, we need the advice of planners, engineers, and policy analysts. Even in a legislature made up mainly of lawyers, professional legal counsel is normally employed to aid in drafting bills.

The policy analyst or adviser need not be a specialist. Frequently, such a person is a "generalist," a professional public servant. The policy adviser is familiar with the workings of government and with the backgound and peculiar characteristics of a particular field of public policy. Neutrality and imparitality are reflected in his ability to work with a succession of partisan policymakers—to give them the best possible judgment and to cooperate in achieving their distinctive policy objectives. The task is to clarify problems, to delineate options, and to work out detailed programs for achieving the policy objectives that are set by policymakers.[5]

When we reach the stage of formulating concrete proposals in the policymaking process, we often opt for efficiency and competence over democratic principle. Yet there are dangers here. Experts and professionals are not without their own biases. Policy advisers can structure the information that policymakers receive in such a way as to make the options they prefer seem especially attractive and to exclude other possibilities. Furthermore, the power to appoint the professional staff can be an important political resource. Unless "neutral competence" is a strong tradition in the organization, advisers may feel that their primary loyalty is to those who appointed them rather than to the "public interest." Top officials appoint experts who agree with what they want to do, and expect them to provide a justification for the policies they are trying to advance. They select attorneys who will "make their programs legal," and find economists or professors who will "prove" that their policies are "scientifically correct."

Apart from trying to create a career civil service, protected against partisan pressures by permanent appointments, a tradition of impartiality and objectivity, and the expectation that they may have to serve the interests of one party today and another tomorrow, there are other ways of trying to get around this problem in the design of decision-making syttems. Each involves balancing an element of democratic process and participation against the principle of expert competence and efficiency.

The first of these is adversary planning. Instead of delegating the detailed study of policy alternatives to a single staff of advisers, we create rival groups of experts, each with different biases, preconcep-

[5] Hugh Heclo, "The OMB and the Presidency–the Problem of Neutral Competence," The Public Interest 38 (Winter 1975), pp. 80–98.

tions, and favored policy proposals. Each group works out the rationale for a different plan of action, and the rival proposals are argued before the policymaking body. The object is not to select a staff on the basis of neutral competence but to seek out, intentionally, advisers and specialists with strong ideas and different points of view. In some sense, we represent the divisions of opinion that exist in any profession in the planning process.[6]

Adversary planning recognizes that experts are seldom neutral. They have their own values and goals for public policy. Many enter government service because they want to see their views prevail. The civil servant who carefully cultivates neutrality and avoids controversies may not be the best policy adviser. In fact, passionate commitment may often be the mark of a really dedicated and well-informed professional. After all, when it comes to formulating programs, we want the help of someone who is able to make up their mind. It is less helpful to receive a report that says "on the one hand this, and on the other hand that." Adversary planning may be a way of making the commitments and sharply divergent views of specialists useful in the policy process, while ensuring that we do not get just one side of the story.

Adversary planning may also be useful in assuring that various interests in the community get a hearing in policy formation. Perhaps as public problems become more complex, democratic process can only be assured if different interest groups are provided with professional advisers as skilled and competent as those who work for government itself. To be sure, powerful interest organizations in business, labor, and other fields already employ not only lobbyists but also large research staffs of lawyers, economists, and other professionals. However, many have argued that it is also essential to provide "advocate planners" to groups that are normally unrepresented in the political process. Just as indigent defendants are entitled to have a public defender represent them in court, the poor and minorities might be assisted by competent professionals, paid for by public funds, to "take their side" in their relationships with government agencies. For example, trained policy analysts might aid welfare clients in developing a technically competent statement of their interests to counter the analyses made by the advisers to welfare agencies. Or small towns might be assisted by transportation or land use experts who could scrutinize and challenge the proposals of state or national planning authorities when these affect local interests.[7]

---

[6] *See Alexander L. George, "The Case for Multiple Advocacy in Making Foreign Power,"* American Political Science Review 66 *(September 1972), pp. 751–785.*

[7] *Lewis C. Mainzer,* Political Bureaucracy *(Glenview, Ill.: Scott, Foresman, 1973), pp. 132–135.*

Adversary planning might also be applied to the relationships of legislatures and executive agencies. Many congressmen complain that today's public programs are so complex and hard to understand that the legislator and his few assistants are at a great disadvantage when trying to evaluate the detailed testimony provided by staff experts from government bureaus who appear before them to justify their budget requests or policy proposals. In the field of military policy, for example, few congressmen have the expertise to challenge and question the proposals and priorities presented by the Defense Department. Is a new missile system really needed? Could it be built more cheaply or efficiently? Such questions require a detailed knowledge of military strategy, intelligence estimates of the capabilities and intentions of possible foes, technical sophistication about the engineering problems of advanced weaponry, and a thorough understanding of military contracts and the economics of the industries that provide the weapons. Perhaps Congress can only play its role in a representative system of controlling and checking the executive branch if it has the advice of staffs of experts who are the equal of their counterparts in the government agencies.

"Participatory planning" is a second method of balancing democratic procedure against professional competence. Here, planners are required to meet with citizens' groups throughout the process of formulating policy proposals. In planning a shopping mall or a housing development, for example, consultation might begin before initial proposals are drafted and continue throughout the planning process. The planners have to argue out their ideas, step by step, with those who will be affected by them, with the businessmen and shoppers who will use the mall, with the tenants who will live in the housing project. The finished product does not reflect only the judgment of professionals but is the joint product of experts and laymen.

Of course, participatory planning means that planners must learn to be politicians. They must develop the skills of building support for proposals, devising compromises and creating coalitions among rival interests, negotiating with the leaders of various factions, and so on. It can be argued that this is not their job, that planners should be hired to provide their best professional judgment, and that the political issues should be left to politicians.

Another objection would be that participatory planning enables the planner to develop a constituency for his own ideas and proposals, and that this gives him a base of power to be used against those who have formal authority in the political system. The planner should work for the policymakers, opponents will argue, and not become an additional contender in the political process. Once again, no definitive answer can be given to the question of which is the best way to structure this phase of the decision-making process, but these are some of the arguments and factors that should be weighed in making decisions about procedure.[8]

deliberation

But the experts are not the ones who make the final decisions. They "report back" and their recommendations are discussed, debated, revised, and finally accepted or rejected. But to whom should they report back? The next step in the process might be consideration of plans and proposals by the final policymakers—the legislature, board of directors, and the like. But sometimes we want to introduce *more* participation into the process before a final decision is taken.

When facing a difficult or controversial problem, with the recommended course of action on the table, we often feel that it is wise to involve more people in the process of deliberation before taking action. So we say, "This is such an important matter that we should hold a general meeting to discuss it." Or we decide to publicize the idea and wait for responses from the community. Or we provide for a "public hearing" on the matter, and invite anyone who wants to make their views known to appear.[9]

The purposes of deliberation are distinct from those of enactment. We are not yet coming to a conclusion but examining alternatives from the point of view of different interests, criteria of choice, and possible consequences. In a sense, deliberation is a kind of laboratory experiment. Rather than simply putting a policy into effect and seeing what happens, we try to learn how various interests feel they would be affected *if* a particular public action were taken. In this way, we anticipate difficulties, and we may become aware of possible consequences that may have escaped our attention. Perhaps we did not realize that a proposed change in the zoning ordinances would be militantly opposed by a certain group in the community. Perhaps we were not aware that a minor change in the minimum wage laws might mean economic disaster for the state's tourist industry, which depends on part-time or seasonal employees. Through public hearings, general meetings, or publicizing policy proposals, we stimulate various interests to consider how *they* might be affected by a new policy, encourage them to react and add to the store of information available to policymakers.

So it may not be that the body that will *make* the decision is the only body that should participate in debating and deliberating it. By making

---

[8] Paul Davidoff, *"Advocacy and Pluralism in Planning,"* Journal of the American Institute of Planners 31 *(November 1965), pp. 331–338.*

[9] *In many cases, public hearings are legally required before formal action by local governments and other public agencies.*

a distinction between deliberation and decision making and urging the creation of additional institutions in the policymaking process, we are arguing for a more democratic, participatory mode of choice than would otherwise have been the case.

enactment

There comes a point in the affairs of any council or committee when a subtle transformation takes place. The issue has been discussed and debated. It has been assigned to a subcommittee for study, and this group has reported back with a detailed proposal for action. This recommendation has been gone over carefully. Everyone has had their say. All the controversies have been thrashed out. Now there is a pause. The chairman then says, "Well, are we ready to take a vote?" At this point, the nature of the body changes, and the roles of all the members in it. The council is no longer a forum for debate but the center of authoritative choice. The members are no longer advocates. They have become policymakers.

In designing a political system, we have to decide *who* will make final, binding decisions. Will it be the whole membership, a representative assembly, an executive board, or the officials at the top of a hierarchy—the president or manager? Will the rule of decision be consensus, majority, or a qualified majority? Will there be a procedure for *referendum* by which, on petition of a certain number of voters, an issue can be removed from the assembly and the power of decision vested in a majority of the entire membership?

Some of these decisions were no doubt made at the time the organization was founded and are embodied in the charter and constitution. Yet, this is seldom the end of the matter. Deciding on the appropriate mechanisms of choice is an ongoing and recurrent issue. In the course of debating a concrete policy issue, the point will be made that "an issue like this is so important that we should take a vote of the full membership" or "the chairman should take care of minor and routine matters like this." The substance of policy is then put aside while we decide on a matter of procedure. Out of such piecemeal decisions, the constitutional form of the organization evolves and develops.

Here again we face a choice about how much democracy and how much authority we want in the organization. We measure the alternatives against the criteria of efficiency and participation. The chairman *should* make routine decisions if the expectations of the group are fairly clear to everybody. There is no sense wasting time on matters where the outcome is obvious. There is no question that his decisions will be accepted and obeyed. But if the issue is controversial, we fear that the decision of the executive committee or the council might not be accepted as legitimate. Its authority might be questioned, the structure of the organization might be endangered, there might be a schism in the community. Would the decision be more acceptable if it were made by vote of the entire membership? Would this protect the integrity of existing institutions? Would the dissident minority be more likely to see this as a "fairer" way of making the decision and be less likely to leave the organization? Would the general vote really settle the matter? Or would the members feel that the council was avoiding its responsibilities?

The objective is to create viable mechanisms of conflict resolution. Where the stakes are low, or agreement apparent, or there is a high level of support for the authority structure, we can afford to "streamline" the process of decision by referring more and more decisions to the judgment of officers. But when there are important differences of opinion, and mistrust of "the establishment" is becoming apparent, then we may want to increase the level of participation in policymaking.

implementation

Once we have decided *what* to do, we have to organize to get the job done. In planning for the administration of policy, there is usually an initial presumption in favor of efficiency and competence over participation. We assume that the issues have been debated and the various interests heard. We feel that we have reached a final decision through the appropriate processes. Now the problem is to execute the policy. We want administration to be effective, and we want it to be impartial. Rules should be applied and services provided without favoritism. Things should run smoothly, without foul-ups or unnecessary delays. The task of the administrator should be to carry out the expressed will of the community. He or she has no authority, we assume, to decide whether the policy is desirable or not. The job is to find the best way of accomplishing the purposes laid down by the policymakers.

In any large-scale political system—a nation, a state, a big city, or a corporation—we normally associate the task of administration with bureaucratic organization. Bureaucracy is perhaps the dominant form of political organization of our age. Most of us work, or will work, for them, and they affect almost everything we do. The defining characteristic of a bureaucracy is its "rationality." It is like a machine, a systematic organization of people "put together" in relationship to one another to accomplish an overall purpose. As Max Weber, the distinguished German political scientist, wrote, "The decisive reason for the advance of bureaucratic organization has always been its technical superiority over any other form of organization."[10]

---

[10] *Hans Gerth and C. Wright Mills, From Max Weber: Essays in Sociology (New York: Oxford University Press, 1946), p. 214.*

Authority in a bureaucracy is organized from the top down. The overall task is broken down into specialized functions. One individual is in charge of each. The subordinates, in turn, are responsible for particular tasks within that office and so on through the organization. Each individual is accountable to a specific superior. The job of the administrator is to coordinate the work of subordinates so that a specific part of the overall mission of the organization is accomplished efficiently.

In theory, at least, bureaucracy has a variety of virtues. It is efficient. Personnel are selected on the basis of their competence at a particular specialized task. The whole organization is designed to take a complex function, break it down into its component parts, and coordinate a variety of particular tasks in an overall integrated performance. When something goes wrong, the source of the problem can be pinpointed and corrected through the chain-of-command. Bureaucracy is responsible and predictable. Administrators do not make policy but apply known rules according to established criteria. (If the applicant is over sixty-five years of age, and persons over sixty-five are entitled to social security benefits, then the applicant is entitled to benefits.) Ultimately, the top administrator is accountable to the decision makers and, through them, to the community.

Such is the case for bureaucracy in the abstract. In practice, things may work out differently. Bureaucracies may become incompetent and mindless, so bound up in their own rules and procedures that policies, however intelligently formulated, become arbitrary and irrational when they finally reach the citizen. When the individual encounters government, it may be in the person of a bored, impersonal official who has little interest in the needs or rights of the citizen. To get anything done, to actually receive the benefits you are entitled to as a matter of public policy, it may be necessary to penetrate labyrinthine layers of officialdom. The citizen comes to visualize contacts with government as frustrating, time-consuming, and oppressive.

Bureaucracies may become irresponsible. Officials become expert in protecting themselves and their positions, covering up mistakes, avoiding responsibilities. They refine the arts of delay and evasion. "Channels" become not means of control and accountability, but long dark corridors down which many items of public business disappear, perhaps forever. It is not only the citizen who is frustrated but policymakers as well. They cannot control the agencies established to carry out their decisions. Bureaucracy takes on a life of its own. Officials have their own purposes, which may or may not be those of the community.

To check the potential abuses of bureaucracy we might want to introduce elements of democratic practice into the system of implementation, as a safeguard against arbitrariness and irresponsibility in what are otherwise relatively pure authority structures. In designing institutions for the implementation of policy, then, it is worthwhile asking the following questions.

How Are We Going to Ensure that the Actions of Administrators Are Consistent with the Intentions of Policy?

How can policymakers exercise effective control over administrators? There are a variety of possibilities. One is to specify the content of policy in exact detail, to attempt to write regulations that provide for every contingency, and give the administrator little latitude for discretion or choice. The danger here is that we may make policy heavy and inflexible with "red tape." Policymakers cannot anticipate all the detailed implications of what is going to happen in practice. It is, in fact, administration that is most burdened by rules and regulations that leads to irrationality and impersonality in application. Furthermore, the official most bound by detailed rules is the one who is apt to become mechanical and arbitrary in carrying out his job. If the administrator is going to act like a human being, he has to be treated like one—his job has to offer him the opportunity for taking initiative, for exercising judgment, for creativity and growth. The administrator cannot be treated simply like part of a machine. He is part of the process of government. He too is required to make decisions and to exercise political judgment.

Ideally then, political discussion and argument does not end with the policy decision but becomes part of the administrative process as well. It is useful to think in terms of creating "forums" where policymakers and administrators can discuss and debate ongoing policy. The administrator "gives reasons" for the decisions he has made in designing a program for the execution of policy. Close to the impact of policy, the administrator becomes a source of ideas for new programs, or he can point out weaknesses and imperfections in the original policy decision.

In recent years, the budgetary process has become a central focus for this deliberative encounter between policymakers and administrators. The idea of "planning-programming-budgeting" (PPBS) is that the annual budget review be made an opportunity for appraising the programs and progress of government as a whole. Administrators when submitting budget requests for their agencies, are called upon to review their work and to justify their requests. What approach have they been taking to accomplishing the mission of their agency? What are possible alternatives to the existing program? Would any of the alternatives be more efficient or effective? What is the rationale for continuing existing programs and procedures or adopting new ones? The approach is supposed to serve as a check on bureaucratic inertia and routine. Administrators are called upon to think like policymakers, to reconsider their segment of public responsibility, to propose creative alternatives and innovations.

"Pure bureaucracy" envisions the administrator as simply carrying out policy decisions. In a theory of "participatory bureaucracy" the administrator would be seen as part of the policymaking process. The official becomes a source of initiatives, a party to the formulation of alternatives and the deliberation of policy options. Thinking back to the ideas of adversary and participatory planning, we begin to see the possibility of creating institutions—boards, committees—that bring together legislators, top executives, administrative specialists, and perhaps citizens in the process of policy deliberation. The design of the political system becomes less a straight line from initiation to implementation and more a process that folds back on itself, in which each of the processes becomes intertwined with all the rest.

Should Elements of Democratic Participation Be Introduced into Administrative Decision Making?

Many policy decisions do not provide the administrator with detailed criteria and regulations to follow in executing policy. Rather, they offer broad guidelines, and leave it to the administrators to "work out the details." The administrator has considerable latitude and discretion in execution. He or she is very much part of the decision-making process itself.

When this occurs, agenda setting, the formulation and deliberation of alternatives, and actual policy choice is taking place within the bureaucracy. Many decisions of great importance to citizens are made in this way. Safety regulations for airlines, licensing requirements for various occupations, admissions standards for universities, pollution-control regulations, and facilities in public parks are examples of policy decisions that may be made entirely inside bureaucracies. So the question arises of whether, when administrators are in fact making policy decisions, the process of choice should be designed to incorporate the participation of citizens and affected interests. Some states and some federal agencies require public hearings when administrative regulations are being made. (Federal law requires that proposed regulations be published in the *Federal Register* and that interested parties have the opportunity to present written opinions, but there are liberal provisions for exemption even from this minimal provision for participation.)

Some administrative institutions provide for "advisory councils" of citizen groups who participate in important administrative decisions. However, there are dangers here. The detailed, technical work of administrative regulation is of little interest to the ordinary citizen, and those most likely to participate in such councils (or to appear at public hearings) are those who have a direct interest in the work of the agency. Such "representative institutions" may do little more than create a comfortable and cooperative relationship between the regulators and the regulated. There is always a danger that government agencies will serve the interests of their "clients" rather than the community as a whole. Participatory institutions may only legitimate the kinds of informal influence between administrators and affected interests that often undermine the integrity of the administrative process.

Sometimes the appropriate mechanism for introducing participation into bureaucracy will be not an advisory council or a hearing procedure but a judicial process. Many federal regulatory agencies (such as the Interstate Commerce Commission of the Federal Communications Commission) operate very much like a court. In applying rules to specific cases, the administrator is, in effect, interpreting law. His actions will impose penalties on individuals or provide them with benefits. Especially when the policy guidelines are broad and vague, the administrative agency may in fact be making law, much as a court does. Decisions in one case will set precedents for later actions. For example, "deceptive advertising" is against the law. But what "deceptive" means in advertising is determined by the Federal Trade Commission, on a case-by-case basis. If a food manufacturer uses the slogan that his product is "better for your health," the question arises, Better than what? Must he prove that the product actually promotes health, and introduce medical evidence to that effect? Or would it be sufficient to show that the product is not injurious to health? Or is the question whether the product is "healthier" than that of his competitor? To answer such questions, an adversary procedure is called for, with both the party protesting against the advertising slogan and the manufacturer given an opportunity to present evidence and testimony—to make their case in a courtlike atmosphere.

How Do We Protect Individuals Against Abuses of Administrative Power?

What can the citizen do if he feels that policies are being applied arbitrarily or unfairly? In any organization, we have to develop procedures to deal with individual complaints, and in so doing, we introduce elements of the democratic principle that individuals ought to have some control over decisions that affect them. Businesses have to create processes for dealing with the complaints of customers, universities procedures for disputes between teachers or deans and students, governments for appeals against the decisions of officials. Once again, we come up against the problem of how we adjudicate fairly in cases of conflict between the powers of the organization and the rights of the individual.

Depending on the nature of the organization, the right of appeal may be directly to the policymakers—to the governing board or legislative body—or special tribunals may be created—a judicial system within the organization—to hear cases on conflicts of this type using procedures like those of a court of law.

In the Scandinavian countries, and in some American governmental units, there is an official called the ombudsman whose job is to investigate and act on complaints by citizens against the performance of administrators. This official is paid by the legislature and is, in a sense, the "citizen's advocate" against the bureaucracy. The ombudsman has the power to investigate and make recommendations for improvements, to publicize instances of administrative arbitrariness, inefficiency, or delay, and in some cases, he may prosecute illegal or corrupt administrative actions in the courts.[11]

In creating structures to carry out policy, then, we have to decide how the rights of citizens will be protected. In small organizations, appeal directly to policymakers may be sufficient. Where there is an effective system of representation, the legislator may be able to act as the citizen's advocate. (In fact, most congressmen in the United States spend a considerable amount of time investigating problems of their constituents with administrative agencies.) However, as the organization grows in complexity, it becomes necessary to consider rights of appeal and hearings procedures—the right to a fair trial in cases of disputes between officials and individuals. And the ombudsman institution suggests the possibility of a special officer whose only duty is to look into complaints and problems of individuals.

mary

Issues of political organization can be heated and controversial. When we have to make judgments on problems of this kind, it is worthwhile first to ask what *aspect* of the decision-making process is being debated. In political argument, such distinctions are seldom clearly made. However, whether we accept the proposition that the organization ought to be made more democratic or more efficient often depends on the particular policymaking function that is at issue, whether we are talking about the initiatory phase, agenda setting, policy planning, deliberation of plans and proposals, enactment, or implementation. In

---

[11] *See Walter Gellhorn,* Ombudsmen and Others: Citizens' Protectors in Nine Countries *(Cambridge: Harvard University Press, 1966); Donald C. Rowat (Ed.),* The Ombudsman: Citizen's Defender *(London: Allen and Unwin, 1965).*

designing political institutions, and in arguments that concern institutional design, it is important to think through *who* should perform these functions, *how* they should be organized, and *what power* they should have. In this way, the big questions of democracy and authority are brought down to earth and can be applied to the practical problems of political architecture.

for further reading

Berman, Daniel M., *A Bill Becomes a Law: Congress Enacts Civil Rights Legislation,* Second Edition (New York: Macmillan, 1966). A study of Congress as a decision-making system.

Fenno, Richard F., *The Power of the Purse: Appropriations Politics in Congress* (Boston: Little, Brown, 1966). Another fine study of Congress as a political system, focusing on Congressional committees.

Mainzer, Lewis C., *Political Bureaucracy* (Glenview, Ill.: Scott, Foresman, 1973). A very contemporary public administration textbook, which puts a great deal of emphasis on mixing democratic processes into the structure of bureaucratic organizations.

March, James G., and Herbert Simon, *Organizations* (New York: John Wiley, 1958). A classic work on the internal dynamics of administrative organizations.

Moynihan, Daniel P., *Maximum Feasible Misunderstanding* (New York: The Free Press, 1969). A critical appraisal of the effort of Community Action Programs to involve the poor in making decisions on community projects.

Seidman, Harold, *Politics, Position and Power* (New York: Oxford University Press, 1970). A realistic study of the political forces that come to bear on the organization of governmental institutions, and how organization affects power relationships.

Selznick, Philip, *TVA and the Grass Roots: A Study in the Sociology of Formal Organizations* (New York: Harper and Row, 1966). A classic study of the interplay between democracy and authority in the design and operation of a government agency.

Thompson, Victor A., *Modern Organizations* (New York: Alfred A. Knopf, 1961). A reexamination of traditional theories of bureaucracy, with emphasis on the role of professional values in organization and management.

Wilensky, Harold L., *Organizational Intelligence* (New York: Basic Books, 1967). A discussion of the problems of organizing information and intelligence in the formulation and deliberation of public policy.

chapter thirteen the politics of constitution making

In the last two chapters, we outlined some principles of political design. But political structure is not only a question of finding the correct balance between democracy and authority. It is also part of the struggle for power and influence. The art of constitution making, then, is not just the search for the best system of government. It also involves a strategic analysis of power relationships, and the skills of bargaining, negotiation, and compromise. Each faction within the organization will be calculating how any proposal will affect the interests it wants to protect or to advance. The problem then is to find political forms that no crucial interest thinks will operate to its disadvantage. The "founding fathers," no matter how venerated, were not only political philosophers who abstractly contemplated the ideal constitution. They were also practical politicians, who were concerned with the concrete issues of their time and place.

A constitution is a form of conflict resolution. It states the terms of settlement of a political conflict of a particular kind. If everyone saw eye to eye on every issue, there would be no reason to lay out a system for resolving differences. On the other hand, constitutions are not written by those who disagree so completely that they must fight it out to the end or decide to go their separate ways. Rather, constitutions are made by those who expect to disagree vigorously, but who also want to form or to maintain a political community. In constitution making, the search is for points of agreement among people who are simultaneously weighing their personal stakes and interests and those of the community as a whole. For this reason, a constitution, closely examined, gives a good idea of the balance of power in a society or organization at the time it was created. (And, for the same reason, it follows that as power relations change, the constitutional structure will become increasingly controversial, and eventually a new settlement will have to be reached.)

An example from the American frontier illustrates the point. In the early nineteenth century, settlers frequently reached the new lands of the midwest ahead of the government. Legally, they could not occupy the land until it had been officially surveyed and registered. In fact, they created governments of their own, "claims associations," to resolve disputes and to protect claims against land speculators. The need for government arose out of the conflict of private interests. The journal of one of the founders of such an association, Jason Lathrop, in the Pike Creek region of southern Wisconsin, speaks of the problem:

> Much conflicting interest was manifest between the settlers, from the first, in making their claims. Some were greedy in securing at least one section of 640 acres for themselves, and some as much for all their friends who expected to settle in the country. Before the lands were surveyed, this often brought confusion and disputes with reference to boundary lines . . . . These contentions often led to bitter quarrels and even bloodshed. . . .

On the one hand, bitter conflict and on the other, agreement to form a political community—the preamble to the constitution of the association they founded states the terms of the bargain at which they arrived.

> Whereas, a union of cooperation of all the inhabitants, will be indispensably necessary . . . for the securing and protecting of our claims; and whereas, we duly appreciate the benefit which may result from such an association, not only in regulating the manner of making and sustaining claims, and settling differences in regard to them, but in securing the same against speculators at the land sale. . . . We, therefore, as well meaning inhabitants, having in view the promotion of the interest of our settlement, and knowing the many advantages derived from unity of feeling and action, do come forward this day, and solemnly pledge ourselves to render each other our mutual assistance in the protection of our just rights. . . .[1]

The settlers created the office of clerk, to record the claims of the members, and a board of censors to adjudicate disputes.

Normally, the politics of constitution making begins with a small group that has a special interest in the creation of a new government or the reform of an old one. They begin a process of negotiation with

---

[1] *James Willard Hurst,* Law and the Conditions of Freedom in the Nineteenth Century United States *(Madison: University of Wisconsin Press, 1967), pp. 3–4.*

those who have power in the community, those whose assent is essential to the success of the project. For the innovators, the stakes of reaching agreement are high. Obviously, they want the new organization. The other powerful groups or individuals may be less enthusiastic. It is then up to the innovators to find the grounds of agreement, to bend and to accommodate to the interests of those who are deemed critical to the outcome.

Seldom is the entire community involved in the process. Not everyone who will be affected participates in the act of creation. As we shall see, the framework of the British constitution was forged over centuries in negotiations between the king and the nobles, later the middle class. The people who would ultimately be governed had little to do with the design. The American constitution was born in the minds of a very small group of advocates of a stronger national system. The details were thrashed out at Philadelphia in a body that was far from representative of the people of the new nation as a whole. Seldom are constitutions made through as democratic a process as happened in the case of the Pike Creek Claims Association, and even here, the system created by the earliest settlers was imposed on the later arrivals. Almost inevitably in the process of constitution making, by the time the people are called upon to participate in the creation of new political arrangements, the stage is set, the crucial bargains have been made, and the basic form of the new system has been decided.

The political arts of constitution making, understood not only as the creation of a total design for government but also as the gradual change and refinement of structure in any organization, is not an exceptional but an everyday part of politics. It is a normal and ongoing part of the process of political choice and judgment for anyone who takes an active role in the life of any organization. But to illustrate this aspect of the art of statecraft, we look to the larger, more epic examples. The experience of the building of the British, American, and Chinese systems of government shows three very different approaches to the work of fashioning political order.

the British constitution

The evolution of the British political system illustrates the point that constitution making is not a once-and-for-all matter. The British do not have a written constitution. There are important documents to be sure—such as Magna Carta (1215), the Acts of Settlement (1701), and the Bill of Rights (1689)—but, basically, for the British, constitution making is understood as the gradual evolution of ancient customs and usages.

The British view their constitutional history as having no beginning. The origins of the distinctive institutions of the nation, the relationship of king and Parliament, the idea of a government under laws established by the community, are deemed to be lost in the mists of the Anglo-Saxon past, before written history. From this point of view, to change is always to restore, and the task of building the political system has appeared as a matter of making repairs and adjustments in an established order, seeking a balance that was supposed to have existed sometime in the past. The key was the tension between king and Parliament. The system always seemed tilted to favor the one or the other. It evolved out of recurrent clashes that led to efforts to restore balance. Each effort leads to the enunciation of principles, rules, and ideals that are preserved and used later to justify subsequent adjustments in the system.

Thus the barons who met on the meadow at Runnymede in 1215 and forced King John to sign the Magna Carta hardly assumed that they were creating a new political system, far less challenging the lawful order. They thought they were doing no more than insisting on historic rights that an unscrupulous king was bent on taking from them.

The central idea of feudalism was contract between lord and vassal. The nation was viewed as a system of such relationships. At the top is the king, whose vassals are the nobility. The lesser nobility are the vassals of the higher nobility. The serfs are the vassals of the lord of their manor. In this context, Magna Carta is hardly a foundation of individual liberty and modern democracy. Rather it is little more than a confirmation of feudal privileges by the nobility who felt that, under John, the king's power had grown too greatly in relation to their own. This is the furthest thing from a revolution, which is meant to change the form of government. Every step confirms established practice. The document itself is in the form of a royal charter. The king's sovereign authority is sustained. It is he who grants the rights and liberties of his subjects. However, there is a further implication. Although the king is the maker of law, he is bound—as is every man—by contracts he had made. Hence the king, though sovereign in his authority, cannot be willful or arbitrary. His government, ultimately, must conform to the laws he has made. The king is under the law.

And, basically, the entire enterprise of Magna Carta is an exercise in practical politics. The fact of the matter was that King John needed money badly. He had lost his domains in France, and inflation had shrunk his real income. His revenue depended on the feudal dues he received through his "contract" with the barons. The nobility were the economic elite of the time. It was they who directly controlled and managed the land. For John to govern, the barons had to be willing to increase their own taxes. Since it was John's fiscal exactions that led the barons to demand the Magna Carta, so it was his financial requirements that led him to acquiesce to their demands.

How could one change taxes to meet new requirements? Obviously, it was not good enough for the king to do so arbitrarily. There were two sides to the feudal contract. A change in a contract requires the consent of both parties. And this requires negotiations between the vassals and the king, a meeting between them. We see in embryonic form the dim outlines of the notion of the "power of the purse" vested in a parliamentary body, the close interdependence between the powers of taxation and representation, the built-in tension between crown and Parliament, executive and legislature, that underlies all of Anglo-American government. But at that moment, the barons of Runnymede hardly thought they were establishing principles of government. They were settling an affair of the moment with the lawful king. And they would hardly have seen Magna Carta itself as the beginning of these ideas. They were reiterating and improving upon the machinery of government that they assumed had been there all along.

It can hardly be said that Magna Carta was signed and the issue then settled. One of John's first acts was to get a papal declaration that the Great Charter was null and void. However, when John died and left the throne to his nine-year-old son, Henry III, it seemed expedient to mobilize support for the young monarch, and one means to this end was to reissue the Magna Carta under his name. But as he grew up, the issue of money once again arose. The king, dedicated to the Roman Catholic Church, engaged in foreign expeditions, in Sicily and France and acquired other obligations on behalf of the pope. By 1258, at the meeting of the Great Council, or Parliament as it was beginning to be called, the nobles required that the king accept a permanent council who "shall have the power to give honest counsel to the king in the government of the realm . . . and to amend and redress all that they see to need amendment and redress . . ."[2] This new assertion of the power of Parliament was solidified and extended under Earl Simon Montfort, a strong and popular leader. In the struggle for balance between royal authority and the nobility, Montfort tipped the scale toward Parliament by introducing a third factor into the situation. He capitalized on his personal support in the country by calling to Parliament, in the king's name, of course, representatives of the smaller independent country farmers and the people of the cities. Later, the lords would sit in one house, the House of Lords, and the representatives of the cities and country districts in another, the House of Commons (1295).

Seen in any period, the British sense for political design is one of making gradual changes in ongoing institutions in response to practical issues of power and policy, generally rooted in the basic problem of

---

[2] *Quoted in Bernard Schwartz,* The Roots of Freedom: A Constitutional History of England *(New York: Hill and Wang, 1967), p. 29.*

finance and taxation. With the passage of time, more and more of the basic relationships of authority and representation were settled.

The crucial idea behind the system is the perennial tension between king and Parliament. In the sixteenth century, the whole of Europe entered a period of national integration and the consolidation of royal power. In Britain, as elsewhere, there was a demand for stronger central authority to advance commerce and economic growth, to curb the excesses of the nobility, to build a national community beyond the parochial limits of the medieval system, and to defend the nation in a period of international power politics set off by the age of empire and the Reformation. But in Britain, the Tudor monarchs (including particularly Henry VII, Henry VIII, and Elizabeth I) consolidated power with the support of active and lively Parliaments, unlike France, where the legislative body ceased to meet in this period, not to be called again until the eve of the Revolution of 1789.[3]

Royal authority grew with the vitality of the Tudor monarchs. Their successors, the Stuarts, attempted to carry the process to its extreme conclusion, declaring monarchical absolutism, attempting to rule without Parliament, and overriding the now firmly established independent courts. Civil war ensued, one king was decapitated and another abdicated. The seventeenth century was one of complex constitutional conflict, which was only resolved in 1689 when Parliament selected William and Mary to occupy the throne. The pattern of constitution making, which essentially settled the form of the modern British state, is by now familiar. Ancient rights were reasserted. The king was restored to his historic prerogatives, but he now was empowered quite visibly by act of Parliament. The king ruled, but he did so by virtue of the will of the people expressed through the legislature. Never again could the king assert a right to rule alone.

The present-day British constitution still reflects the implicit logic of the feudal contract, and the centuries-old process of negotiation and bargaining among the critical forces in the nation. Today, of course, the monarch is a figurehead. His real powers diminished rapidly, especially in the 1700s under George I and George II, who were uninterested in the assertion of royal authority. Today the theory of the constitution is that the monarch rules through her ministers, the cabinet, headed by the prime minister. However, for the cabinet to govern effectively, it must have the support of Parliament. Only Parliament, again, can provide the finances for the operation of government, and of course, no government is legitimate that does not rest on the assent of Parliament.

With the Industrial Revolution, the holders of the concrete resources essential to the operation of the state changed dramatically.

[3] Ibid., p. 105.

The old nobility, controlling agricultural wealth, diminished in influence, and with it, the power of the House of Lords, which in our time plays little more than a symbolic role in the making of law. As the finances of the realm came more and more to depend on industry and business, and later, on the organized working class, as democracy came more and more to be the dominant ideology of Western society, the House of Commons became the center of parliamentary power. Modern political parties emerged in the nineteenth century to organize and mobilize the new voters who were progressively admitted to citizenship. The ancient forms remain, but their significance in the system changes. Today, the British citizen normally votes for one of the two major parties, Labour or Conservative. The leaders of the party that has a majority in the House of Commons are almost automatically chosen by the queen to form the new cabinet, or "government." (If there is a bitter division in the majority party, the queen may have some discretion in the appointment of the new prime minister.) The cabinet governs as long as it enjoys majority support in Parliament, or until the next election, which must occur at least once every five years.[4]

Again following historic usage, the monarch formally "calls" and "dismisses" Parliament. But now she does so at the request of her ministers. The cabinet, then, the executive committee of the majority party, decides when during its five-year tenure is most favorable for their party to have new elections. However, should the cabinet lose its majority in Commons, perhaps because of a split over the policies of the incumbent leaders, the "government"—effectively the prime minister—has two choices. Either it may resign and permit the new majority group to form a government or the prime minister may go to the queen, state that "Her Majesty's Ministers" no longer "enjoy the confidence of Parliament," and ask her to call for new elections, to determine whether the existing cabinet or the opposition majority in Commons actually represents the will of the people. By such alchemy of interpretation has a system based on monarchy and nobility become a democracy. In theory, nothing has changed. In practice, everything has.

The British experience illustrates the nature of constitution making as an ongoing, evolutionary art. The skill of the British has been to maintain unity by settling changes in power relationships by adaptations and new interpretations of historic forms. The ancient formulas are already accepted and legitimate. They constitute a point of agreement among contending parties. The element of craft is the discovery of new formulations of these principles, the seeing of new implications in the legacy of the past, that fit the terms of the problem to be solved.

[4] *Grame C. Moodie,* The Government of Great Britain *(New York: Thomas Y. Crowell, 1971), pp. 1–19.*

Behind the success of this process of sustaining unity among those forces critical to the survival of the political order (for the British, culturally and historically are no less prone to conflict and bitterness than anyone else) is an implicit assumption—that there will never be absolute winners and losers among the critical parties to the debate. The king and nobility are not overthrown, though their influence and relevance gradually diminishes. The result, despite Britain's ups and downs as a world power, is a singular success story in the creation of political structure, the fashioning of a flexible order for society, highly legitimate, that endures over long spans of time.

the framing of the American constitution

If Britain illuminates the arts of constitution making over an extended period of time, the framing of the American constitution displays the skills of politics involved in settling the form of a new government within a specific assembly of men, at a given time and place. However, the distinctiveness of the two cases should not be overstated. It would be wrong to see the Philadelphia Convention of 1787 as operating in an historical vacuum. The delegates were profoundly influenced by British political ideas and institutions; this was their own cultural legacy of government, and they had experienced it in the state governments that had emerged from the British colonial system in America. The tension between executive and legislature was an idea they found "natural" and progressive. In British practice, and in the ideals of the radical Whigs for parliamentary reform in the late eighteenth century, they saw the model to be imitated in visualizing the overall structure of government.

Also like the British, the American constitution makers did not see themselves as philosopher-kings handing down abstract principles for an ideal system of government. Rather, they appeared to themselves as practical men, attempting to solve an immediate, concrete problem. As Gouverneur Morris, one of the authors, said of the final product, "While some have boasted it as a work from heaven, others have given it a less righteous origin. I have many reasons to believe that it is the work of plain, honest men, and as such, I think, it will appear."

The "initiators" wanted a stronger national government. To a small group of prominent Americans—the best known included Washington, Hamilton, Madison, and Jay—the Articles of Confederation, under which the new republic had been governed after 1781, were inadequate to the needs of the new nation. Because the national government under the Articles was essentially an alliance of states (not totally unlike the modern United Nations), its Congress, made up of delegates appointed by state legislatures, paid by them, and serving at their pleasure, could make resolutions and recommendations, but it had little power to enforce them. Its budget was dependent on contributions by the states, often given reluctantly. There was no national executive or court system. The states raised armies and could independently decide whether or not to dispatch troops to support the national government. The consequence, in the eyes of the nationalists, was that the affairs of the American political order that had emerged from the revolution were coming apart at the seams. Internationally, America was weak and European powers could easily take advantage of it. Financially, the central government was chronically in trouble, unable to meet its debts both to foreign and domestic creditors. The country was not even a common market. Each state had its own distinctive commercial and business law, which it enforced in its own courts. Some states enforced tariffs against the others. Doing business with Maryland out of Boston was very much like trading with a foreign country.

The problem for the nationalists was that the people generally did not feel these problems, or at least, they did not feel them very strongly. For most of the people in America, the states were the critical arena of politics that affected their lives. The Confederation Congress was a remote and somewhat vague authority. Given the transportation and communications of the time, the affairs of Georgia were as remote from the interest of a New Englander as those of Europe —perhaps more so. For politicians, the issues that mattered were settled in state legislatures. Only those whose wealth, prestige, or interests permitted could afford the indulgence of being concerned with the relatively remote affairs of the union. Furthermore, born out of revolution, there was a strong suspicion of powerful central governments divorced from the direct control of the people. However, in good measure, the prevailing attitude toward the central government was one of indifference and apathy. What went on in the Confederation Congress was a matter of concern, of course, but the practical stakes were much lower for the average politician than were those of his own state. This relative indifference and ambiguity about national affairs would be critical to the strategy of the nationalists.

The nationalists had to account for those whose power was critical to the achievement of their objectives. These included the state governments, and the political groups centered in them, and, given the democratic bias of the country, popular opinion itself. The two would be played off against one another before the task was done. The process began innocently enough with a meeting sponsored by Washington at Mount Vernon between political leaders from Maryland and Virginia to consider problems of free commerce on the Potomac. The narrower issue, as it was thrashed out, suggested the larger problem, and at the initiative of Washington and Madison, an invitation was extended generally to the other states to meet at Annapolis in September, 1786, to consider mutual problems of interstate commerce. Little was accomplished of substance at Annapolis, but in casual way the meeting came around, or was brought around, to the subject of the Articles of Confederation. Madison and Hamilton persuaded the delegates to recommend to the states that a convention be held in Philadelphia the following summer to consider revision of the Articles.

The delegates to the convention represented varied interests.[5] Different states saw the national enterprise differently. Georgia, as a remote frontier state, was concerned about national power as a defense against Indian attack. Virginia, the state of Washington and Madison, saw itself as a natural leader of the union. New York, except for Hamilton, was secure in its support for the *status quo*. Although some of the delegates were adamant states' rights supporters—at least three of the fifty-five left the convention in a huff, and at the end, five more refused to sign—there was a common universe of discourse and concern. Thirty-nine of the delegates had served in the Confederation Congress. They shared, as John Roche says, a "continental frame of reference."[6] They had become accustomed to thinking about the problems of the United States, as well as the affairs of their own particular states. This made the task of the initiators in working toward a basic understanding on the nature of the problem and a concrete proposal of a new system of government somewhat easier. The convention was not a real cross section of attitudes on the relative power of the national and state governments. This initial commitment of a great majority of the delegates to the national experiment was in part due to successful political guidance of the delegate selection process in the state legislatures. However, it is also true that given the low salience of the issue to many state legislatures, those who had some interest in and experience with national affairs, and were willing to take time out from their other business to spend the summer in Philadelphia, appeared to be obvious candidates for the job.

The delegates were, on the whole, an unusually prestigious, influential, wealthy, and well-educated group. No frontiersmen or urban workers were there, and only one small farmer was numbered among the delegates. This too added to the common outlook of the delegates and made the creation of agreement easier than would have been the case in a more representative assembly. However, to view the meeting as a conservative cabal, an upper-class effort to stem the tide of radical democracy in the states, and to protect their investments in western lands and continental securities, certainly overstates the case.[7] In political ideology, the debates prove the delegates were far

[5] *See Carl Van Doren,* The Great Rehearsal *(New York: Viking Press, 1948), p. 35.*

[6] *John P. Roche, "The Founding Fathers: A Reform Caucus in Action,"* American Political Science Review *55 (December 1961), p. 801.*

[7] *Charles A. Beard,* An Economic Interpretation of the United States *(New York: Macmillan, 1913).*

from being exclusively orthodox conservatives plotting on behalf of the propertied class.

At the outset, few of the delegates had clear, predetermined ideas about what ought to be done. They had been appointed to propose revisions to the Articles and nothing more. However, there was considerable ambiguity and vagueness about the concrete steps that would be required to turn the floundering confederation into a going concern. Here the more committed nationalists seized the initiative. The Virginia delegation, which contained many of the leaders of the nationalist cause, introduced their own proposals, to "structure the discussion." The Virginia Plan was significant in two respects. First, it was a proposal for a self-sufficient national government, able to tax, with its own independent executive and judiciary, and a legislature elected by the people directly, not of delegates from the state governments. It was a proposal for a totally new governmental authority, not an improvement of the existing alliance of states. Second, far from being simply a revision of the Articles, it was a total program for a new system of government.

As the only concrete proposal available, it was accepted as the framework for discussion. But this first step gave the committed nationalists the advantage. Control of agenda is a potent weapon in the hands of the leaders of any deliberative assembly. The ambivalent delegates could argue with the particulars, but they had not, until later, any alternative proposal to set beside it. All assemblies take on a life of their own, particularly when they meet over a prolonged period of time, and in this case the idea of the independent national government and the objective of total revision gradually grew within the convention.

The debate focused on the structure of the national legislature. For half the summer, this would be the major topic. Its ramifications and implications almost caused the negotiations to break down. When this issue was finally resolved, the rest of the pieces of the puzzle fell readily into place.

The controversy had several sides to it. First, there was the issue of democracy itself. In the late eighteenth century, the idea that the people as a whole were competent to decide on public affairs was hardly a settled matter. In the political discourse of the day, the word "democracy" did not have the respectable tone it has today. Rather, in many minds, it connoted something like "mob rule." For some of the New England delegates in particular, the recent experience of Shay's Rebellion made them suspicious of a popularly elected legislature, as proposed in the Virginia Plan. But, on the other side, such wealthy and seemingly aristocratic spokesmen as George Mason of Virginia were as eloquent as the absent Jefferson in defense of the right and capacity of the common man to rule himself. The second dimension of the debate over the legislature had to do with the question of equality of representation for the states. The Virginia Plan, proposing representation by population directly and without qualification, would have enabled the larger states—Massachusetts, New York, and Virginia—to control the legislature. The smaller, less populous states reacted vigorously. This was a complete reversal of the philosophy of the Articles, which gave each state the same power in the legislature. In fact, the Delaware delegation was under instructions from its legislature to accept no proposals that would change the existing system of equality of representation.

Now the more reluctant nationalists were capable of putting together an alternative proposal. The New Jersey Plan began with the interests of the smaller states and proposed a legislature in which each state had an equal vote. It also provided for a plural executive, a governing committee, which was an appeal to those who feared a concentration of "monarchical" power. But significantly, the New Jersey Plan was not merely a case for the preservation of the philosophy of the Articles. It too called for the establishment of an independent and effective national government.

The nationalists by this time had the votes, and when a formal roll call was held, the New Jersey Plan was defeated by nine states to three. But the object of the nationalist leaders was not merely majority control. Constitutional negotiation must account for all the critical forces, and, hence, the reluctance of any state or sizable body of opinion was crucial. The overall objective was an effective national union, not a framework of government that would leave several critical states embittered and outside. The debate continued until a formula for reconciliation was discovered.

Sherman of Connecticut had early suggested a formula that pulled the several pieces of the puzzle together. As a form of compromise, this was not merely a matter of splitting the difference, but an insight into how the points at issue could be reformulated. The legislature would have two houses, one directly elected by the people, according to population, in which the large states would have an advantage. The second house, the Senate, would have equal representation of the states and would be selected by the state legislatures.[8] The claims of the large and small states, of those who wanted a democratic system and those who preferred election by the allegedly more prudent elites in the state legislatures were equally accommodated. When this solution was finally adopted, the end was in sight.

Three other compromises illustrate the process of accommodation in the convention. The electoral college system of selecting the president was a makeshift arrangement, hammered out in committee, in an

---

[8] *Since the Seventeenth Amendment, in 1913, of course, senators have been directly elected by the people.*

attempt to find some way of satisfying those who insisted on a strong executive and those who feared a popularly elected, democratic Caesar; those who wanted the president directly elected by the people and those who advocated selection by the state legislatures; those from the small states demanding equal rights and those who wanted the "one man, one vote" principle. The result was an agreement, which has never worked the way it was designed, for the people in each state to directly elect a special "college" for the sole purpose of selecting the president, each state to have a number of electors equal to their representation in the House of Representatives and the Senate.

A second fundamental compromise grew out of the general conflict over representation. The South wanted to count slaves as well as free citizens in determining the number of congressmen from each state. The North hardly was enthusiastic about increasing the legislative strength of the South on the basis of that region's peculiar institution, already morally suspect to many Northerners. Finally, it was decided that slaves would count three-fifths of a free citizen for the purposes of representation.

As we recall, the initial impetus for the convention grew out of problems of interstate trade. North of the Potomac, most were eager for the national government to have extensive powers in this area. The South, less interested in internal trade, but critically concerned about agricultural exports, especially cotton, feared that the North would take advantage, raising revenue through taxes on such products. Finally, it was agreed that the national government would have broad powers over trade and navigation, but that no taxes on exports would be imposed.

It would be a mistake to see the convention only in terms of bargaining, compromise, and give and take. It was also a deliberative body, and its members were not only adversaries but also leaders searching for a workable system of government. The nationalists did not enter with a comprehensive solution to every problem and then merely give in when and where they had to in order to gain support. At first, there was considerable fuzziness in the minds of all on many points. The "practical" men of the convention, in settling the basic issues among them, were also grappling toward the comprehension and development of unusual ideas about government.[9] At that time, republican institutions were new in the world and democratic theory mainly a matter of abstract principles. Madison defended the secrecy of the meetings and the lack of a formal record, "Because opinions were so various and at first so crude that it was necessary they should be long debated before a uniform system of opinion could be

---

[9] *Catherine Drinker Bowen,* Miracle at Philadelphia *(New York: Bantam Books, 1968), p. 32.*

formed."[10] Federalism, the idea that two governments can exercise jurisdiction over the same area and population for different purposes, is usually considered the prime innovation of the convention, and Madison is often called "the father of federalism." But it is clear that he had no real conception of this when the convention started. The idea that there could be a system in which two governments *both* had sovereign powers was hard to comprehend, especially for eighteenth-century minds attuned to the notion that sovereignty must inevitably focus at a single point in a political system. As Gouverneur Morris insisted, he could not "conceive of a government in which there could be two supremes." The process of debate in the convention was more than just rhetoric designed to marshal support. Read carefully, it is obvious there was much tentative probing of ideas, advancing of opinions to test their plausibility. The convention was an arena of both negotiation and political creativity.

With the document signed, the politics of the constitution were still not complete. The nationalists now had to sell their product to the states and to the people. The states, having been persuaded to send delegates to this convention, who were then persuaded to adopt a new system of government rather than a revision of the Articles, now had to be convinced to create ratifying conventions, directly elected by the people. The problem, as John Roche put it, was to "induce the states, by democratic means of coercion, to emasculate themselves."[11] Finally, the nationalists had to win the assent of the ratifying conventions themselves.

The process took almost three years. Once more the arguments were long and bitter. Basic questions of philosophy of government and of private and sectional interest were rehearsed, as leaders once more weighed the things they had in common against the particular factors that divided them. The nationalists lobbied and "politicked" in the ratifying conventions. Assurances were given and bargains were struck. One problem, the absence of a Bill of Rights from the Constitution led to strong promises that this would be rectified by the new government. The first ten amendments, introduced and ratified in the first years of the federal government, made good on this pledge. Some of the votes in the ratifying conventions were very close. Although Delaware, New Jersey, and Georgia accepted the constitution unanimously, in Massachusetts the vote was 187 to 168 and Virginia ratified by 87 to 79. The critical contest was in New York. Here the nationalists unleashed all their powers of persuasion. One document that resulted from the debate, *The Federalist Papers*, a defense of the constitution by

---

[10] *Van Doren, The Great Rehearsal, p. 28.*
[11] *John P. Roche, "The Founding Fathers: A Reform Caucus in Action," p. 800.*

Hamilton, Madison, and Jay, stands to this day as a basic discussion of the political principles and philosophy of the American system, and is a model of the arts of political argument and advocacy at their best.

On July 2, 1788, the constitution formally went into effect with the ratification by nine states. While the Philadelphia convention is a study in the politics of constitution making, it hardly ends the story of the development of the American political system. Constitution making in America, as in Britain, has been an ongoing art. The basic forms designed and fashioned at Philadelphia have evolved through interpretation and usage, by amendment and that constant process of choice in concrete situations that shapes the character of any political organization.

the search for political structure
in the People's Republic of China

Constitution makers always seem wiser in retrospect, particularly when their work endures, as it has in the British and American cases. However, the process of creating political form is best appreciated in the present, when the situation is still inchoate and we have no idea how the story will develop. In the People's Republic of China, as political order is being fashioned, the stable form it will eventually take is by no means evident.

From one point of view, the first twenty-five years of the history of the People's Republic of China can be interpreted simply as a struggle for power among the Communist party; the technicians, managers, experts, planners, and administrators of the new regime; and the People's Liberation Army. However, at a deeper level, the record of this period is also one of a search for the terms of accommodation between the forces that in the long run, are essential to the survival and success of a regime.

There is always a dominant metaphor behind every exercise in constitution making. The British system of government, basically, still has the form and logic of the feudal contract. The United States Constitution imitates the British system as it existed in the eighteenth century and the colonial governments of America, but it was also influenced, as was much of eighteenth-century democratic theory, by the ideas of Newtonian mechanics, at that time the most advanced scientific style of thought. Thus, the United States system appears as an equilibrium of opposing forces, as in the system of "checks and balances." The argument of *The Federalist* contains many similes to physical principles. One prominent element in the Chinese vision of political form has been the dialectical process of history as described by Marx. Another is the experience of a revolutionary army, struggling, fighting, retreating, seeking to mobilize the peasantry, planning strategy for over a generation to overthrow the Nationalist regime. The skills of the first generation of Communist China's leaders were those of destroying a political order, not creating and running one. And what they valued and sought to perpetuate through politics was the struggle, the epic achievement and heroism, the flexibility and fluidity, the direct mass action, that had brought them to power.

But every revolution must eventually become a going concern. It often comes as a surprise to revolutionary leaders, whose whole conciousness and effort has been directed to the overthrow of a ruling class and a system, that once the struggle has been won they are now the ruling class and must create a system of their own. When the Communists came to power in 1949, they had to maintain law and order, deliver public services, administer the country, and provide for the organization and coordination of the economy. To achieve these goals, the revolution had to become institutionalized. They had to create organization, managed by trained administrators and specialists.

These new elites were critical to the experiment in government. In a sense, the Communist leaders, with their vision of politics as guerilla war are the initiators, but to complete the design of government, they must find a place for the specialists in organization and technology. The conflict between "red" and "expert" became central to the process of finding stable form and political order in the People's Republic of China. Franz Schurmann describes the issue as follows: "One can see the relationship between the two values in the question of proletarianization and industrialization. Proletarianization is essentally a human goal; it calls for the transformation of human beings. Industrialization is a technical goal; it calls for the transformation of things. . . . The value of expertise is essentially a technical goal, in the sense that the educated individual aspires to acquire specialized skills and knowledge. The value of "red" is essentially a human goal, in that it requires the total transformation of the individual. . . ."[12]

These tensions were acknowledged in Chinese Communist ideology. The model for the constitution maker is perhaps best stated in Mao Tse-tung's speech, "On the Question of Correctly Resolving Contradictions Among the People." Marxist-Leninist thought, of course, is based on the process of dialectic, on the reconciliation of opposites. For Mao, there are antagonistic and nonantagonistic "contradictions." Antagonistic contradictions occur with "enemies" and must eventually be settled by force or the working out of the logic of history. This would apply, for example, in the relations of China with capitalist, imperialist powers. Nonantagonistic contradictions occur among the people and must be settled amicably. Before all conflicts are

Franz Schurmann, Ideology and Organization in Communist China, *Revised Edition* (Berkeley: University of California Press, 1968), pp. 51–52.

finally resolved in the eternally harmonious Marxist utopia of perfect communism, it is to be expected that differences will arise among the revolutionary forces, between the peasantry and the proletariat, between the claims of industry and agriculture, between the experts and organizers and the party cadres. Even within the party organization, such disputes will arise. They should not be deplored but must be seen as a natural part of the dialectical process.

The art of statecraft is that of finding correct solutions to these contradictions. Hence, they must be expressed and not hidden, in the councils of the party, as in the deliberations among the managers of a factory or the workers of a collective farm. Discussion must go on until the path of reconciliation is found. On the larger scene, the implicit contradictions among social classes and forces must come into the open, be analyzed, and the correct "nonantagonistic" solution found. [13]

The search for a solution to the contradiction between red and expert is visible in the major episodes of politics in China during the first twenty-five years of the People's Republic. Initially the task of economic and political institutionalization seems to have been considered paramount. The model to be emulated in the building of China was that of the Soviet Union. The problem was to create an industrial society, to "proletarianize" a peasant culture. The structure of the state, the economy and society was borrowed from the USSR. In this vision of the building of communism, the role of manager and expert came before that of party mobilizer. An inevitable consequence was that the "distance" between the leaders and the masses increased. A new contradiction appeared, that between the leaders and the led, the government and the people. A "new class," a Communist elite was being created. This was not compatible with the vision of revolutionary society in the mind of Mao Tse-tung or Liu Shao-Ch'i.

The "Great Leap Forward," from 1957 to 1960, replaced the rationality of the expert with the enthusiasm of the party cadres. The Maoist reasserted their authority. The objective was to replace planned step-by-step development with a sudden thrust, which would bring China's power alongside the major industrial powers in a few years. Change would come up from the bottom, from peasants and worker whose leaders were engaged in the work process itself. The contradiction between leader and led, red and expert, would be obliterated by removing the distinction between them. Specialists were ruthlessly attacked and derided. Managers were told to go out of their offices and directly lead production teams. Natural leadership should prevail over routinized authority. The ideologically inspired "red" should be the

[13] For a study of this idea of "Resolution of Contradictions" applied to concrete economic policy issues, see Michael C. Oksenberg, "Policy-Making Under Mao Tse-tung, 1949–1968," Comparative Politics 3 (April 1971), pp. 323–360.

same person as the technically qualified expert. The "three-unification campaign" implied that cadres, technicians, and workers should be welded together in the organic unity of the production team.[14]

Economically, the Great Leap Forward was a disaster. Production advanced or fell whimsically and chaotically, the country lost developmental momentum rather than crashing through to industrial maturity. Eventually, the party leaders called upon the managers to return to their offices and restore order. By 1961, the balance of critical forces had shifted once again.

During the 1960s, the organizers became preeminent in all institutions of Chinese politics. Power shifted to managers in the economy, to administrators politically. The People's Liberation Army, urged in the Great Leap to put aside its specialized role and become revolutionary activists, became a greater force in domestic affairs. And the Communist party itself took on the forms of a stable, hierarchic institution.

Once more, in the Cultural Revolution of 1966–1969, Mao Tse-tung and his allies tried to restore the sense of mass action which he believed must be the operating dynamic of a revolutionary society. His faction of the party, in the army, and most importantly the Red Guards, a militant youth movement, were sent into the country to attack the "bureaucrats" and the "capitalist roaders." The contradiction would be resolved in a larger pattern of social struggle.

By the end of the 1960s, China was seeking a new settlement among the basic political forces. The People's Liberation Army had become a new and central factor in politics, and around it were arrayed the managerial and administrative elites and the cultural revolutionists. Implicitly, the accommodation seemed to be that the "red" component of the revolution would be honored symbolically while the "experts" would dominate the conduct of affairs. The cult of Mao blossomed, the great leader venerated in the most lavish ways. Everything that was done in China was supposed to be accomplished by emulation of Mao or in accord with his thought, particularly as recorded in the *Little Red Book*.

We still do not know the settled form that government will eventually take in China. By the mid-1970s, power seemed increasingly to be concentrated in the hands of the conservatives—those dedicated to the maintenance of a stable, structured order. The star of the "perennial revolutionaries" seemed to be on the wane. Efforts were being made to establish a formal, constitutional order for the regime. Does this mean that government as a dialectical process was an idea for a transitional period now passed and that the regime will become increasingly prosaic and bureaucratized? Or will the "resolution of contradictions," like the image of the feudal contract in Britain and the

---

[14] *Franz Schurmann,* Ideology and Organization in Communist China, *pp. 69–73.*

picture of opposing forces that must be checked and balanced in the United States, become the ancient and revered formula for conflict resolution, one that the Chinese will accept as automatically as we accept majority rule? All the evidence is not yet in, and clearly the Chinese are still a people in search of a settled set of political institutions and practices.

conclusion

These three case studies illustrate much about the arts of statecraft. It is apparent that constitution making is a matter of choice on behalf of other people. It is the leaders who impose design and structure on the process of government. In doing so, they define how interests will be expressed, how policies will be deliberated and decided, how the society will come to conclusions about its public purposes and carry them out.

In each of these cases, we see the conflict between the principles of democracy and authority, and the effort to blend and mix them in a system of government. The British tension between the powers of king and Parliament, the American system of checks and balances between executive and legislature, the Chinese dialectic between red and expert are all expressions of this theme.

It is apparent that constitution making involves the arts of bargaining and compromise, as well as coalition building, that in essence, political architecture is a matter of the creation of agreement among forces who disagree on particulars, but have a common stake in political community and political structure. In all three cases, constitution making was a process of finding a formula of accommodation among forces whose cooperation was essential for the success of a regime.

The politics of constitution making are part of the struggle for power and influence in a political system. The facts of power within the community must be acknowledged and analyzed.

Finally, constitution making requires an *idea*, an overall concept of political order, an image of how contending forces can work together, and a formula for conflict resolution that all interests acknowledge as legitimate and binding. The ideas of the contract between sovereign and subjects, the equilibrium of forces expressed in the American system of checks and balances, the dialectical resolution of contradictions, are all expressions of a common theme—that there are distinctive and contending interests in the community, that none should dominate the rest, and that a process can be defined whereby these contending interests can work together for common purposes to found a political community.

The British Constitutional Experience

Bagehot, Walter, *The English Constitution* (London: World Classics Edition, 1928). Many other editions are available. This is by now dated, but gives a fine interpretation of the logic of the British system and its historical development.

Lovell, Colin Rhys, *English Constitutional and Legal History* (New York: Oxford University Press, 1962). Thorough, comprehensive and well written. Emphasizes the emergence of the modern constitution from Medieval institutions. Gives a real sense for historic continuity.

Jennings, Sir Ivor, *The British Constitution* (Cambridge: Cambridge University Press, 1961). A standard interpretation of contemporary British political institutions.

Schwartz, Bernard, *The Roots of Freedom: A Constitutional History of England* (New York: Hill and Wang, 1967). A very readable survey of British constitutional development.

The American Constitutional Convention

Beard, Charles A., *An Economic Interpretation of the Constitution of the United States* (New York: Macmillan, 1913). Many other editions available. A controversial interpretation of the Constitution as the work of a conservative and propertied elite.

Bowen, Catherine Drinker, *Miracle at Philadelphia* (New York: Bantam Books, 1968). A popular, easy-to-read discussion, but one that gives attention to the process of creative intellectual search and discovery among the delegates.

McDonald, Forrest, *We the People: The Economic Origins of the Constitution* (Chicago: University of Chicago Press, 1958). An attempt to refute Charles Beard's thesis, noted above.

Roche, John F., "The Founding Fathers: A Reform Caucus in Action," *American Political Science Review 55* (December 1961). An interpretation of the politics of constitution making. I drew on it heavily in this chapter.

Van Doren, Carl, *The Great Rehearsal* (New York: Viking Press, 1948). A good, popular discussion of the politics of the Philadelphia convention.

Maoism and Political Order in China

Schram, Stuart, *Mao Tse-tung* (Baltimore: Penguin Books, 1970). A biography of the Chinese leader, but some attention to his philosophy and role as political architect.

Schurmann, Franz, *Ideology and Organization in Communist China,* Revised Edition (Berkeley: University of California Press, 1968). A very useful discussion of the search for principles of political orde in the formative years of the Chinese People's Republic.

chapter
fourteen
the process
of law

Every political organization must develop institutions for the settlement of disputes. As we have already noted, *how* we make decisions about conflicts of rights, about the application of general rules to particular cases, about the adjudication of controversies between individuals and between individuals and government, is an important part of the problem of political architecture.

The design of the legal process is a major source of political argument. What are the requirements of a fair trial? How can we assure that the process of adjudication we create not only does justice but is in itself just?

In this chapter, we examine the basic underlying logic of the Anglo-American law. There are of course many other legal systems in the world. This is not the only way of thinking about the principles that should be applied in constructing procedures for the adjudication of disputes. However, this particular conception of law is a fundamental part of our civilization. It provides the framework of ideas and ideals that we normally employ in analyzing the design of legal institutions and evaluating them.

The law is a specialized language of political argument. It contains specific standards of evaluation that define what counts as a good case and what does not. The fundamental principles of the common law not only provide guidelines for structuring the legal process but they also enable us to evaluate and to criticize the existing structure of legal institutions.

Law can be understood in a variety of ways. It is a mechanism of social control and it provides the framework of political order.[1] I establishes rights and duties. It is the rule-making and rule-enforcing aspect of public policy. However, most fundamentally, law is a technique of conflict resolution. It provides a process for the settlement of disputes that do not get resolved by other means.[2]

As a means of conflict resolution, law can be seen as an alternative to combat, dueling, vendetta, or other means by which a person who felt himself wronged by another might try to settle accounts. The idea of law is that disputes should not be settled simply by a test of power. The common law does see the trial as a contest—but one in which the contestants are deprived of all political resources except reasoned argument. Each side should have an equal opportunity to make its case. In the theory of the common law, the power of the state and of the individual is reduced to common ground. Ideally, in a court of law, the state appears simply as a "party" to a case, no different from any individual.

forms of law

There are three principal bodies of law: civil, criminal, and constitutional. They are classified according to the type of conflict to which each applies.

Civil Law

Civil law concerns conflicts between individuals.[3] Civil actions are based on the right of an individual to sue another for damages or restitution when he feels that he has been wrongfully injured by the conduct or action of another. One central principle underlies the entire

---

[1] Roscoe Pound, Social Control through Law (New Haven: Yale University Press, 1968), pp. 1–34.

[2] "What then is this law business about? It is about the fact that our society is honeycombed with disputes. Disputes actual and potential; disputes to be settled and disputes to be prevented; both appealing to law, both making up the business of the law. But obviously those which most violently call for attention are the actual disputes, and to these our first attention must be directed. Actual disputes call for somebody to do something about them. First, so they there may be peace, for the disputants; for other persons whose ears and toes the disputants are disturbing. And secondly, so that the dispute may really be put at rest, which means, so that a solution may be achieved which, at least in the main, is bearable to the parties and not disgusting to the lookers-on. This doing of something about disputes, this doing of it reasonably, is the 'business of law'." K. N. Llewelyn, The Bramble Bush (Dobbs Ferry, N.Y.: Oceana Publications, 1960), p. 12.

[3] There is an ambiguity here. Civil law is the body of rules that regulates private conflicts in English-speaking countries. However, the term is also used to distinguish the civil law systems of continental Europe from the common law systems of the Anglo-American world. The former is based on a system of codes and descends from the Roman law; the latter, based on a much different set of principles, is descended from historic judicial precedent.

idea of civil law—that of personal responsibility. The conscientious person will take "reasonable care" that his actions do not inflict injury or harm on another, that his possessions are not used in such a way as to be hurtful to others. The expectation of the law is that the individual will be careful not to infringe on the rights of others, and that each person is responsible for the consequences of his conduct as it affects others.

The main branches of civil law are tort, property, and contract. The law of tort is concerned with such matters as negligence, slander, fraud, and trespass, with the damage that one person may do to another's person, estate, or reputation. As Oliver Wendell Holmes pointed out, the law of tort is really less concerned with defining certain actions as wrong, and more with asking where the burden of risk should lie. Should the costs of accidents, carelessness, and thoughtlessness fall on those who are affected by them, or on those whose conduct causes them to occur? It would seem fundamentally unfair that the victim of an accident should pay the costs and suffer the consequences. Through law, then, we try to shift the costs of misfortune to those who caused them. And this means that to win a civil suit is not so much to inflict punishment on a person who has "broken the law" as it is to provide compensation to one who has been injured.[4]

The law of property has to do with the rights of individuals to the use of things, and the remedies available to them if another infringes on these rights. Note the subtle implication here. A person, before the law, does not simply own an object. He has specific and defined rights over its use and control. The right of property is not unlimited. For example, a person may have the right to collect the rent from a building though he does not own it. (It might be mortgaged to a bank.) An easement gives a person the right to use property he does not own —say to pass across it to get to his own land.

Contract is a particularly broad and central category of the law. It concerns all agreements between people and the institutions formed by these agreements. Some have described the change from the medieval to the modern world as a passage from status to contract. In earlier Western society, social relations were primarily determined by static, inherited, hierarchic principles. You were born a lord or a serf, and with that status went certain rights and obligations, and that was that. In the early nineteenth century, the view of the relation of individuals to social institutions changed fundamentally. All social institutions were seen as forms of contract, as freely created by the will and choice of the individuals concerned. (In theory, even government rests on a "social contract.") The family, in law, is viewed as a form of

---

[4] *Oliver Wendell Holmes,* The Common Law, *Mark DeWolff Howe (Ed.) (Boston: Little, Brown, 1963), p. 115.*

contract. (And divorce, then, is a question of when a person is no longer committed to a contract he has made. Grounds for divorce, such as desertion or adultery, imply a "breach of contract.") All organizations and associations are forms of contract, as are labor-management relations. The law of contract covers far more than the relations between buyers and sellers in the economic marketplace.

Roscoe Pound once elegantly summed up the basic assumptions of the civil law, the expectations of how a responsible individual will act toward others so as not to cause them harm.

1. In civilized society men must be able to assume that others will commit no intentional aggressions upon them.

2. In civilized society men must be able to assume that they may control for beneficial purposes what they have discovered and appropriated to their own use, what they have created by their own labor, and what they have acquired under the existing social and economic order.

3. In civilized society men must be able to assume that those with whom they deal in the general intercourse of society will act in good faith and hence

   (a) will make good reasonable expectations which their promises or conduct reasonably create;

   (b) will carry out their undertakings according to the expectations which the moral sentiment of the community attaches thereto;

   (c) will restore specifically or by equivalent what comes to them by mistake or unanticipated or not fully intended situation whereby they receive at another's expense what they could not reasonably have expected to receive under the circumstances.

4. In civilized society men must be able to assume that those who are engaged in some course of conduct will act with due care not to cast an unreasonable risk of injury upon others.

5. In civilized society men must be able to assume that those who maintain things likely to get out of hand or to escape and do damage will restrain them or keep them within their proper bounds.[5]

The names of cases usually help in identifying the branch of law to which they belong. Civil cases are disputes between two individuals. The plaintiff, who brings the case and alleges that harm has been done to him, comes first. The defendant, who is accused of causing the harm, is second; thus, *Brown* v. *Smith*, *Fletcher* v. *Rylands*, and so forth.

---

[5] *Roscoe Pound,* Sound Control through Law, *pp. 113–115.*

Of course, the term "person" in the law may refer to an organization as well as an individual. So we may have *Hollywood Silver Fox Farm* v. *Emmett* (in which the defendant was restrained from firing a gun that disturbed the breeding habits of the plaintiff's foxes) or *Ford Motor Co.* v. *Amalgamated Union of Engineering and Foundry Workers.* Governments may also be the subject of civil suits or may bring them.

Criminal Law

In a criminal case, the government (or an individual) alleges that a specific unlawful act has been committed, one that is defined by a criminal statute. At issue here is not compensation or restitution, but punishment—fine or imprisonment. However, in a certain sense, a criminal case has the same form as a civil suit. The government brings the case and appears in the role of the plaintiff. The government, in effect, argues that *it* is the injured party, its laws having been violated or, more accurately, that a specific individual has been harmed by an illegal action and the government is acting on his behalf. The defendant again is the person accused of committing a wrong against a specific party, in this case the state. Thus, the case normally takes the form of *The People* v. *Smith* or *Wisconsin* v. *Smith* or *The United States* v. *General Motors.* [6]

Now the role of the court as a settler of disputes begins to come clear. A criminal case is a dispute between the government and an individual. The prosecutor alleges that a law has been broken. The defendant claims that it has not, or if it has, that he is not the party responsible. The job of the court is to settle the dispute. The idea is fundamental to the Anglo-American conception of judicial independence. Although the state *provides* for the courts, finances and establishes them, the judiciary is not supposed to be an agent of government, carrying out its purposes.

Constitutional Law

Law is often viewed as a mechanism through which government regulates the conduct of people. However, in constitutional governments, the state itself is the subject of law. "Government under law" means that the rights and obligations of the state are defined, just as the rights and obligations of individuals are through civil and criminal law. Constitutional government is limited government.

The constitutional case completes the cycle of the forms of law.

---

[6] *The title of a case is followed by a citation. Thus the last case mentioned, an antitrust action against General Motors for illegal conspiracy in fixing prices, is normally cited as U.S. v. General Motors Corp., 384 US 127 (1966). The "US" refers to the United States Reports, one of a series of volumes of Supreme Court decisions. The 384 refers to the volume and the 127 to the page where the decision appears.*

Here the individual appears as plaintiff. It is alleged that the government has broken the law, and that the individual has been personally harmed thereby. The government now is in the role of defendant. It will argue that its actions were in fact lawful. Again, the name of the plaintiff comes first, and so we have *Brown* v. *Board of Education of Topeka* 347 US 483 (1954) (the famous case in which Brown argued that the maintenance of segregated schools by the Topeka Board of Education deprived him of "equal protection of the laws" as guaranteed by the Fourteenth Amendment) or *Miranda* v. *Arizona* 384 US 436 (1966) (in which the Supreme Court ruled that a defendant had a constitutional right to legal counsel during police interrogation).

The Supreme Court of the United States is the final arbiter of the federal constitution and the state supreme courts of their own constitutions. There is no right of appeal from the Supreme Court when a case is brought on constitutional grounds. Normally, constitutional cases are decided by lower federal courts, and the Supreme Court only comes into the picture when it decides that a major issue of constitutional interpretation is at stake.

Constitutional cases may concern (1) whether a governmental action is consistent with the enumerated powers of the federal government in the Constitution; (2) whether the action is consistent with the powers of a specific branch of the federal government; (3) whether the action is consistent with individual rights created by the Constitution, particularly in the first ten amendments. State government actions may also raise issues of constitutional interpretation when they appear to infringe on powers reserved to the federal government or when they involve issues of individual rights under the constitution. The last is a complex area of judicial interpretation. Basically, the Bill of Rights pertains to actions of the federal government. The first amendment says that "*Congress* shall make no laws affecting the freedom of speech. . . ." The wording poses no limitations on state governments. However, the Fourteenth Amendment provides that "no state *shall* make or enforce any law which shall abridge the privileges or immunities of citizens of the United States. . . ." Now any citizen of a state is simultaneously a citizen of the United States, and the Bill of Rights is certainly among the "privileges and immunities" of citizens of the United States. Through this process of reasoning, many of the provisions of the Bill of Rights have been held to apply to state governments as well as the federal government.

legal argument and the structure of the case

Legal reasoning is a highly structured and systematic form of the general process of political argument that we have been discussing throughout this book. Essentially the law poses the same problems that arise in any form of political analysis. The problem can be stated in more than one way. Various criteria of decision can be applied. Different measures (remedies) may be invoked to accomplish the objectives of policy. Strategic questions arise. The issues of the substance of a decision and procedure by which it is made are part of any legal process. In the law, the roles of the advocates (attorneys) and policymakers (judges and juries) are clearly differentiated from one another.

Of course, extensive training is required to master this form of political argument and analysis. However, it is possible to capture something of the flavor of the problems of choice and judgment that arise in law by considering a case from the point of view of the various actors who have a part to play in the decision-making process.

The Plaintiff

The party claiming injury activates the judicial process. The plaintiff's action is crucial. Until a case is brought, the entire judicial machinery remains silent and inactive. No matter what illegal actions or hurtful practices exist in society, the courts can do nothing about them until an action is brought. We do not know what such phrases in the constitution as "equal protection of the laws" or "freedom of speech" mean until cases are presented by parties who allege that they personally have been wronged by unconstitutional government actions. And it is not the court, but the plaintiff who generally sees the possibility of a new line of constitutional interpretation.[7]

At the outset, the plaintiff (who may be a prosecuting attorney in a criminal action or an individual—and his attorney—in a civil suit) has some crucial choices to make. These involve the nature of the charge, the choice of the court, and the logic of the argument. These are problems of advocacy, and in a sense of power and influence, of how to get one's way in a situation of conflict.

Assume that someone drives a heavy truck into your backyard, plowing up the lawn, destroying bushes and trees. In the process, the driver makes off with some lawn furniture and other objects of private property. Fortunately, you get a good look at the truck before it gets away. What do you do? You may call the police and file a criminal complaint. In this case, the prosecutor takes over and the matter is pretty much out of your hands. The prosecutor now decides whether to bring charges at all, and if so, what charges to bring. Is this a case of criminal trespass, reckless driving, criminal destruction of property,

---

[7] *However, the Supreme Court does seek out cases on points of constitutional interpretation that it thinks should be clarified. For a specific example, and a superb treatment of the process of constitutional interpretation by the Supreme Court generally, see Anthony Lewis; Gideon's Trumpet (New York: Random House, 1964).*

burglary, theft, or larceny? The choice will involve questions of strategy for the prosecuting attorney. What kind of evidence is available? What charges can be proved beyond a reasonable doubt? Might the accused be willing to plead guilty to a lesser charge so as to avoid the expense and trouble of a full-scale trial? Each crime has its own definition in law, and a charge must satisfy each of its "elements." Larceny, for example, generally applies only to the theft of movable objects. The theft of your lawn furniture would seem to fit, but "stealing" your land by moving property stakes in the dark of night would not. Some other charge would have to be brought.

However, other problems of choice for the plaintiff arise out of the illustration. There are not only criminal charges here, but possible civil wrongs as well; the plaintiff might bring a civil action for property damage. The plaintiff can choose to bring a criminal action, a civil action, *or both*. If it seems unlikely that one could collect damages from the driver himself, could a suit be brought against his employer? To what extent is the employer responsible for the conduct of his employees?

A further problem for the plaintiff is the choice of court. Usually this is a technical matter. In the United States, there are two judicial systems, one run by the states and the other by the federal government. In most states, the systems of trial courts include courts of general jurisdiction (typically called district or circuit courts) which handle most kinds of cases. Courts of special jurisdiction include probate, traffic, divorce, juvenile, and other specialized branches of law. Small claims courts hear cases involving small sums—often less than $1000—through informal procedures. The federal court system has jurisdiction over two types of cases, those involving "diversity of citizenship"—where the parties are citizens of different states—and those involving federal laws. Both systems have appellate courts—in federal system, eleven courts of appeals and the Supreme Court.[8]

Often the choice of court is obvious or predetermined. However, in some cases, a choice will have to be made between bringing federal or state charges where both systems of law apply. There may be both federal and state environmental protection laws that apply to a particular situation, and the question is which court is apt to be most favorable to your action. In some cases, you can choose between different courts of first instance. One might be in a position to bring a federal case in any number of district courts. Lawyers get a feeling for the tendency of different courts—the district court of New York has a reputation for favoring business interests, that of Washington, D.C. for being liberal

---

[8] *Carl A. Auerbach, Lloyd K. Garrison, Willard Hurst, and Samuel Mermin,* The Legal Process *(San Francisco: Chandler, 1961), pp. 3–5.*

on civil rights matters—and such factors may enter into the choice of jurisdiction.

The third problem for the plaintiff is how to structure the argument, how to present the facts of the case so that all the elements of law as defined by the charge are accounted for, and point relentlessly toward a specific conclusion. In the above illustration, the plaintiff's property was in fact damaged in the ways specified, the damage was done by this particular truck, and the respondent was in fact the driver of that truck, and his action was in fact willfully negligent. In a trial, the management of the evidence is entirely in the hands of the plaintiff's attorney. The court cannot make the plaintiff's case for him. The court only takes cognizance of the evidence and the charges that the plaintiff brings.

The problem of choice and judgment is particularly important for the prosecuting attorney, for he (or she) has important powers of independent discretion in criminal cases. Not only does the prosecutor determine what charges are to be brought—the choice between murder and manslaughter, for example—but he also has formal authority over other aspects of the legal process. The prosecutor can decide how much bail will be recommended, which has implications for whether a defendant goes free or languishes in jail. He determines whether to press charges or to dismiss, how many counts of each charge will be brought, and whether charges will be reduced if the defendant agrees to plead guilty. All of these the prosecutor does with little direct supervision or control. Furthermore, the prosecutor may pursue investigations of his own into specific areas. The way a prosecutor uses this discretionary power has a significant impact on law and law enforcement in any community. He may, if so inclined, "overlook" illegal activities by the solid, substantial citizens and bear down hard on minorities or particular feared and troublesome groups. He may emphasize some areas of criminality and neglect others. While background, ideology, community attitudes, and political ambitions may all influence the prosecutor's judgment, he may also be calculating the "conviction rate." No prosecutor wants to be known as a loser, and the ratio of convictions to cases is important in the way attorneys in this field evaluate one another. Consequently, there is an interest in bargaining for guilty pleas and bringing charges that he feels he can win.[9]

The Defense

Hypothetically, the defendant does not have to prove anything. The

---

[9] *James Eisenstein,* Politics and the Legal Process *(New York: Harper and Row, 1973), pp. 102–105.*

burden falls entirely on the plaintiff. In theory, at least, the parties to a case in the Anglo-American system of law do not start even. The court is expected to be biased in favor of the defendant, who is presumed innocent until proven guilty. This is, however, an attitude that is often hard to accept or sustain. Many jurors will feel that anyone who has gotten into so much hot water must surely be guilty, and part of the defense attorney's responsibility is to assure that the basic principle of the presumption of innocence is thoroughly ingrained in the jurors' minds. To this extent, the job is an educational one.

The task of the defense is to cast doubt on the plaintiff's case. The three key strategic considerations are legal relevance, the statement and interpretation of the facts, and the element of excuse or mitigation.

For the first, the attorney examines the logic of the charge and the principles of law invoked by his opponent. Even granting that the facts are as stipulated—so what? The accused might have said some unkind things about the plaintiff in the newspaper, but they were not slanderous—not designed to injure the plaintiff's reputation—they were rather the kind of legitimate criticism that any public official must expect and that is protected under the first amendment right of free speech. The defense brings an alternative principle to bear, and introduces precedents—decisions from earlier cases—to show that the kind of language used by his client has previously been considered appropriate in the exercise of this right. The ground of argument has been shifted. The problem is to be defined not as one of slander but of freedom of speech.

For the second, the defense examines the plaintiff's statement of the facts. Did the driver of the wayward truck actually steal the lawn furniture? The plaintiff identified the truck, but did he actually see the driver, given that he was not able to record the license number? Someone else, of course, could have been driving the truck.

The question of mitigation or excuse is the third facet of defense advocacy. Law rests on what "a reasonable person would do," and this urges the questions of what reasons can be given for the defendant's conduct. It is the right of the defendant to explain himself. Yes, the defendant did drive the truck onto the lawn, but he was trying to avoid hitting a child who had suddenly run out into the street. Yes, the candidate was responsible for an undercover investigation of the personal habits of his opponent, but he did not authorize illegal entry into his home or his psychiatrist's office, and he was far too busy with the affairs of state to supervise every detail of his campaign.

Attorneys and Conflict Resolution

The trial, culminating in a verdict, is the classic model of legal process. However, most legal disputes are not settled that way. The largest number of cases are settled before they come to court. As high as 90 percent of felony cases are settled by guilty pleas, which do not involve the full adversary process. In some respects, the trial is the exceptional form of legal process.

Much of the process of conflict resolution in law goes on between attorneys and their clients through techniques of compromise and bargaining. In civil matters, an agreement may be negotiated between the principals after each has consulted with lawyers, with no need for formal judicial proceeding. Many cases, such as settlements for debts, do not reach trial simply because the defendant does not appear. Some cases are settled in pretrial proceedings, when initial motions are made in the presence of a judge.

In criminal cases, plea bargaining is a characteristic conflict resolution process. Here, the defendant agrees to plead guilty to a lesser offense rather than defend himself against a more serious charge. From the prosecutor's point of view, this procedure assures certain convictions rather than expensive and time-consuming trials where the outcome may be doubtful. For the defense, the risk of long imprisonment or a serious criminal record is reduced. Some suggest that plea bargaining is a necessary part of the criminal justice system. If all cases went through a full trial proceeding, the courts would be swamped. However, others argue that the procedure results in serious miscarriages of justice and a weakening of legal order. Many innocent people may be encouraged to plead guilty when caught up in a process that is intimidating and confusing. We create a system of legal fictions which is not the same as justice. Manslaughter and reckless driving are not the same thing, and to claim that they can be freely exchanged is a perversion of justice.

Plea bargaining calls for shrewd strategic calculations by both parties. Defense and prosecution estimate the strength of the case of the other side. If the defense can persuade the prosecution that there are serious flaws in the case, a bargain for a substantial reduction of charges is possible. If the prosecutor's case is strong, there is less latitude for bargaining. In either case, there is both an element of bluff and of the mutual exchange of information and confidence involved.[10]

The Judge and the Jury

The judge's role is both that of umpire and policymaker. He or she guides the procedure of a trial, as the head of a committee guides the process of policy deliberation. In trial by jury, the judge determines the principle of law and the jury the facts and the verdict. Where jury trial does not apply, where it is waived, and in appellate cases, the judge or judges are the sole decision makers.

---

[10] *For a fine discussion of the process, see James Eisenstein,* Politics and the Legal Process, *pp. 110–118.*

As decision maker, the judge's role is the same as that of anyone else in this position. The problem is that of authoritative choice from among alternative possibilities, each of which has some plausibility. And the problem is one of justifying an authoritative decision—of giving good reasons for the conclusion reached.

In theory, the task of the judge is to enunciate the legal principle that corresponds to the facts of the case. This is called the *ratio decidendi*, the point on which the decision turns. The written opinion is an argument justifying the choice of a particular "turning point." It gives reasons to show the correspondence of the principle to the facts, and it provides grounds for eliminating alternative possibilities. Consider the reasoning of Chief Justice John Marshall in the case of *Marbury* v. *Madison*,[11] which legitimated the practice of judicial review in the American political system.

When there is a charge that the Constitution has been violated, who should decide the question? Congress cannot have the power, for its powers are defined and limited by the Constitution. Clearly it was not the intent of those who provided a written constitution that it should be overruled by those whose powers it defined and limited. Similarly, the power cannot reside in the president, for in that case, this branch would be the sovereign, it could overrule any act of Congress, and once again, the written constitution would be meaningless. It is the function of the judiciary to interpret law. The Constitution is a form of law. If an act of Congress is in opposition to the Constitution, should the court disregard the Constitution? Clearly not. Therefore, the power of constitutional interpretation resides in the judiciary and the Supreme Court.

However, the definition of the *ratio decidendi* is itself a matter of choice and judgment. There are many facts in a case, and the ones that are material to the decision can appear quite differently to different people. As Julius Stone points out, there are, in fact, as many possible *rationes decidendi*[12] as there are logically possible combinations of the facts. The judge's decision then represents one possible pattern of relationships between facts and principles. The opinion is, in fact, an argument for interpreting the matter before the court this way rather than some other. If appealed, this is the argument that a higher court will examine in relation to other plausible interpretations.

Where does the judge find the law that is to be applied to cases? As Benjamin Cardozo says,

There are times when the source is obvious. The rule that fits the

---

[11] *1 Cranch 137 (1803).*

[12] *Julius Stone, "The Ratio Decidendi" in Auerbach, Garrison, Hurst, and Mermin,* The Legal Process, *p. 62.*

case may be supplied by the constitution or by statute. If that is so, the judge looks no farther. The correspondence ascertained, his duty is to obey. The constitution overrides a statute, but a statute, if consistent with the constitution, overrides the law of judges.[13]

The "law of judges" is basically that of precedent. (For example, Justice Marshall's reasoning in *Marbury* v. *Madison* stands as a precedent justifying the Supreme Court's authority to interpret the Constitution in all subsequent cases.) To argue from precedent involves seeing analogies between previous cases and the one presently at issue. For example, the law of larceny was developed basically to deal with cattle theft in early Anglo-Saxon England, around the thirteenth century. But to steal a horse is like stealing a cow, and an automobile is like a horse, hence the law of larceny applies to auto theft, whether or not the legislature has specifically mentioned automobiles in the criminal statutes.[14]

The principle behind precedent is that the law should be consistent, that similar cases should be decided by the same standard, so that the individual knows where he stands in relation to the rules of society. This is stated as the rule of *stare decisis*, that previous judgments should be followed unless there are absolutely compelling reasons to do otherwise.

Nonetheless, argument from precedent is an act of choice, perception, and judgment. Is a labor union 'like' a conspiracy, in that it deprives an employer of his right to freely hire and fire who he wishes? Or is it like a voluntary association among workers which must be protected by the laws of free association? Or is collective bargaining a form of contract, and should this body of law apply? Such issues were hotly contested in Anglo-American law throughout the nineteenth and early twentieth centuries, and the problem was only really settled in the United States with the National Labor Relations Act of 1936, which finally legalized and regulated labor organization and collective bargaining.

There is some discretion in every judicial decision. To be sure, in the great majority of cases, the weight is heavily on one side or the other. As Cardozo once said, the decision in 90 percent of cases is predetermined from the outset. But when the law does not point firmly in one direction, the judge is thrown back on his own resources. Here the judge not only applies law but also creates it. ("Of course judges make law," one once said to me, "I made some myself this morning.")

---

[13] *Benjamin Cardozo,* The Nature of the Judicial Process *(New Haven: Yale University Press, 1921), p. 14.*

[14] *Jerome Hall,* Law, Theft and Society, *Second Edition (Indianapolis: Bobbs-Merrill, 1952), p. 259.*

The judge makes a decision in a concrete case. But that decision may stand as a precedent in later cases. The decision may shape the legal system itself.

In this situation, the judge faces all the fundamental questions of public choice. Matters of political principle arise. The courts are deciding what rights will be recognized, what conceptions of equality, freedom, and justice will be embodied in law. The ideological convictions of judges become significant. A more "liberal" Supreme Court, like the Warren Court, will move the law in the direction of greater emphasis on equality and individual rights, particularly where the "underdogs" are affected, in such areas as segregation and defendants' rights. The more conservative Burger Court retrenches a bit in its reading of the idea of equal protection of the laws and on such issues as pornography and defendants' rights.

Similarly, the way judges assess their responsibility, their conception of their role, has a bearing on how they will decide. Some see themselves as "activist" judges, explicitly acting as policymakers on major public issues. This is the tradition of Cardozo, Brandeis, Holmes, and Douglas. Others, such as Frankfurter, and some members of the Burger Court, define their responsibilities in terms of "judicial self-restraint," confining themselves more to the craft and the interpretation of law in the technical sense.

Of course, the environment of power affects judicial decisions. Political ambition and community and peer group pressures all bear on the way in which judges make decisions.[15] Should judges be political realists? Should they calculate the chances of enforcement or compliance with the law when they make decisions? Or should they decide only on facts and principles and let others cope with the issue of practicality?

At some level, judges must be aware not only of the legal but also of the social and economic implications of their choices. When a judge issues an injunction against the construction of the Alaskan pipeline, or rules on a complex issue of antitrust law that affects a corporation like General Motors or IBM, he or she is dealing with fundamental issues of public policy. Here judicial decision deals not just with the law but also with such issues as the relative priority to be given environmental protection and energy supply, or the productive potential and competitive capacity of the nation in world trade. To what extent judges should be concerned with the social consequences of their decisions is a standing argument in legal theory. To what extent

---

[15] Jack W. Peltason describes the pressures brought against southern Federal court judges who made pro-integration decisions in the 1960s in Fifty-Eight Lonely Men (New York: Harcourt, Brace and World, 1961), Chap. 8.

their decisions are based on ideological or public policy preferences is a heated controversy in political science.

Some argue that in effect judges make up their minds on the basis of their own views and that the written opinion is a form of rationalization. Others feel that the opinion is a search for consistency between what is a policy choice and the logic of the law. Of course, like the rest of us, judges think about the disputes they must settle in different ways, and the same judge may go at different cases in different ways. What distinguishes judges from policymakers in general (at least at the higher levels) is that they have in common the experiences of legal education, and that their public choices must be argued and justified in the language of the law. Thus, in addition to the considerations that enter into any problem of policy choice, judges must be aware of the implications of their decisions for the legal system itself. Furthermore, their opinions will be tested by the "invisible college" of the legal community for consistency with the basic premises of this form of political argument and choice. Finally, of course, the legitimacy of law itself, in the long run, depends on the belief of the community that this form of conflict resolution is on the whole reasonable and fair.

ideal of a fair trial

Like all other aspects of political order, the organization of the legal process is a subject for argument and public choice. The law poses its own problems of political design and structure. Foremost among these is the ideal of a fair trial. As stated earlier, the central point of the adversary proceeding is that both parties appear as equals before the court, differences in status, power, and resources being reduced to reasoned argument through the procedures of law. Yet this ideal is not often fully realized in practice. And to the extent that it is not, questions arise of reform and change.

Like the political order in general, law can be envisioned as a system of rights. In the United States, basic constitutional rights provide a framework for the evaluation of legal institutions.

1. *Rights against the imposition of sanctions before the trial.*
   a. Arrest on warrant or sufficient cause.
   b. Right to indictment by a grand jury.
   c. Habeas corpus.
   d. No excessive bail.

The state has no right to impose punishment. Only a court can do that. From the point of view of the law, the judgment of the police or the prosecutor that an individual has broken the law begins a dispute between government and the individual, it does not resolve it. Certain fundamental rights then apply against the use of coercive force to impose sanctions on individuals. The requirement that the government prove to a court or grand jury that reasonable grounds exist to suspect an individual of a crime is a check on potential arbitrariness by officials. The writ of habeas corpus requires that a person held by authorities be brought before a court so that inquiries can be made regarding the grounds of his detention. Like the right against excessive bail, the intent is to prevent law enforcement agencies from imposing punishment without a judicial proceeding. (For similar reasons, the police are legally required to show that they have used no more than "reasonable force" in apprehending a suspect.)

2. *Rights against the use of power to give government an advantage in the trial.*
   a. No unreasonable searches or seizures.
   b. No forced confessions.
   c. Right to counsel and to remain silent.

Differences in the power of the parties should have no bearing in law, including the power of the state. A second category of rights is intended to reduce the possibility that the police and prosecution will use their authority and power to build their case against a suspect. Thus the law should protect against the use of force to obtain evidence or to get a confession. However, psychological pressure may be just as important as coercion or brutality. For the average person, the experience of being arrested and questioned is highly intimidating. He feels guilty, whether he is or not. Those who have learned positive attitudes toward the police may be inclined to be helpful, to cooperate even as a case is built against them. Others simply feel helpless against the power of government. Disoriented and frightened, the person simply wants to escape from the present dilemma, and so he "goes along" with his captors or is unaware of the implications of what he is saying. For such reasons, the law has come to the view that the adversary process begins at the point of first apprehension and not with the trial itself. The individual has the right of counsel and against self-incrimination from the time of arrest. As every fan of detective programs knows, the police are required to "give the suspect his rights" at the time he is taken into custody—though many doubt that this is a sufficient safeguard.

3. *Rights within the trial.*
   a. Right to counsel and against self-incrimination.
   b. Right to "due process of law."
   c. Right to a speedy trial.
   d. Trial by jury.
   e. Rights of appeal.

Again, the problem is to assure that both sides are reduced to equality in argument. The right to legal counsel and against self-incrimination continues from the pretrial period. The right to due process of law includes the numerous technical rules of procedure embedded in the common law notion of a fair trial—the right to make various motions, to present evidence and testimony, to confrontation with hostile witnesses, to cross-examination—all rights that should be equally available to both parties. The right to a speedy trial is of course based on the notion that "justice delayed is justice denied." Trial by jury is a right, not a requirement of judicial process. The parties may waive the right and be tried simply by a judge, but the court itself may not decide to dispense with a jury in cases where the right applies.

    4. *Rights against the power of the court.*
        a.   No cruel or unusual punishments may be imposed.

The court then, and not the state, has the right to impose punishment. But this power too must not be used arbitrarily. In recent years, this standard of justice has again become controversial. Is capital punishment in itself "cruel and unusual"? Some argue that the chance of mistake is so great in capital cases, the possibility that the extreme penalty will be applied in a reasonable and consistent manner so small, that it must be eliminated.

Issues of legal reform

It is remarkable how recently some of these rights, which seem so essential to the idea of a fair trial, have actually become part of American judicial procedure. Until 1963, for example, there was no requirement that defendants be represented by counsel before state courts in noncapital cases. A person without funds could be sent to jail without having representation by a lawyer in many states. In the case of *Gideon* v. *Wainwright*, [16] the Supreme Court unanimously held that a state must furnish counsel to indigent defendants. In subsequent years, the right against self-incrimination and the right to confront witnesses was also made obligatory in state courts. Only in 1966, in *Miranda* v. *Arizona*, [17] was the idea that the adversary process begins with arrest and that the individual has a right to have counsel present during interrogation recognized in law. These and other developments in legal process usually go under the heading of "defendants' rights." As always, emphasis on one set of rights raises issues of others. Some feel that such reforms have tipped the balance too much in favor of the defendant and have hampered police work; they urge that more atten-

---

[16] *372 US 335 (1963). This case was also the subject of Anthony Lewis'* Gideon's Trumpet *referred to above.*
[17] *384 US 436 (1966).*

tion be given to the rights of the community and to the victims of crime. If the state has an obligation to enforce law, does it owe compensation to those who suffer loss or injury as a result of crime? Attention is also being given to the rights of prisoners, and some feel that this is a neglected area in our discussions of legal fairness.

The judicial process, like all other political institutions, is perennially under construction. The idea of a fair trial is an ideal, not an assurance. As such, the procedures of law are always a source of argument. In recent years, new questions have been raised about the quality of justice provided by the legal system.

One basic criticism is that the law is apt to be applied more severely to the poor, to minorities, and to the ignorant than to the more prosperous, respectable, and better educated. Students of judicial reform have begun to collect statistics, and they consistently find that the middle class citizen is likely to receive a suspended sentence or probation, while the poor or the nonwhite go to jail for the same offense. At the lower levels of the court system, prejudice may be the rule rather than the exception. Some criminal court justices see themselves essentially as part of the law enforcement system, rather than as impartial adjudicators. Many laws—against loitering, public drunkenness, vagrancy, and the like—are designed to be applied only against one class of the population. (When did you last hear of a banker being arrested for sleeping in a railroad station? But some do, when they miss trains.) The Supreme Court has ruled that capital punishment is often cruel and unusual, simply because it is rarely invoked, and when it is, the condemned is normally from a group out of favor with the "respectable" community.

Another problem is that of the quality of legal representation. Both parties may have counsel, but the dice are loaded when one side can generally get the better attorneys. The poor and indigent must rely on the services of inexperienced, overworked public defenders, who confront the collective resources of the police and the prosecutor's office. But the problem can, in fact, cut either way. The district attorney may also be understaffed and overworked and no match for the expensive and celebrated defense lawyer, backed by a platoon of legal researchers. When two forces of "harried justice" meet, the young, inexperienced prosecutor with a long docket of cases to prepare and try confronting the public defender in the same situation, the chances of adequate justice being done are very small indeed.

The high cost of justice lurks behind many issues of judicial reform. Some argue that only the very rich and very poor can afford justice in the present system. A major trial may very well cost over $100,000. The working class or middle class litigant is priced out of the market. If accused of a crime, an adequate defense may lead to bankruptcy. And a person with limited resources is hardly likely to use the law to resolve civil conflicts with other individuals and companies.

Some begin to take the law into their own hands. The small contractor is tempted to throw a rock through a window rather than go to court to collect a bad debt. Equality in law seems a very remote ideal for the individual contemplating taking on a giant corporation in a civil suit, with its full-time staff of highly paid attorneys.

What are the remedies? Public service legal organizations have emerged in some areas, prepared to support litigation in specific fields, such as consumer protection, environmental affairs, or civil liberties. But such services are sparse and even in principle do not answer the question. Organizations like the American Civil Liberties Union select cases at their own discretion (and must do so with an eye to their own limited resources). They cannot, in the nature of things, assure that the right to adequate representation will be met. A more extensive system of small claims courts, where adequate justice could be provided for routine and minor matters without need for expensive legal assistance, is another possibility. The streamlining and simplification of judicial procedures, the elimination of minor and prejudicial crimes, could reduce both the cost of justice and the burden on police, the courts, and the legal profession alike.

The ideal of speedy justice is also not always met in practice. Justice in America is often extremely late and normally time-consuming. In many jurisdictions, months and sometimes years pass before cases come to trial. Where criminal courts are clogged, defendants may sit in jail for long periods before their cases are heard—a denial of justice that goes to the heart of the system. Attorneys become expert in protracting litigation in civil matters, hoping that plaintiffs will give up eventually or settle out of court for less than they had claimed simply to get the matter over with. There is a fine line between a system of justice that is scrupulous and painstaking in its concern for rights, for fair procedure, and full hearing, and one that becomes so complex, convoluted, and ponderous that it defeats its own objectives.

●nclusion

The process through which we make public decisions is seldom defined once and for all. Rather, political organization and structure is an ongoing problem for decision making in itself, perennially open to argument. What is true of the political system in general applies as well to the processes of law. The idea of a fair trial is that parties in conflict will have equal ability to present their case before an impartial tribunal. This is a central criterion of political evaluation against which existing systems of law may be appraised and which provides grounds for possible reforms and changes. Fundamental issues of choice become apparent. Does plea bargaining simplify the system of justice, or does it create greater injustice, as innocent parties agree to plead guilty to some charge to avoid further frustrating involvement with the law? Does equal justice imply not only the right to counsel but also the right to counsel of approximately equal ability as your opponent? And if the latter, how can the goal be reached in practice? If the law is applied unequally to different groups and classes, how can greater equality be achieved, while avoiding the extremes of a law that is too lenient to protect the safety of the community and the rights of individuals, and on the other side, a law that becomes rigid and unreasonable by treating everyone with harsh severity?

The law, basically, is a means of conflict resolution provided by government to citizens as a public service. As such, it is a part of the political order, a means of promoting peace, order, and personal security. It is also essential to the realization of individual rights, against the state as against other individuals. But what if this system is not in practice available to all citizens as a means for resolving conflicts and enforcing rights? On grounds of equality, it is hard to justify a service of this kind that is more available to some than to others simply for reasons of ability to pay. It is hard to argue that the enjoyment of rights should be contingent on having the economic means to see that they are enforced. And on grounds of efficiency, it is difficult to defend those aspects of the system that, through delay, complexity, and simple bad practice, defeat their own objectives.

for further reading

Bickel, Alexander, *The Least Dangerous Branch: The Supreme Court at the Bar of Politics* (Indianapolis: Bobbs-Merrill, 1962). A thorough discussion of the role of the Supreme Court in the American political system.

Casper, Jonathan, *American Criminal Justice: The Defendant's Perspective* (Englewood Cliffs, N.J.: Prentice-Hall, 1962). A realistic analysis of the system from the point of view of those who get caught up in it.

Eisenstein, James, *Politics and the Legal Process* (New York: Harper and Row, 1973). Probably the best of a number of recent books looking at the legal process as a problem of politics and political behavior.

Friedman, Wolfgang, *Law in a Changing Society*, Revised Edition (Baltimore: Penguin Books, 1972). The relation of law to contemporary social change and public policy. Excellent treatment of law and economic affairs. Deals with Europe as well as America.

Hall, Jerome, *Law, Theft and Society*, Second Edition (Indianapolis: Bobbs-Merrill, 1952). The best book I know on the growth of law over time and the use of analogy and precedent in legal reasoning.

Holmes, Oliver Wendell, *The Common Law* (Boston: Little, Brown, 1963), Mark Dewolff Howe (Ed.). An excellent statement of the basic assumptions and principles of the Anglo-American common law.

Lewis, Anthony, *Gideon's Trumpet* (New York: Random House, 1964). A superb treatment of the process of constitutional interpretation in the Supreme Court. As pleasant to read as a good novel.

Llewelyn, K. N., *The Bramble Bush* (Dobbs Ferry, N.Y.: Oceana Publications, 1960). The introductory lectures of a great law professor to his students, outlining the idea of law and the principles of legal practice.

Mermin, Samuel, *Law and the Legal System* (Boston: Little, Brown, 1963). Like the above, designed as a beginning book for law students. Solid and packed with information. Takes a sample case to discuss its legal ramifications.

Pound, Roscoe, *Social Control Through Law* (New Haven: Yale University Press, 1968). The relationship of law to the problem of political order.

Pritchett, C. Herman, *The American Constitutional System*, Second Edition (New York: McGraw-Hill 1967). A brief survey of American constitutional law, somewhat dated.

Shapiro, Martin, *Law and Politics in the Supreme Court* (New York: The Free Press, 1964). Discusses the impact of the Supreme Court in public policymaking, particularly economic affairs.

chapter
fifteen
the "system"

We must finally confront the most formidable problem of all, that of political order for society as a whole. The political system of a nation is more than its constitution—the formal arrangement of the offices of government. It includes all the processes by which public opinion is mobilized and expressed, the relationships of economic and social institutions to politics, the values, myths, and beliefs that tie a people together to form a community. The political system is nothing less than the overall pattern of power and authority relationships in society as a whole.

Just classifying the political systems of the world is a perplexing task. We start with the conventional polarity between democracies and dictatorships—between those regimes that rest on free, competitive elections and those that do not. But when we look closely at particular cases, all kinds of problems become apparent. A variety of different systems appear in the democratic category. The nations of the English-speaking world and Scandinavia seem to have one kind of democracy, but France is something else again. France has democratic institutions, but also a tradition of strong, centralized, bureaucratic power. Parliament seems less important in France than Great Britain, and the administration more so.

There are multiparty, two-party, and one-party democracies. There are nations like Mexico, which have all the trappings of democracy, but where one party, the PRI, has been in power consistently since the 1920s. Are democratic institutions only a facade here, and should the Mexican system really be classified as an authoritarian regime? After all, the Soviet Union also has a democratic constitution and holds regular elections for the Supreme Soviet, but it would obviously be stretching the point to call Russia a democracy. But if we exclude Mexico, what are we to do with Sweden, where the Social Democratic party has been dominant since the early 1930s, or Japan, where the Liberals have held power since World War II?

Still it seems possible to distinguish "authentic" democracies from nondemocracies by asking whether an opposition party could plausibly win the next election—whether it would be permitted to take power. That seems to distinguish the Soviet Union from Japan and Sweden, but it is hard to be sure about Mexico. Such a test becomes a matter of the personal opinion of the observer. There is no objective way of making the distinction. And if we use party competition as the test of democracy, how do we compare two-party and multiparty systems? The more extreme parties, both of the right and the left, are stronger in such nations as France and Italy than they are in Britain or the United States. In these nations, the Communist party may win up to one-quarter or more of the votes in a general election, and they have a real chance of coming to power by themselves, or in coalition with other parties. Does this mean that France and Italy should be considered *more* democratic than Britain or the United States?

The category of dictatorships also raises problems. There are military dictators, civilian dictators, and party dictatorships, and they all have different characteristics. Another distinction that can be made is between authoritarian and totalitarian systems. In an authoritarian regime, for example, Franco Spain and Brazil, the dominant elite monopolizes political power but does not try to restructure society completely. In a totalitarian system, the object is to use political power to create a completely new social order. The aspiration is to totally politicize society, while in an authoritarian system, a clear separation between private and public life remains. Nazi Germany, the Soviet Union, and the People's Republic of China are the usual examples of totalitarian systems. But once again, these distinctions are arguable, and much depends on the overall "atmosphere" of the regime in the mind of the observer. Both authoritarian and totalitarian systems deal ruthlessly with opposition. But both find that power has its limits. China and the Soviet Union alike eventually had to make compromises in their plans for overhauling society. The Soviet leaders found that they could not totally change the values and institutions of the Russian peasantry, and Mao learned that he could not do without the "experts." Totalitarianism is an aspiration, but is it ever an achievement? We do not want to classify political systems merely according to what the rulers think they are doing. We want to define how the system actually works. At this point, the clear-cut distinction between authoritarian and totalitarian systems begins to blur.

In evaluating and classifying political systems, we also have to deal with the problem of continuity. Because a nation has had one free election in a century does not make it a democracy, and a short-term military dictatorship may be a temporary aberration in a basically democratic nation. We want to know how to characterize the *system*, not merely the current government. How deeply rooted are democratic institutions—or nondemocratic ones?

Stable political order, either democratic or nondemocratic, is an unusual achievement. Political turbulence and change has been the rule in human political affairs over the past two centuries, stability the exception. Of the democracies, only the United States, Great Britain, Australia, Canada, New Zealand, Sweden, and Switzerland have consistently and without exception structured governments according to the same constitutional rules since the 1930s. (If we except the Nazi occupation period, Norway, Denmark, the Netherlands, and Belgium would also be included.) Of the nondemocratic regimes, only the USSR, Nicaragua, and Paraguay predate World War II (assuming that the restoration of the Spanish monarchy in 1975 marked a change of regime). All the rest of the political systems of the world have come into existence, been interrupted, or changed fundamentally in the last thirty-five years.

We also know that the structure of government alone does not give a full picture of the political dynamics of society. We have to take the economic system into account as well. Once again, we start with a simply dichotomy. We classify systems as capitalist or socialist depending on whether the principal means of production are privately or publicly owned. Now we confront further ambiguities and paradoxes. We begin to make a distinction between democratic and nondemocratic socialist states. Conventionally, Sweden is an example of the former, the USSR of the latter. Similarly, there can be democratic and nondemocratic capitalist systems—the United States and Spain.

Once again, the neat system falls apart on close examination. Sweden may be defined as a "social democracy," but its economic system is capitalistic. On the other hand, France, which we could hardly describe as a socialist system on any grounds at all, has a very large government-owned industrial sector. Over one-third of all industrial investment in France is in the hands of the government. The state owns or has a large share of ownership in many key industries—including electricity, oil, transport, and automobile and aircraft manufacture. France also has a planned economy, relying far less on the free play of market forces than would seem to be characteristic of a capitalist system. Yet, except for a brief period in the 1930s, France has never had anything resembling a socialist government. In many ways, the relationship of state and economy in

France is precapitalistic, a tradition that goes back to mercantilism and absolute monarchy.[1]

When we try to define our own political system, when we try to capture the essence of how the American system works in fact as well as in theory, the problem becomes particularly acute. Formally, the United States is a constitutional democracy, but to what extent is it actually so? Some recent political science textbooks—bearing titles like *The Irony of Democracy* and *Democracy for the Few*[2]—raise large questions about the system. They argue that America may not in fact be a democracy, that, as in some other societies, democratic institutions may be a facade behind which "real" power relationships operate. Economically, America has a capitalist system, yet we know that government and the economy are intertwined in complex and intricate ways. This is not precisely what Adam Smith—or Thomas Jefferson—had in mind.

the system: choice and judgment

We do make judgments on the nature of the political order as a whole. We try to find overall pattern in the complex and contradictory workings of our society. Then we define and characterize "the system" and compare it favorably or unfavorably with other societies, and with certain idealized conceptions of political order that exist in our minds. (America is not a *true* democracy, or *really* capitalistic, and the Soviet Union does not *actually* practice socialism—perhaps the system is better described as one of "state capitalism.") Such judgments stand as presumptions in political argument. They are first premises from which follow appeals for reform or social reconstruction; arguments for solidarity, thankfulness and the preservation of existing institutions; or perhaps nostalgic longing for a return to an historic golden age.

The fact that all such judgments are suspect is obvious. Social reality is complex and multifaceted. It admits to many possible patterns that can plausibly be taken to characterize the whole. But the fact that we cannot *accurately* characterize a political system as a whole

---

[1] *An excellent discussion of the "varieties" of capitalism in the modern world is Andrew Shonfield,* Modern Capitalism: The Changing Balance of Public and Private Power, *Revised Edition (New York: Oxford University Press, 1969).*

[2] *Thomas R. Dye and Harmon Ziegler,* The Irony of Democracy, *Second Edition (San Francisco: Wadsworth Publishing Co., 1972); Michael Parenti,* Democracy for the Few *(New York: St. Martin's Press, 1974). Perhaps the best of the revisionist texts is Kenneth M. Dolbeare and Murray J. Edelman,* American Politics, *Second Edition (Boston: D. C. Heath, 1974).*

does not mean that we have been asking the wrong question. When we define form and pattern, when we classify political systems, when we make judgments on the nature of political order as a whole, we are engaged in the very important business of political myth making. Every society needs an image of its collective identity. The image may take a variety of forms. It may be an historical one, a picture of the evolution and development of a people through time. It may be a logical construct, a systematic view of how the pieces of society fit together in a pattern and how various processes operate in relation to one another to create an organic whole. It may be an image phrased in terms of values and ideals, of approximation to some perfect form.

How the myth is formulated makes a great deal of difference.[3] Depending on which version of the myth is accepted, a people may become traditionalist or rational and interventionist, optimistic or pessimistic, supportive of their institutions or estranged from them. In everyday political argument, we do evoke various images of our collective identity, and the pictures that we create and endorse are not without their effect. Furthermore, the picture in our mind of the system as a whole has a very direct bearing on practical decision making.

It might be argued that overall political structure is not a problem of political choice at all, or at least not a choice in the same sense as deciding on a welfare program, a local zoning ordinance, or the operating rules of a committee or an administrative agency. Public choice takes place *within* a civilization, but it does not create it. The social order is not a consciously contrived artifice of human effort. Civilization is a product of custom and mores and traditions; it evolves organically over time and is not susceptible to rational direction. The point is well taken. Creating a blueprint for comprehensive social change does not seem like a very promising undertaking. We are very unlikely to reduce Western industrial civilization to its component parts and put it back together again in an entirely new way.

At the same time, however, we do recognize that much of the world we live in is, in part, a product of intentional, deliberate action by people in the past, who in a sense chose the institutions we live in for us. And there is no particularly good reason to believe that this process is over, that advanced industrial society has reached its final, finished form. If we phrase the questions correctly, we may find that we do face relatively concrete decisions about the design of major social institutions, and that the way we make these choices can have a large bearing on the further development of our political system.

---

[3] *E. J. A. Pocock,* Politics, Language and Time *(New York: Atheneum, 1971).*

Part of the problem with using simple categories like democracy and dictatorship, capitalism and socialism, to describe and define complex modern societies is that these concepts come from social theories that were designed for earlier, simpler societies. The classic theory of capitalism, like that of representative democracy, is a product of the late eighteenth century. Socialism is a product of the nineteenth. Each of these models of political and economic order emerged in a social system that no longer exists. As *principles* of political order, each retains a certain validity. The idea of the market still has persuasive force as an organizing principle in some situations. The values of constitutional democracy are still crucial in our appraisal of political institutions. Socialism is an ideal endorsed by many. But as a *description* of the order of modern industrial society, none is fully adequate.

What has changed fundamentally in the nature of political order over the past century? Many possibilities could be cited, but the most fundamental for our purposes is the growth of the large, complex organization. To a large extent, advanced industrial society is a more recent creation than we at first suspect. Most of the characteristic institutions of our age are developments of the last 100 years. Mass political parties only began to emerge in the second half of the nineteenth century. Before that time, "democratic process" was quite a different thing than it is today. The trade union began to develop in about the same period, but in the United States, it really only became a powerful political institution in the 1930s. The major trade associations and modern interest groups also began to multiply rapidly about the turn of the century. The corporation is an institution of ancient lineage, but the modern corporation, as many have noted, is an institution quite unlike its ancestors.[4] Peter Drucker captured the essence of this transformation in the following words:

> Only a lifetime ago, at the turn of the century, the social world of Western man might have been represented as a prairie on which man himself was the highest eminence. A small hill—government—rose on the horizon, but while it was larger than anything else there it was still quite low. Today, by contrast, man's social world, whether East or West, resembles the Himalayas. Man seems to be dwarfed by the giant mountains of

[4] *Adolf A. Berle and Gardiner C. Means,* The Modern Corporation and Private Property, *Revised Edition (New York: Harcourt, Brace and World, 1968); Edward S. Mason,* The Corporation in Modern Society *(New York: Atheneum, 1969).*

large-scale organization all around him. Here is the Mount Everest of modern government. Then come the towering cliffs of the large business corporations,and scarcely less high and forbidding, the peaks of the large powerful labor unions; then the huge universities, the big hospitals—all of them creatures of this century.[5]

Throughout this book, we have been aware that every organization has a political dimension. In modern society, government is a function of many institutions and associations besides the state. Corporations, unions, universities, foundations, and interest groups are part of the political order in at least three respects.

First, they attempt to influence public decisions, and in many areas they are part of the policymaking system of government.

Second, complex organizations themselves make what are, in effect, public decisions. The major institutions of our "mixed economy" are part of the process of planning and decision making for society as a whole. They decide what products and services will be produced and at what prices, how work will be organized and capital used. They share in that characteristic function of government, the allocation of scarce resources among competing wants and needs. They have a strong (some would say a preponderant) voice in determining the overall goals and direction of the society.

Third, complex organizations are, in effect, private governments.[6] They have rule-making authority, backed by sanctions, that is binding on their members. We are in many ways more intimately governed by organizations than by governments. Our everyday activities are normally more directly influenced by the regulations, by the rights and duties created by corporations, unions, universities and similar institutions than by the laws of the state.

The political system of a modern nation includes all such complex organizations, the connections between them, and their relationship to the state. We will have to be concerned about not only the political system that is created *within* such organizations but also the total political order that is made up *of* complex organizations. Now certain fundamental questions become apparent. What is the balance of power between these organizations? Is government still the overall source of policy direction for the society, or do the institutions of the economy, the corporations and trade unions, rival the state for power? Or do the complex organizations form an all-pervasive inte-

---

[5] Peter F. Drucker, The Concept of the Corporation *(New York: New American Library, 1964), p. vii.*

[6] *On the idea of private government see Sanford Lakoff and Daniel Rich (Eds.),* Private Government *(Glenview, Ill.: Scott, Foresman, 1973).*

grated system of coordination and control? Or do these organizations check and balance one another so that none becomes predominant? And then there are further issues to be considered. How are individuals to exert control over organizations that have grown remote, impersonal, and unresponsive, yet have tremendous power over their lives? How do we apply the theory of democracy to the institutions of modern society? If complex organizations make what are, in fact, public decisions, to whom are they responsible and for what?

To come to terms with such questions we need to establish criteria for decision. We need to make up our minds about what is problematic, if anything, about the institutional arrangements of our society as a basis for political argument. The first step might be to examine certain rival theories of political order that relate government to other organizations.

four models of political order

There are four basic models of the relationship of the state to other organizations and associations: pluralism, corporatism, social democracy, and totalitarian statism. Each of these can be used either as an empirical or a normative theory. As an empirical model, we can ask which of these better *characterizes* modern industrial society. As a normative ideal, we can ask which provides a more desirable *design* for political order.

Pluralism

The pluralist ideal is one of a political order in which authority is not vested in the state alone but is divided among a multitude of overlapping and competing groups and associations.[7] The complete political system is not the product of conscious plan. The associational life of the society is not directed by the state. Rather, institutions and organizations emerge autonomously in response to changing individual needs and aspirations. The social order is always in flux, constantly changing, as new institutions arise and become prominent, others decline, some persist as the preserve of small groups or subcultures. The trade union arises as a counterpoise to the power of the corporation. Interest groups emerge in a wide variety of fields. Some become permanent fixtures of the political landscape. Others complete their task—or fail—and disappear. Affiliation with organized religion ebbs

---

[7] Harold J. Laski, *"Authority as Federal,"* in A Grammar of Politics (London: Allen and Unwin, 1967), pp. 241–286.

and flows with the temper of the times. The great universities and research foundations occupy center stage for a time, then draw back and blend in more with the rest of the setting. Cooperative societies grow rapidly, then stabilize and persist as a minor but significant organizational form. All of this happens without any overall image of how society should be organized or should develop.

For the pluralist, association is a matter of individual choice. All organizations are forms of contract. The individual is free to enter an organization—or to leave it. A pluralist society contains a multitude of organizations, reflecting the diverse needs and interests of its inhabitants. The total social order reflects the sum total of individual decisions to affiliate with others in common undertakings. The organization can never tyrannize the individual as long as he is free to take his business elsewhere—to join a rival group or organize a new one.

Pluralism is to political order as the market is to the economy. Association is a product of the forces of supply and demand in the same way that the production of goods and services is organized by competition among a variety of manufacturers of similar and different products. In such a system, the structural tasks of government are limited. The better society results from a *laissez-faire* policy. The main role of government in social organization is to preserve freedom of association and to protect the contractual rights of individuals with regard to organizations. Beyond that, government serves to coordinate the institutions that are created in the society and to adapt them to one another. The government's role in the design of order is essentially responsive rather than creative.

Within the political order, voluntary associations act as interest groups. In a fully pluralist society, policy will reflect the balance of power within groups in the society. Should one interest become too powerful, "countervailing forces" will develop. Farmers' organizations rise to challenge the railroads, labor unions to confront the corporation, minority groups, conservation and consumer protection movements come into-existence to champion neglected issues. Over time, the system becomes more highly differentiated. The argument is joined. The policymaker must devise a program that satisfies the heterogeneous interests of society. The state becomes, in effect, an umpire among the claims of competing interests.

Pluralism, it is held, is a check on the exercise of governmental power, one more effective than the effort to create "limited government" by constitutional law. Where power is divided among a variety of groups and associations, no small elite can dominate society. Political loyalties run to private organizations as well as to the state. The individual may take the side of his union, or his church, against the government. But the individual belongs to a variety of groups. He is not only a union member, or a Catholic, or a Mason. Hence, no private body has an exclusive claim on his fidelity.[8]

Historically, America has generally been regarded as a close approximation of the pluralist ideal. Power is fragmented and divided, not only between levels of government, but among a variety of groups and associations. There is an ethos of voluntary organization in the country, noted since Alexis de Toqueville first remarked on the propensity of Americans to cooperate voluntarily for common purposes over a century ago.

However, in recent years, many have begun to question America's reputation as a pluralist society. Large, mass organizations come to displace smaller, more differentiated ones. The individual has less choice among competing alternatives. He is less free —sometimes quite unfree—to join a competing group or form a new one.

The rise to predominance of certain forms of organization—the giant corporation, the industrywide union, the "peak" interest group association (e.g., the national confederation of smaller bodies, like the United States Chamber of Commerce or the AFL-CIO)—brings into question the natural balance between interests. The more powerful institutions are closely linked to government. Large organizations play a powerful role in the representative process. They are accepted as spokesmen for their interests, though they may in fact represent no more than a minority of their members. Government, as in the pluralist model, may be responsive to group pressures, but it does not reflect the full spectrum of views and interests. Rather, public policy takes the direction desired by the predominant institutions, and the total political order takes a form consistent with the purposes and goals of such organizations.[9]

For those who take such a view of the overall structure of the American political system, the order as a whole cannot be described as pluralistic. It may have a closer resemblance to some form of corporatism, or democratic statism.

Corporatism

The word "corporatism" often has pejorative connotations. It is as-

---

[8] *The classic version of the ideal of interest group democracy may be found in David B. Truman,* The Governmental Process *(New York: Alfred A. Knopf, 1958), and Robert A. Dahl,* A Preface to Democratic Theory.

[9] *On the criticism of the pluralist model of American society, see Henry Kariel,* The Decline of American Pluralism *(Stanford: Stanford University Press, 1961); William E. Connolly (Ed.),* The Bias of Pluralism *(New York: Atherton Press, 1969); Theodore J. Lowi,* The End of Liberalism *(New York: W. W. Norton, 1969).*

sociated with fascist political systems, like those of Mussolini's Italy or Franco's Spain. However, corporatism can be understood simply as a general framework for political order. Corporatist institutions are present in many nations. Although they are more characteristic of Mediterranean and Latin American nations, they can be identified in many Western European nations and in Scandinavia. Some American institutions have corporatist overtones. As will soon be apparent, corporatism has nothing to do with "government by corporations," meaning business enterprises.[10]

In corporatist thought, the state is expected to play an active role in the design of political order. The government is not indifferent to the overall form of the associational life of the community. Organizations are something more than voluntary contracts among individuals. They are part of the organic life of the society. Classic corporatism has its roots in Aristotle and medieval Christian thought. There are certain natural associations that are essential to human well-being and development. Among these are the family, economic organization, the political community, and religion. The problem of government is to devise just and harmonious relationships among these institutions, and to assure that they play their proper role in human affairs.

The distinction between corporatism and totalitarianism is that the state is expected to respect the essential autonomy and integrity of other institutions. They are not just instruments of the state, but part of the social order that the state must nurture and protect. For example, the state must protect the family. It is not simply a private contract between individuals. Nor is it a means for making good citizens. It is a necessary part of the social order. (This outlook, in part, accounts for the fact that divorce laws are normally stricter in Latin nations.)

Perhaps the easiest way for an American to grasp the point is to consider our tradition of academic freedom in the university. The state is expected to support higher education. But it is not supposed to use the university as an instrument of political purposes. The university should be autonomous from the state, and the state should respect its integrity. The university, and not government, should define the purposes of the institution.

Corporatism does not have to rest on any particular philosophy. Classic corporatism, most often found in Latin nations, is the most articulate about its underlying principles. There are many other ways of arriving at the basic idea. For example, in the United States and

---

[10] Frederick B. Pike and Thomas Stritch (Eds.), The New Corporatism (Notre Dame: University of Notre Dame Press, 1974); Andrew Shonfield, Modern Capitalism (New York: Oxford University Press, 1969); Samuel Beer, British Politics in the Collectivist Age (New York: Alfred A. Knopf, 1969).

northern Europe, corporatism is often associated simply with rational management. The model of coordinating functionally diverse activities that is part of good business management is applied to the organization of the political order as a whole. Such ideas interested Herbert Hoover and other American leaders in the 1920s and were part of the New Deal policy of Franklin Roosevelt.

In corporatism, the role of the state is to rationalize the relationships between critical organizations. Although we may define them as capitalistic, nations with corporatist institutions (including at least France, Spain, Germany, Sweden, and, to some extent, Britain and perhaps the United States) do not rely on market forces entirely in structuring economic relationships. Rather, the state plays a role in organizing the economic system. Wages and prices, the terms of competition, the planning of production, are all functions that involve structured negotiations between economic organizations —corporations and trade unions—and the state. In France, for example, national economic planning is a political process, in which the government, the large firms, interest groups, the banks, and (in theory at least) the trade unions participate. In Sweden, prices and wages are, to a large extent, determined by formal meetings between the national employer's organization and the national trade union federation, with participation of the government.

In corporatist systems, major economic interest groups have a legitimate role to play in policymaking. "Pressure group influence" does not seem vaguely suspect and corrupt, as it does in the United States. Rather, the major organizations and associations are formally part of the decision-making process. Similarly, competitors are often actively encouraged to meet together and make plans for their industry as a whole. What would be regarded as "collusion" or "cartelization" in the United States, and prosecuted under antitrust laws (as, for example, when competitors get together to fix prices and to determine shares of the market) is often considered an appropriate way of rationalizing the economy in corporate systems.

As a system of interest representation, corporatism differs markedly from pluralism. In corporatist systems, interests are organized in a limited number of compulsory, noncompetitive, and functionally differentiated associations. They are licensed or created by the state and granted a deliberate monopoly of interest representation in their field. In pluralism, groups are multiple, voluntary, and competitive. They emerge autonomously, without state sponsorship, and are not granted specific representational authority.[11]

---

[11] *Philippe Schmitter, "Still the Century of Corporatism?" in Frederick Pike and Thomas Stritch, The New Corporatism, pp. 93–96. This article has an excellent bibliography on corporatist theory and practice.*

Thus, in a fully corporatist society (Franco Spain being a close approximation), there are *official* trade unions, industrial and professional associations, and interest groups. Those who practice a certain trade or work in a particular field must belong to them. Only these "licensed" groups have a right to participate in policymaking. Others that arise in society are suspect; they may be defined as "illegal associations" and suppressed.

Some would characterize America as a society moving from pluralism to corporatism. In many areas, private organizations are intimately involved with government. Transportation, energy, the stock market, and health care are all areas where the important trade associations and industries are expected to play a role in policymaking. The government agencies that regulate these fields have close connections with leaders of the industries, and in some cases, industrial organizations have a virtual veto power over appointments to the regulatory bodies. Some interest associations have a semiofficial policymaking status, as in the case of bar associations and medical associations that supervise licensing and professional practice in many states. However, it is important to keep in mind the distinction between such specific examples of corporatist practice and the idea of corporatism as an explicit philosophy of political order, one that the state attempts to impose on the organization of society as a whole.

Social Democracy

In defining a third position on the relation of the state to complex organizations as "democratic socialism," we again face the problem of the differences in European and American ideological labels. Many in the United States who define themselves as "liberals" or "populists" would subscribe to the general position outlined below.

To the democratic socialist, private institutions should be responsive to the will of the people, manifested through democratic processes, and acting through the power of government. Private organizations are essentially the creatures and instruments of popular will. Private power is a corrupting force in the political order.

For advocates of this position, the crucial problem of advanced capitalist society is that it takes its direction from the policies of giant organizations rather than from the will of the people. These private bodies in fact plan for society as a whole and use their influence over the leaders of government to advance their own purposes rather than those of the public. The problem of statecraft is seen as that of liberating the state from the control of private interests and ensuring that corporate enterprise, trade unions, and powerful interest associations are made responsive to popular sovereignty.

From this point of view, overall government planning of the economy and society is legitimate when the state itself is organized in a democratic manner. The people, through political action, should be able to control the direction and objectives of the society. The democratic socialist does not believe in complete government ownership of the means of production. Nor does he believe that private organizations should be reduced to agencies of the state. Whereas many democratic socialists would endorse some measure of direct government ownership and control of basic industries, in such fields as transportation, energy, and the like, most believe that the independence and vitality of private associations and businesses is essential to democratic society. The important problem is that private institutions should be responsive to the will of individuals and that the overall policies of the society should be determined democratically.

In achieving this end, a variety of means may be employed. Government ownership of industry is a policy option, not a dogmatic imperative. The state may regulate the economy through a variety of instruments. It may plan; it may use fiscal and budgetary policy to provide incentives to private enterprise compatible with democratically defined policy objectives; it may regulate the conduct of private bodies through law. It may attempt to make private organizations more internally democratic, through such measures as "worker's control" of industry.

The important point is that unlike the pluralist, the democratic socialist does not believe that the associational order of society should emerge autonomously, with only such government direction as is necessary to ensure that the system remain open and voluntary. Unlike the corporatist, he does not believe that there is a "natural order" of associations that the state should define, organize and protect. The democratic socialist shares with the pluralist the view that private associations should arise as a product of popular will. But the total order formed by such associations should be given political direction and planning through the democratically constituted powers of government.

Totalitarian Statism

Here the political order arises from a vision of the ideal society. The state is the exclusive organizing and directing force in society. The distinction between the state and society, private life and public life, disappears. The function of every organization—from the family to the athletic team to the factory and club—is essentially political. Its purpose is to advance the purposes of the state. All private associations are seen essentially as instruments of political action. Unlike pluralism, organizations do not emerge autonomously according to the interests and desires of individuals for affiliation and common purpose. Unlike corporatism, organizations do not have a distinctive function that the state is obliged to nurture and defend. Unlike democratic socialism, the state's role is not merely that of coordinating and directing an order that rests fundamentally on a highly diverse and differentiated universe of private organizations and assuring that the system remains responsive to popular will. Rather, every private body is legitimate and acceptable only insofar as it advances resolutionary purposes and serves to enhance the design for a "new order" of society.

Practical Problems of Political Order

Most of us will probably reject totalitarianism as a desirable model for the further development of our civilization. (And it should be noted that neither the Soviet Union, nor China, nor Cuba is fully totalitarian in its approach to political organization.) However, we do not really have to make a decision as to whether society should be organized along pluralist, corporatist, or social democratic lines. Every advanced industrial society contains elements of all three, and those who espouse one of these views frequently incorporate aspects of the others into their thought. These basic models can best be seen as a basis for political argument, as a point of departure for defining concrete problems and deciding on what to do about them. The issue is not only how we want to characterize society, but how we want to apply these principles when we face a dilemma of choice.

Thus, if you were a faculty member or an administrator of a public university, how you might respond to—and intervene in—the deliberations of the state legislature on the budget of your institution might depend on which of these views you endorsed. If you were a pluralist, you would think it appropriate for the university to actively defend its interests, to lobby for its budget and academic program in competition with other interest groups that were also trying to get the greatest support possible for their programs from the legislature. If you took a corporatist view, the most important principle might be to defend the autonomy and academic independence of the institution. To be sure, the legislature has the right to set the budget, but decisions on the academic program should be made by the faculty and not by the government. If your position was that of the democratic socialist, you might decide that the university was a public service to the citizens of the state and that the people, through their representatives, had a right to decide what the university should do and teach. If the legislature decided that more emphasis should be given to preparing students for jobs needed in the economy rather than in the liberal arts, then the university's responsibility is to change its program to meet that goal.

It is relatively easy to criticize the system. We all feel some estrangement from the regime of giant organizations. The problem is to find
remedies for its defects. It is often said that large organizations have
grown remote and impersonal. They exercise great power but are not
held accountable to the public through democratic process. They profoundly influence the lives of individuals, but they may not be sufficiently responsive to those who are affected by them. We need not
accept all the critical arguments against the giant institutions of our
society. There is, after all, much to be said for them. Normally, they
do meet high standards of efficiency and adaptability. We depend on
them to sustain our way of life. So we need not take the view that
large-scale institutions are in themselves a bad thing. Rather, the
question is whether there is room for improvement in their *political*
performance. There are at least four practical public policy options
that should be considered as we deliberate such matters.

Increasing Pluralism

In pluralist theory, the individual's ultimate power over an organization is his ability to leave it. The employee quits; the customer takes
his business elsewhere. The sanction of "exit" is an important
mechanism for assuring the responsiveness of organizations. The
threat of defection will often make leaders more solicitous about
the interests and grievances of those they serve.[12]

However, this sanction can only be effective when the individual
can leave an undesired relationship for an equivalent one without
great sacrifice or hardship. One policy option to be considered then
when we suspect that an organization has become oppressive, inefficient, or indifferent is the intentional creation of competition, perhaps
by government action.

There are a variety of ways in which government can encourage
organizational pluralism. It can provide incentives for the creation of
rival institutions. In some states, cooperative societies have lower
rates of taxation and looser legal regulation than private corporations,
and usually such laws were enacted in an effort to create competition
for private business. Government can actively encourage new forms
of association—the Community Action Programs, the Farm Bureau
Federation, and the United States Chamber of Commerce are all interest groups whose organization was at least in part a matter of
government initiative. Another alternative is for government to create
an enterprise that will compete with private enterprise. In the United

---

[12] *Albert O. Hirschman,* Exit, Voice and Loyalty, *pp. 1–29.*

States in the early 1970s, suspicion of the power of giant petroleum companies led some to suggest that government organize a public energy corporation that would compete against the major oil companies and provide a yardstick for policymakers in evaluating the price and profit performance of the large corporations.

Antitrust laws have a similar purpose. In a pluralist economy, it is government's responsibility to sustain competition. Monopoly is a public problem. When one firm, or a group of firms, can force out smaller competitors and dominate an industry, government may bring charges under the Sherman and Clayton Antitrust acts. If the courts find that an "unreasonable restraint on trade" exists, or that the dominant firms have engaged in illegal activities to control competition, the large firm may be broken up into smaller competing units. Over the years, antitrust laws have been used with varying degrees of vigor, depending on the sentiments of various administrations toward private enterprise. Some suggest that the laws should be made much stronger, and that dominance of an industrial sector itself, as well as illegal actions to restrain competition, be made subject to law. However, the important point is that there is a standing case in our public debate for government to assume the responsibility for sustaining competition, and that giant organizations are only legitimate when effective individual freedom of choice can be demonstrated.[13]

Whenever organization power seems arbitrary or oppressive, the creation of pluralistic competition can be considered as a policy alternative. Milton Friedman has advocated this as a remedy for what he sees as the authoritarian structure of the public schools. Education is legally compulsory and virtually a legal monopoly. The individual has little choice over the kind of education he receives. The values of professional educators, rather than the needs or interests of individuals are dominant in the schools. To the extent that citizens can influence school policy, it is through the cumbersome and imperfect process of school board elections. Private education suffers "unfair competition" from state-supported schools. Those who choose it must nonetheless pay taxes for public institutions.

For Friedman, the remedy is simple. We only have to change the basis of public financial support for education—from supporting the schools to supporting the students. Instead of using tax money to build school buildings and pay teachers, each individual would receive a comprehensive, lifetime grant for education. Beyond a stan-

[13] *For further details on antitrust policy, see Mark S. Massel,* Competition and Monopoly: Legal and Economic Issues *(Washington: The Brookings Institution, 1962); Marshall A. Robinson, Herbert C. Morton, and James D. Calderwood,* An Introduction to Economic Reasoning, Fourth Edition *(Garden City, N.Y.: Doubleday, 1967), pp. 51–79.*

dardized elementary education, each would decide how to use his educational "vouchers" in a marketplace of competing private educational institutions. Since each person would receive the same grant, equality of opportunity would be assured. Private entrepreneurs would have the incentive to develop varying educational programs responsive to the needs and desires of "consumers." Instead of mass, lock-step education, the system would become highly differentiated and experimental. In such a free market system, there would be competitive checks on the quality of instruction. Superior teaching and excellence in educational programs would be rewarded through the laws of supply and demand.[14]

Of course, Friedman's proposal is highly controversial. It assumes that society has only a very limited stake in the kind of education its people as a whole receive. It assumes that the individual, rather than society, should make the final judgment on what would be taught in the schools. Furthermore, it puts a great responsibility on the individual. If the individual chooses an education that proves worthless, or squanders his opportunities, he has no one to blame but himself. Nonetheless, Friedman's ideas are being taken seriously in educational policymaking circles, and they do illustrate one way of thinking about the problem of political order and individual freedom in a complex society.

Public Planning

A second response to the problem of political order in modern society is that the state take an active, dominant role in coordinating and regulating the system of private corporations and organizations. As we have noted, the democratic socialist (and many others as well) does not believe that pluralist competition can assure the responsiveness of the system. Modern society is too complex to be left to the laws of supply and demand, to the imperfectly synchronized decisions of major economic organizations. Shortages and bottlenecks occur, too much is produced in some areas and not enough in others. Some basic human needs—health care, housing, the quality of the environment—are neglected when basic decisions on what will be produced and how the product of society will be distributed are left to corporate enterprise and organized labor. The system is, in fact, planned and regulated. But the question is, who should do the planning? Should it be the dominant economic institutions or the democratic state?

Public planning is compatible with a democratic system of gov-

---

[14] *Milton Friedman,* Capitalism and Freedom *(Chicago: University of Chicago Press, 1962), Chap. 6.*

ernment and capitalistic economic organization. All modern nations practice some form of government planning, ranging from general Keynesian economic management through fiscal and monetary policy to the more comprehensive planning exercises of such nations as France.

If the power of large organizations seems to be a problem in considering the total political order of modern industrial society, one possible solution is to give government the authority to plan, to give overall direction and guidance to the system. The complex organization is not merely a private activity. It is also an instrument of public purposes. The ultimate source of authority in society must be government which is responsive to the public will. The complex organization must be integrated into an overall conception of public purposes.[15]

The primary dilemma is how democratic planning could be made to work in practice. The state, after all, can have purposes of its own. The institutions of government are not always responsive to the will of the people. What does it really mean to plan democratically? How can the "will of the people" be expressed in the planning process? The democratic socialist, and the populist, often seem to argue that the "public interest" is simply expressed through free elections that bring a party to power with a mandate to put its program into effect. In fact, when we start to consider the complexity of planning for a society like the United States, the problem of making planning truly democratic begins to appear quite formidable. How can the average citizen express an effective opinion on such matters as energy policy, airline rates and service, or wage and price policy? Are these issues so technical that they require expert judgment? In that case, how are the planners to be held responsible to public will?

When we begin to consider the difficulties of a conception of planning based simply on "majority rule," we may begin thinking of a more pluralist or corporatist conception of national planning. What is important is that society's goals be set not only by the interests of corporate enterprise but also through confrontation and negotiation among all the interests that are present in modern society. Much of what is called democratic planning is, in fact, corporatistic planning. In France, for example, a very elaborate participatory process has been created. The central government planning staff sets overall targets and priorities and then holds extensive consultation through a system of committees representing various economic sectors (steel, coal, agriculture, etc.). Government planners, trade associations, industrialists, bankers, labor unions (in theory at least—the French

---

[15] *The best statement of this position is John Kenneth Galbraith,* Economics and the Public Purpose *(Boston: Houghton-Mifflin, 1973).*

unions have been less than enthusiastic about the program), local governments, and community organizations meet and deliberate together to work out detailed programs for the different economic sectors and regions of the country.

Once we begin talking about how the public would be represented in any effort at democratic planning, we begin to realize that we are back in the world of the complex organization once again. Parties, trade associations, interest groups and labor unions are complex organizations in the same way as corporations. In a large society, consent must be organized to be effective. But the institutions through which consent is organized can also take on bureaucratic features, can become impersonal and uncompetitive, committed to their own expansion and to essentially private purposes. The quality of representation *within* such organizations now becomes crucial. And that problem leads us to a third way of looking at the problem of political order and the complex organization.

Democratizing the Complex Organization

Not many of the large organizations of our society are notably democratic in their internal political structure. That they should be made more so is an old idea that has been recently revived. Ralph Nader has urged that consumer or public interest representatives be appointed to the boards of large corporations (and many have, in fact). He also proposes that the federal government charter major corporations (most are now incorporated under fairly lenient state laws) and that these new corporate constitutions provide for a more representative system of management. European experiments in workers' control and industrial democracy are attracting new interest in America. Student protest movements of the 1960s advocated the radical democratization of the university.

This is another approach to change in the political order of modern society. We look at the large organization as a form of private government and ask how it can be made more responsive to those who are affected by its decisions. Instead of trying to control the organization through pluralist competition or public regulation and planning, we look to the political system of the organization itself and ask how it can be made more responsible.

In theory, the corporation is a representative political system. The stockholders elect the board of directors, who appoint the management. To the critics, there are two things wrong with the theory. First, in practice, shareholders control is not often effective. The annual meetings of large companies are largely ceremonial. Real control lies in the hands of the directors and the managers. (For most stockholders, voting power is unimportant. What is crucial is the power of exit—the ability to sell shares quickly in the stock market.)

The second problem is that the interests of investors are not the only ones affected by corporate policies. Employees, consumers, suppliers, citizens of the communities in which the corporation operates, and the public generally are all part of the constituency of the corporation. Yet they have little formal voice in the policies of the firm.

Here again, the corporation is viewed not merely as a private organization but as part of the political order. As such, it should be accountable to the public in the same way as government. As Ralph Nader says, "Corporations are effectively like states, private governments with vast economic, political and social impact. A democratic society . . . should not suffer such public power without public accountability. . . . It makes no public sense to apply the constitution to Wyoming and West Tisbury, Mass., but not to General Motors and Standard Oil of New Jersey."[16]

Precisely how corporate accountability can be brought about is another question. One approach is through the existing structure of the corporation. In the early 1970s, Ralph Nader's Project on Corporate Accountability sought to create what was in effect a second political party within General Motors. Stockholders can turn over their voting rights to others through the device of the proxy. When a proxy fight for control of a corporation takes place, the existing management and their rivals make appeals for the votes of uncommitted stockholders. Nader's idea was to appeal for proxy votes among General Motors' 1,300,000 shareholders on behalf of his public interest organization. He hoped to win a sufficient share of voting power to add three directors representing the public interest to the corporation's board. However, this proposal won less than 5 percent of the vote of outstanding shares in four successive years.[17]

Another approach would be to revise the constitution of the corporation so that the governing board would represent not only investors but also other affected interests. Some foreign nations practice tripartite control: the investors, the government, and the employees each have one-third of the representatives on corporate boards. In Germany, the managing board of all corporations is equally divided between labor and management.[18]

It is possible to visualize a more representative system of corpo-

---

[16] Ralph Nader, "The Case for Federal Chartering," in Ralph Nader and Mark J. Green, Corporate Power in America (New York: Grossman Books, 1972), p. 82.

[17] David Vogel, "Contemporary Criticism of Business: The Publicization of the Corporation" (paper presented to the American Political Science Association. New Orleans, La., 1973), mimeo, p. 39.

[18] The German system provides for a two-tiered structure. The top board is like the American board of directors, represents the shareholders, and deals with financial affairs. The management board representing labor and management governs the internal affairs of the company —work procedures, factory design, wages, operating rules, employee benefits, and so forth.

rate political organization. But again, the problem is how democratic such a system would be in practice. How would consumer or public interest representatives be elected? It is hard to imagine individuals voting directly for representatives to all the corporations with which they do business or which affect the communities in which they live. (I own a Volvo, a Grumman canoe, a Sears refrigerator, and a Sylvania television set. How much of a voice should I have in the governance of these firms? How informed a voter am I apt to be?)

What the proponents of such a system visualize seems to have more in common with corporatism than democracy. The important point is that interests affected by corporate policies share in its governance. But how such representatives would be accountable to their constituencies is not clear. I am not convinced that Ralph Nader would always be speaking for me were he on the board of directors of General Motors any more than the existing leadership of the firm does. On what basis would he support his claim to represent the consumers of General Motors' products, or better yet, the "public interest"?

The question of workers' representation in the governance of the corporation is a little more straightforward, but it also raises serious problems. The employees of an organization are of course most directly part of its political community. They are immediately subject to its rule-making authority. Here the case for representation in the formal political structure would seem to be most compelling. Yet many American workers would argue that they do participate in those aspects of corporate policy that affect them through their unions, that in fact the government of the corporation as it affects workers does rest, through collective bargaining, on the consent of the governed. It is true that the "law" of the corporation as it affects worker's rights and benefits, with regard to working conditions and operating rules, is made through a process in which both labor and management participate. Whether formal representation on governing boards would make the corporation more responsive to the "governed" or whether it would weaken the bargaining powers of unions seems to be an open question.[19]

All complex organizations raise similar questions about the legitimacy of their political systems and the accountability of their powers. Many associations and interests groups claim to represent their memberships before government. But does the AFL-CIO really speak for a majority of carpenters or machinists? Do the American Medical Association's positions on health care accurately reflect the view of American doctors?

---

[19] *Philip Selznick,* Law, Society and Industrial Justice *(New York: Russell Sage Foundation, 1964), p. 151.*

Many such groups are not exposed to the pressures of competitive pluralism. The lawyer or doctor has no real alternative to membership in the bar or medical association. Often, the official organization has a semigovernmental role in regulating the profession. In many areas, interest group representation is not pluralist but corporatist in nature. One association is recognized *de facto* as the appropriate spokesman for a specific interest by government bodies. In only a few areas of society are there really adversary interest groups in operation. We accept the notion that competition between parties is essential to democracy, but we do not apply the same norm to interest organizations. In true pluralism, it will be recalled, the individual's ultimate source of power is the existence of a competitive alternative.

There is an interesting precedent in American public policy for dealing with this problem. In the common law of associations, government need not be concerned with the political order of voluntary groups. Their systems can be democratic or authoritarian—it is not an issue for the state so long as the organization is truly voluntary and the individual is free to leave.

But when a private organization is involuntary, the theory does not hold. Then it may become the responsibility of the state to *impose* a democratic system on the private organization. This is exactly what has happened in the case of trade unions. Under union shop rules, an employee must join the union. He cannot make a private employment contract but must accept the one that is bargained collectively. For American law, this means that the union is involuntary and must therefore be organized democratically. Through the National Labor Relations Act and the Landrum-Griffin Act, most of the procedures of constitutional democracy—periodic elections, secret ballot, freedom of speech, the right to nominate and to oppose—are required of unions by federal law and the democratic conduct of unions is enforced by federal agencies.

This precedent raises interesting questions about other organizations and associations in the American political order. When an organization can be shown to be involuntary in some significant sense—perhaps that the choice to leave it is not truly costless for the individual—does government have an obligation to require that the political system of the organization be structured democratically?[20]

In considering the democratization of the complex organization, we have returned to the problem of political judgment which we raised in Chapters Eleven and Twelve. What is the appropriate bal-

---

[20] *Charles W. Anderson, "Public Policy and the Complex Organization," in Leon N. Lindberg
(Ed.),* Politics and the Future of Advanced Industrial Society *(New York: David McKay,
1976).*

ance between democracy and authority in any organization? Some would argue that democracy is not an appropriate standard for judging the political system of the corporation or other organizations. The test of the corporation is its performance. Its purpose is to organize people and resources as efficiently as possible to produce goods and services. The corporation is not a political community or a government. The analogy is misleading. The appropriate test is not whether it is representative but whether it is efficient.

Extending the Rule of Law

There is yet another way of approaching the question. Political order is a system of law. In modern society, both governments and private organizations are sources of law. Perhaps we should view this rule-making authority of private bodies as an extension of the legal system. We then begin to think about the consistency of the system as a whole. Private organizations, as well as governments, should acknowledge fundamental personal and political rights and should live up to basic standards of procedural fairness. As Philip Selznick says

> In recent years, we have seen a transition from preoccupation with freedom *of* association to concern for freedom *in* association. This renewed awareness stems from a realization that the private association can be more oppressive than the state. The loss of a job, the right to pursue a profession, or the opportunity to continue one's education, may be far more hurtful than a jail term.[21]

For the employee, the freedom to go elsewhere or participation in management is probably less important than protection against arbitrary layoffs, transfers, or oppressive working conditions. For the consumer stuck with a bad product—say a car or major appliance —there is not much satisfaction in resolving never to buy from the company again or attending a protest meeting. He feels that he has a *right,* and the company a duty, to set matters straight.

Historically, corporations and other private bodies were virtually autonomous in their internal authority. They could hire and fire whom they pleased and place whatever conditions they wanted on their employees' conduct, both on and off the job. The employee could claim no rights against the organization. As long as he had "contracted in," he had to accept its rules. Gradually, over the years, this autonomy of the organization has been reduced. Wages and hours legislation and industrial health and safety laws create rights for individuals within the organization. The employee wins the right

---

[21] *Philip Selznick,* Law, Society and Industrial Justice *p. 38.*

to bargain collectively. Consumer protection laws establish rights for the purchaser, enforceable in the courts.

Increasingly, the law of the state penetrates and becomes part of the law of private government. Basic questions arise about the respective rights of the association and of the individual. Should the private organization have the right to select its own "citizens"—for the corporation, to hire and fire employees; for the university, to admit and expel students; for the club, to determine who shall be members? Or does the individual have rights against the private government? Many feel that the law of private bodies, like the law of the state, should conform to the constitution and the fundamental norms of the legal order. Laws against racial and sex discrimination should apply to both public and private institutions. So far, the law has stopped short of imposing such standards on purely private bodies. But public universities, regulated corporations, or those that hold government contracts are subject to civil rights legislation and affirmative action programs in selecting their employees.

There has been a tendency in recent years for the courts to look more closely at the problem of "due process of law" in the private organization. In labor unions with union shop contracts, in public universities, in some other institutions, an employee or member has a right to something very much resembling a fair trial before being fired or expelled. While the courts have hesitated to make the principle universal, many would argue that basic rights of procedural fairness should apply to all organizations—that the individual should be protected against arbitrary authority wherever it is encountered. Should a student have a right—enforceable in the courts—to a hearing before being expelled from a university? Should a professional association be required to bring charges against a member before an impartial tribunal before imposing sanctions? Again, the question is not whether private organizations should create their own judicial processes, but whether they should be *imposed* on private organizations as a matter of public law. To what extent should government create "constitutional law" for the private organization?

Our views on this subject will depend in part on our attitude toward the relation of government to private associations. The pluralist might be concerned to preserve the essential independence of private associations. They are not merely instruments of the state. Those who see public power as generally more responsible than private power will be more sanguine about extending the domain of governmental authority. But the larger issue is a conflict of rights—of the rights of private associations against the state, and the rights of individuals against arbitrary power, whether by public or private governments. The position we take finally will depend on how we strike a balance between these two principles.

One writer at least sees the extension of the domain of law as the key to political order in modern, complex society. Theodore Lowi suggests that the essential function of government is to make and apply general rules, authoritatively binding on all individuals and institutions in a society. The aim of government is justice. Interest-group pluralism corrupts the integrity of law and public authority. Internal democracy in the private association is merely an extension of the idea of pluralism, it does not answer the question of legitimate authority in society as a whole. Comprehensive planning endangers personal freedom. The detailed regulation of all aspects of life by government can only lead to bureaucratic control and inefficiency. The problem for government is to establish a viable legal order of general rules and rights. Lowi's vision of what he calls "juridical democracy" seems to be a quest for a formula of political order that lies between what he perceives as the anarchy and corruption of full-scale pluralism and the heavy-handedness of the all-pervasive state.[22]

nclusion

The political system is one of divided loyalties. We are not just citizens of the state but of many other organizations and communities. We are forced to make choices. We can be with our church and against the state, with our union and against our employer, with the national government and against the government of the city in which we live. We can define our responsibility in terms of the interests of the organization we work for or the society as a whole.

It is too easy to say that we should always put the public interest first. There are a variety of publics, and a variety of public interests. Should the university accept government funds, or would the strings attached to research grants "corrupt" an educational institution, make it a tool of the state, divert it from its essential purposes? Should the corporation executive work for the best interests of the company or endorse a larger conception of the public responsibility of the corporation? Should the lawyer or doctor defend the right of professional self-regulation or fight for the public's right to supervise the practice of medicine or the law? Should there be "public" representatives on the governing boards of bar and medical associations?

Such dilemmas are part of normal, everyday political life. The stands that we take on such issues may not seem crucial in determining the overall form that our political system will take. But they are an important kind of political activity. They are, in essence, choices

[22] *Theodore Lowi,* The End of Liberalism *pp. 287–314.*

made on behalf of other people. How we define our loyalties to groups, associations, and organizations is part of the process by which we create the total political context in which we all live.

Similarly, the judgments that we make, and the views we endorse, about the "system" as a whole are not without impact. They affect the views of others, and contribute to the process by which a society creates an image of its collective identity. How then, seriously, would we want to envision the future political order of our civilization? As we think about what America might become in its second 200 years, are we more attracted to the pluralist, the corporatist, or the democratic socialist vision of political order? Are there other alternatives that have not yet been imagined? Our image of the future will influence the reforms and changes that we will champion and support. Faced with a specific issue of institutional change, are we more likely to argue for a vital and lively pluralism, for public planning, the democratization of the complex organization, the expansion of the domain of law? Or are things quite all right the way they are—is the institutional fabric that we have developed through centuries of development and growth one that should be nurtured and protected?

In the course of this book, we have moved from the simplest to the most complex forms of political decision making. Deciding on how to act as a member of a student-faculty committee, deciding on the rights of those who want to build fences around their property and those who want unobstructed views, and deciding on an image of the future for American society are all issues that we talk about and occasionally have to face as real problems of public choice.

The "political moment" comes at different points in a person's life, often unexpectedly. For months, perhaps years, we can go about our business with little concern for public affairs. Talking politics is simply a pastime. But eventually we are on the spot—we have to take a stand or make a judgment. When the time comes, all the theoretical knowledge we have about government, all the information we have acquired about public affairs, may do little good. The circumstances that call for political decision, the forms that political issues can take, are too diverse to be predicted. Often we will be under fire and strongly pressured. We will have to be able to wait, for politics takes time. The most important lessons of political decision making can only be suggested in a book and can only be learned through practical experience. Keeping your wits about you in the face of conflict and asking the right questions when the situation is unclear are habits of mind and character, not formulas and techniques that can be learned and applied. Only with time and practice does the most fundamental principle of all really sink in—if it ever does—that we learn to mistrust our deepest certainties—that we know how to think that we might be mistaken.

Connolly, William E. (Ed.), *The Bias of Pluralism* (New York: Atherton Press, 1969). A collection of articles that reviews the controversy over democratic pluralism as a viable model for political order.

Epstein, Edwin M., *The Corporation in American Politics* (Englewood Cliffs, N.J.: Prentice-Hall, 1969). A very good study of corporations and politics, dealing both with their relationship to government and their role as private governments. Excellent bibliography.

Galbraith, John Kenneth, *Economics and the Public Purpose* (Boston: Houghton-Mifflin, 1973). A good statement of the case for democratic planning in modern industrial society.

Galbraith, John Kenneth, *The New Industrial State* (New York: New American Library, 1967). The role of corporations in planning the American economy. A classic on the political role of complex organizations.

Kariel, Henry S. *The Decline of American Pluralism* (Stanford: Stanford University Press, 1961). A full treatment of the history of pluralist ideas in America, a critical discussion of the decline of American pluralism and an appeal for a return to the pluralist idea.

Lakoff, Sanford A., and Daniel Rich (Ed.), *Private Government* (Glenview, Ill.: Scott, Foresman, 1973). An excellent collection of articles on the subject of private government, with original essays appraising the pluralist system from the point of view of democratic theory.

Lindblom, Charles E., *The Intelligence of Democracy* (New York: The Free Press, 1965). Very technical, but an exhaustive cause for the superiority of pluralism over comprehensive planning.

Lowi, Theodore J., *The End of Liberalism* (New York: W. W. Norton, 1969). A criticism of interest-group pluralism and a defense of juridical democracy as the key to political order in complex society.

Mason, Edward S. (Ed.), *The Corporation in Modern Society* (New York: Atheneum Press, 1969). A very good collection of articles on all aspects of the politics of corporations.

McConnell, Grant, *Private Power and American Democracy* (New York: Alfred A. Knopf, 1966). A critical view of the role of complex organizations in the American political system.

Merriam, Charles E, *Public and Private Government* (New Haven: Yale University Press, 1944). The classic work on private government.

Nader, Ralph, and Mark J. Green (Eds.), *Corporate Power in America* (New York: Grossman, 1972). Contains some of the best materials on the case for democratizing the corporation.

Pennock, Roland J., and John W. Chapman (Eds.), *Voluntary Associations: Nomos XI* (New York: Atherton Press, 1969). Theoretical essays on the private association and its place in pluralist theory.

Pike, Frederick H., and Thomas Stritch (Eds.), *The New Corporatism* (Notre Dame: Notre Dame Press, 1974). Good comparative discussions of the theory and practice of corporatism. See particularly the essay by Philippe Schmitter.

Shonfield, Andrew, *Modern Capitalism* (New York: Oxford University Press, 1965). An excellent comparative study of the various forms of capitalism in the modern world. Very strong on the relation of complex organizations to government and the variety of approaches to planning present in these nations.

Truman, David B., *The Governmental Process* (New York: Alfred A. Knopf, 1958). This book effectively started the argument about interest group pluralism, both as an empirical and normative theory.

Webb, L. C. (Ed.), *Legal Personality and Political Pluralism* (Melbourne: Melbourne University Press, 1958). A good discussion of classic theories of pluralism, and the law of voluntary associations in Anglo-American nations.

index to tables

index to names

index to topics

313